Clinical Sociology
An Agenda for Action

CLINICAL SOCIOLOGY
Research and Practice

SERIES EDITOR:

John G. Bruhn, *Pennsylvania State University/Harrisburg*
Middletown, Pennsylvania

CLINICAL SOCIOLOGY: An Agenda for Action
John G. Bruhn and Howard M. Rebach

1

Introduction
The Application of Sociology

The Field of Clinical Sociology

Historical Roots and Development

In the century or so that sociology has existed, the field has gone through many changes. Perspectives, approaches, and theories have emerged and passed away. Leaders in the field have asserted that sociology should be a "pure science." Some sociologists have emphasized quantitative approaches and the mathematical statement of theory with the objective of constructing general principles supported by data and models of social reality. Innovators have called for interpretive understanding of the social world, an exploration of subjective realities, and critical analyses of power relationships. Through it all, from Comte to Marx and Durkheim, to the Chicago School, to the present, a common theme keeps bubbling to the surface demanding attention.

The theme we refer to here is the practical application of sociology. Our theme of action echoes the long-ago call of Albion Small (1896/1985) and the contemporary call of Harold Cox (1994) for scholarship combined with action. That is, the use of sociology for positive social change and development, and as a basis for active intervention that addresses current social problems.

Today's problems demand attention. Crime and delinquency; violence, both individual and collective; family violence; absent fathers; drug and alcohol abuse; homelessness; a changing job market; ethnic conflict; health and mental health care; and political discord are but a partial list. The times call for action. Like the sociologists of the Chicago School, we cannot ignore the fact that sociological studies have a direct bearing on the issues that face contemporary society. Sociological studies can help uncover the causes of social problems and suggest solutions.

This volume and our previous work (Rebach & Bruhn, 1991a) stem from the belief that, to be useful and viable, sociological knowledge must be actively applied to human social problems. This is not a new or original theme; but sociologists, generally, have seldom considered it mainstream. The members of

1

the Chicago School saw their city and its problems as a laboratory for developing and testing sociological knowledge, yet Robert Park and other members of the School believed "the sociologist's task was to pursue disinterested knowledge" (Bulmer, 1984:123). Traditionally, most sociologists have preferred to assume a detached, "scientific" role. In recognition of this fact, Fritz (1991:17–18) wrote:

> Too often [practical sociology] has been presented as if it were, by its nature, unscientific. Some have also incorrectly treated practical sociology as if it were only an interest of the earliest sociologists—or the students—and an interest that needed to be left behind.

Fritz concluded that, "Labeling practical sociology as *borderline* or *non-academic* encourages the view that sociological practice is peripheral to the discipline." We hold that application and practice are decidedly not peripheral.

At least three labels are used to designate the practical application of sociology: *applied sociology*, *sociological practice*, and *clinical sociology*. The labels do not designate rigid differences in role performance. We apply sociology when we practice it; when we practice it, we attempt to change things for the better. Clark (1990) defined "sociological practice" as an umbrella term covering all forms of practical sociology. She also stated that:

> ... applied sociology employs sociological perspectives to assist in problem solving, and the applied sociologist is generally a research specialist who produces information that is useful in resolving problems in government, industry and other practice settings. (p. 109)

Applied sociologists take on many roles such as management, planning, program evaluation, and social impact studies. Though they address practical issues, their role generally is advisory. The term *clinical sociology* refers to active intervention that is rooted in the perspectives, theory, and methods of sociology. Though the activities of clinical sociologists are diverse, their active intervention as change agents sets them apart from other practicing sociologists. Like other disciplines that are engaged in intervention, clinical sociology is active, humanistic, and change oriented (Freedman, 1982; Rebach & Bruhn, 1991b:4). Clinical sociology is distinctive in that it relies on sociology for its perspective and knowledge base. Gardner (1979:2), cited by Clark (1990:104), acting for the Clinical Sociology Association, formally defined clinical sociology as follows:

> Clinical sociology brings a sociological perspective to intervention and action for change. The clinician is essentially a change agent rather than a researcher or evaluator. Clients may be individuals, groups or organizations. The clinical task involves a redefinition of self, role, and/or situation, using a variety of techniques or methods for facilitating change. The value-orientation is humanistic, holistic, existential, and multi-disciplinary.

Hall (1991:49) stated that clinical sociology "provides a broad, substantive base and conceptual context for intervention work at different levels of social organization...." with perspectives that "range from individual reflection to community change," and that "it allows for the consideration of more individual and social facts in assessing behavior than traditional mental health disciplines." The distinguishing feature of clinical sociology is its emphasis on action. More and more, sociologists are taking active roles as change agents.

The construction of the term *clinical sociology* to designate sociologically based interventions, dates to about 1930 when Ernest W. Burgess introduced courses entitled "Clinical Sociology." Wirth's article (1931) introduced the term to the sociological literature. The ferment and social problems in Chicago during that era prompted the sociologists of the Chicago School to direct attention to their city. While their contributions to research and theory are heralded, they did not completely confine their activities to research and theory.

Current Trends

The term *clinical sociology* has been kept alive since 1930 by occasional articles and other references (Dunham, 1964, 1982; Gouldner, 1956; Lee, 1955; Lennard & Bernstein, 1969; McDonagh, 1944). The field reemerged, as a social movement, among practicing sociologists in the mid-1970s. This movement was led by John Glass, nourished by the writings and other activities of Alfred McClung Lee, Jan Fritz, and Elizabeth Clark, found a following, and led to the establishment of the Clinical Sociology Association, a newsletter, and an annual journal, *The Clinical Sociology Review*, which began publication in 1982.

A number of elements have been responsible for the persistence of the theme of practical sociology and the reemergence of clinical sociology. Like the sociologists of the Chicago School who saw the relevance of their work to urban problems, we cannot help but notice the relevance of sociological theory and research findings to contemporary social problems. Neither can we fail to recognize the ineffectiveness of individually oriented approaches to what, essentially, are social problems.

Lundman (1993:27–53) reviewed four decades of individual treatment programs for juvenile delinquents and concluded that individual treatments for delinquents, such as counseling, have proven largely ineffective as delinquency prevention measures. Critics of the individual approach in the mental health field have tried to call attention to the role of social interaction, both as a source of problems and a locus of intervention (Ackerman, 1958; Swan, 1984; Watzlawick, Beavin, & Jackson, 1967; Watzlawick, 1990). Fein (1990a, 1990b, 1991) suggested that personal distress stems from dysfunctional social roles, and offered a resocialization approach to treatment. Fein specifically reformulated personality disorders as difficulties in role negotiation, deemphasizing the personal characteristics of distressed persons. Ferguson, Ferguson, and Luby (1992) offered an integration of psychodynamic, cognitive, and interpersonal therapies in terms of role performance and social functioning. Their formulations provided tools for assessment and intervention. Although May and Kelly (1992) turned their sociological attention to paranoia, their analysis may serve, more generally, as a critique of assessment and intervention that is oriented toward individuals. May and Kelly (1992) noted the "tendency to locate the problem within the individual."

> ... the appeal is ultimately and invariably to some unpleasant attribute or condition that in some way attaches itself to the individual. Whether the villain is a malfunctioning brain cell, some psycho-sexual trauma of early childhood, or a particular constellation of personality factors, the clues to the problem lie buried deep within the individual, recoverable only with professional assistance. It is this commitment to individualism that prevents a shift away from the medical model towards a more thoroughly social explanation. At the same time, it reinforces the tendency to view as disease, or at least the symptoms of disease, what may more usefully be seen as strategic behavior. (p. 53)

May and Kelly perceived the individual orientation to be fostering a highly deterministic model of human behavior in which action is the result of "forces," rather than deliberate choices made by rational actors who are trying to cope with and adapt to their environment. They stated that "we would expect to locate its [paranoia's] genesis and development in the network of relationships and interaction patterns that constitute the sufferer's social world" (p. 54). Similarly, drug and alcohol prevention programs work best when individual, family, peer, and community risk factors are addressed. Community based prevention programs are complicated; they involve identifying the target population, gaining trust and continued participation, and adapting the intervention to the specific community (Lorion & Ross, 1992).

Anderson and Rouse (1988:135) proposed a sociological approach to domestic violence against women. Their approach

> emphasizes the origins of wife beating in the social structure of patriarchy [and] efforts of the battered women's movement ... have always been mindful of the need for social change and not simply individual therapy. More generally, the sociological perspective on family violence has emphasized social psychological and sociocultural over psychological causes.

A third factor in the reemergence of clinical sociology was the changing career roles of persons with sociological training and backgrounds. Originally, graduate students were prepared for academic positions, but by the mid-1970s, there existed a pool of sociologists who could not, or chose not to find academic positions. These individuals coalesced, in 1978, to form a formal organization, the Clinical Sociology Association. The process has been carefully chronicled by others (Clark, 1990; Fritz, 1991), who noted that the changing career paths of sociologists, and the formation of an association, were significant factors in the reemergence of clinical sociology.

Clinical sociologists practice in diverse settings at all levels of social organization. Stoecker and Beckwith (1992) described citywide work with community based development organizations in Toledo, Ohio. Their work, and their contact with all levels of government and other funding sources resulted in increased

Contents

Preface

Our previous contribution to the field of clinical sociology was an edited book, *Handbook of Clinical Sociology* (1991), in which several colleagues presented an overview of the field. While our experience, and that of our colleagues, was that the collected essays were useful in teaching, we felt that there was a need for a textbook that presented the field, its methods, examples of how clinical sociology is practiced, and its opportunities for the future: hence the present volume.

Our intention was to make the book as practical as possible for both under-graduate and graduate students in clinical sociology and related fields. Both of us have practiced sociology in different ways and at different levels. We have written the book from our respective clinical experiences, which tend to complement each other; yet we do not assume that we are experts. In an evolving field like clinical sociology, the methods of practice are always being tested and refined, and the effects of planned intervention are documented and assessed. Therefore, we have written as we practice. Other practitioners put sociology into practice in different ways. Differences can provide a source of rich debate inside and outside the classroom and contribute to shaping the theory and practice of clinical sociology.

We feel that the field of clinical sociology is exciting because it offers such a broad range of ways in which a sociologist can practice, and the need for practitioners with broad perspectives continues to expand. We have tried to reflect this breadth and excitement in examples throughout the text. We hope that we have been able to interest students looking for a way to practice a variety of skills to consider clinical sociology in making a positive difference with respect to societal problems. We also hope that we have provided ideas that will challenge our colleagues who practice sociology to explore new ways to use their sociological skills in solving problems.

Acknowledgment

We are grateful for the services of Paula Levine in editing and indexing the book and to Jan Russ for her assistance in typing.

definition? By what value system? The authors help the reader clarify the role of values in clinical sociology, pointing us in the direction of "doing the right thing."

Finally, while sociology has its roots in the enormous changes that have identified the nineteenth and twentieth centuries, Bruhn and Rebach's clinical sociology is focused on the twenty-first century. The demographic shifts that have occurred in the twentieth century are setting the stage for the twenty-first. The demands for the practice of clinical sociology will likewise to be grounded in the present and past; but they must adjust to the future. This text sets the agenda for clinical sociology through this century and well into the next.

W. DAVID WATTS
Former president, Sociological Practice Association
Editor, *Clinical Sociology Review*

Foreword

As we enter the twenty-first century, the social world is experiencing rapid and profound change. Sociology as a discipline has its roots in social change. Sociologists continue to search for answers to the problems in living that we confront on the individual, group, and structural levels. *Clinical Sociology: An Agenda for Action* provides a solid grounding in clinical sociology and sociological practice. It provides an organized overview of the extraordinary changes taking place in sociology today: the actual application of sociological knowledge, research, and theory to intentional intervention.

There are two kinds of textbooks: those that tell the student what he or she needs to know to pass a course and those that take the student and the instructor another step into the world surrounding the classroom. This book is the second kind. It tells us what we need to know about a the theory and practice of clinical sociology, and it helps us to think and act well beyond what would normally take place in the classroom or course of study. Clinical sociology is revolutionizing the discipline of sociology. This text takes that revolution one step further.

As Bruhn and Rebach show us in this ground-breaking book, sociology and its practitioners have the opportunity to make substantial and successful contributions to conscious and intentional improvement of social life. Whether the sociological practitioner or clinician is working with individuals or families to develop more effective ways of dealing with each other and the world around them, or designing and executing interventions that are intended to improve the productivity and performance of public or private organizations, or helping to design and implement policy that can affect an entire nation, this text has something to offer.

Clinical Sociology: An Agenda for Action applies sociological theory. It does not engage in "abstract empiricism" or "grand theory." A range of theoretical approaches are discussed, by adopting a problem-solving approach to the clarification and resolution of problems. This is theory in action, not theory in the classroom.

Bruhn and Rebach take us into territory where mainstream sociologists are frequently uncomfortable. Clinical sociology is distinguished by its emphasis on intervention to improve a social situation. But what is improvement? By whose and what does not and to continue to build upon, expand, and test existing theories. We welcome texts that explore in detail the many facets of the increasingly popular and useful field of clinical sociology.

JOHN G. BRUHN
Middletown, Pennsylvania

Series Preface

Sociology is currently perceived to be a generalist field without clearly definable outcomes, and its graduates are often perceived to have indefinable skills. Some sociologists feel that there will be continuing pressure on sociology to become a practice-oriented profession. A recent study of sociological practitioners' views of the most important issues facing sociology now and in the future indicated that sociologists need to help intervene in a variety of societal and organizational problems, especially those within the domain of sociology, e.g., human abuse, violence, substance abuse, poverty, and equity in the delivery of health and human services. The yield for clinical sociology in the future lies in the hands of clinical sociologists themselves. There is no limit to the field or its satisfactions for engaging in actions that are intended to bring about positive change. As John Schaari has said, "The future is not some place we are going to, but one we are creating."

In the last decade there has been a reemergence of interest among some sociologists in the application of sociology to social issues. This had led to the organization of groups, such as Applied Sociology and Clinical Practice, within the ranks of sociology. This movement to create an "action sociology" that intervenes to improve social conditions has become increasingly popular among students who want to do more than observe, study, and comment on social issues.

The field of clinical sociology is in its adolescence. There is a growing awareness among sociologists to examine their methods of study and apply findings from their research to improve the common good, as well as to work with colleagues in related disciplines to solve complex social problems. Clinical sociology needs to share its experiences in research and practice and thereby begin to develop a scientific framework to guide the education of future researchers and practitioners.

This book is the first in a new series entitled *Clinical Sociology: Research and Practice*. There is a need for practitioners to share "best practices," to discuss the complex legal and ethical issues of client relationships, to refine techniques of intervention and evaluation, and to explore the uniqueness of clinical sociology in specific settings such as schools, prisons, organizations, and treatment facilities. There is also a need for more research in clinical sociology to discover what works funding for redevelopment, as well as coordination and cooperation among neighborhood groups. Bryan (1992), a clinical sociologist who was director of a community based substance abuse prevention program, described a school based intervention with African American youth who were the children of substance abusers. The intervention, in which Bryan used a resocialization approach, resulted in an improvement in academic performance and a drop in absenteeism among participants. Van der Merwe and Odendaal (1991) reported their involvement in mediation and conflict resolution in South Africa, which helped open lines of communication between the white government and the various racial and ethnic groups. Watts (1989; Watts & Wright, 1991) described community intervention to combat drug abuse, which included getting communities to acknowledge drug abuse as a community problem, and to "awaken a community to action." His next step was to "assist a community to recognize, plan, and take steps to solve a drug abuse problem." Watts (1989) described helping the community form a task force that involved community leaders in constructing specific, targeted, peer-based interventions, and helping the community obtain outside funding for programs. Abbott and Blake (1988) reported on a program of intervention for homeless street youth, which addressed the structural factors that prevented these youth from entering the "mainstream." Their intervention called upon housing, food, health, educational, and employment services to help stabilize the youth, provide a support network, and involve the youth in "useful and personally gratifying work." Eleven of the 16 participants in their program left street life for more stable work or school settings. Bruhn (1987:169) discussed an active role for clinical sociologists as "health brokers ... facilitating change in the health behaviors of individuals or families; or helping to ameliorate intraorganizational or interagency problems which affect the availability or quality of health care."

A number of clinical sociologists have reported on their work with groups. Brabant (1993) developed a group intervention for children who were grieving over the death of a sibling or parent. Cuthbertson-Johnson and Gagan (1993) developed an education–support group intervention for the families of patients with bipolar disorders, which was based on research and theory on the sociology of emotions. Billson and Disch (1991) described their work with women's groups "... to help women find support, sanity, growth, and empowerment...." They presented strategies for group facilitation based on their 15 years of experience working with such groups. Rebach and Johnstone (1992) described group work with persons who had been diagnosed with psychiatric disorders as well as chemical dependency. These are but a few examples of the diverse nature of sociologically oriented small-group work conducted by clinical sociologists.

Clinical sociologists also have reported sociological work with individuals, traditionally the domain of social workers, psychiatrists, and psychologists (Fein, 1988; Glass, 1992; Straus, 1982, 1984; Swan, 1988). Some clinical sociologists have reported working in forensic settings (Gordon, 1986; Thoresen, 1993; Thornton & Voigt, 1988). These few examples illustrate both the diversity and the variety of levels of clinical sociology practice.

The Macro–Micro Continuum

Definition

Social life, and thus sociological analysis, proceeds on many levels. We use the concept of the sociological spectrum, the *macro–micro continuum*, to describe this variability. Table 1.1 explains this continuum.

Table 1.1. Macro–Micro Continuum

	Types of systems	Examples of structures	Issues for clinical sociology
Macro	World systems	World economy	International trade relations and international conflict resolution
	National systems	Societies, social institutions (e.g., education, the political–legal order, the economic order, etc.	
	Large corporate structures	Political subdivisions (e.g., states, counties, cities), nationwide or multinational corporations	Intra- or interinstitutional conflict: territorial conflicts; culture clashes; interdisciplinary activities
Meso	Smaller corporate structures	Businesses, schools and universities, communities	Intergroup conflict; resource development including human resources; community organization and action such as drug and alcohol or delinquency or crime prevention; or general community improvement
	Secondary groups	Work units, neighborhoods, civic organizations	Improving intra- and intergroup cooperation, communication and relations; political action; problem solving; group solidarity
	Primary groups	Families, couples, peer groups	Improving family and group functioning and relationships; interface with agencies; conflict resolution
Micro	Individuals	Individuals in a social context, e.g., physician–patient	Behavior change

The macro end of the continuum deals with large social units on the societal and intersocietal level. Macrosocial structures include national or world economic systems, media systems, or stratification systems, or social institutions, such as legal structures, religions, education, social welfare, and science. The organization and change of political economies or ethnic group relations are examples of topics addressed at this level. Other examples include interrelationships among and changes of social institutions, such as religions, communication media, social welfare, political orders, and economic orders. Macrosociological topics may also include changing norms or role definitions over time. In general, the macrolevel incorporates a broad sweep of large structures and may include long-time segments.

At the micro end of the continuum are small social units, the smallest of which is the individual as a social actor. Beyond the individual, the microlevel refers to social units that are characterized by the face-to-face interaction and primary group relationships among their members. Couples, dyads, and families are examples of microsocial structures. Microsociological topics include role relationships, interaction processes, dominance structures, and socialization processes. Sociological approaches to intrapersonal processes—self-esteem (Rosenberg, 1990), and emotions (Hochschild, 1979)—are additional microsociological topics.

In between the macro and the micro ends of the continuum is the broad area containing what we label meso, or midlevel, structures, such as networks and organizations. Clinical sociologists may more often be involved with mesolevel issues than with issues at either extreme. Mesolevel structures range from small secondary groups (e.g., a work unit, a club, etc.) to corporations, government agencies, universities, and communities, as well as kinship networks, occupational networks, or friendship networks. Topics for study may include the nature of organizational structure, the organization of work, the influence of organizations on individual behavior, social ties, and the nature and effects of hierarchical relationships. Mesolevel issues often involve interfaces between social units; for example, boundary conflicts between groups or organizations, or between organizational levels. Wolf and Bruhn (1992) documented the relationship between community and family, on one hand, and individual health, on the other. They found family solidarity and community cohesion to be positively associated with indicators of health, while rapid social change and the breakup of family and community solidarity were associated with an increase in illness.

Stephenson (1994) also provided an example of a mesolevel phenomenon when she analyzed the influence of gender and ethnicity on the interaction patterns of managers and professionals within a department. She noted that, while the department appeared, "by the numbers," to be well mixed—40% men, 60% women; 56% white, 44% other—women and minorities were not well integrated into the firm, to the detriment of its efficiency and profitability. Stephenson demonstrated intervention strategies for working with the problem to the mutual benefit of the individual employees and the firm.

The distinctions between macro- and microsociology have been debated for some time (Eisenstadt and Halle, 1985; Knorr-Cetina & Cicourel, 1981). As Huber (1991) pointed out, there is controversy among sociologists about the meaning of the terms *micro* and *macro*. There is a tendency to equate micro with individuals and macro with collective events. Whether efforts are focused at the individual or personal level or at a broader social systems level, the two are linked. The nature of the macro–micro linkages is increasingly important as the etiologies, prevention, and solutions to contemporary social problems in the United States and elsewhere lie in understanding the interfaces and linkages between individual behavior and societal factors.

The Clinical Sociological Approach

Definition

Clinical sociology has its basis in the field of sociology. Sociology, broadly defined, is the systematic study of the social behavior of individuals, the work-ings of social groups, organizations, cultures, and societies, and the influence of these human institutions on individual and group behavior (Kammeyer, Ritzer, & Yetman, 1994:2). In other words, scientific sociology is the study of human behavior.

Clinical work focuses attention on behaviors that some person or group has defined as problematic. But the sociological perspective teaches that all behavior, problematic or not, arises from similar processes, that these processes are essen-tially social, and that even the process that results in behaviors being defined as problematic is social as well. The purpose of this section is to offer a sociological perspective on behavior that influences clinical work.

The basic perspective on behavior is called *biopsychosocial*, recognizing the contribution of the major action systems. Figure 1.1 provides a partial list of influences on behavior under three major headings.

While the list in the figure is not meant to be exhaustive, it suggests factors under each heading that influence behavior. For example, under genetic inheri-tance are such obvious factors as race, size, and looks. To this we must add genetic influences on rate of development; some children are "early bloomers," while others are "late bloomers." We must also add disorders that appear to have some genetic component, for example, hyperactivity (ADHD), and genetic predisposi-tions, for example, multiple sclerosis. In general, biological factors set the parame-ters for what is possible, not in a deterministic sense, but in establishing possi-bilities or constraints.

In addition to genetics, prenatal events also can have a profound effect on individuals' development. Substance use—drugs or alcohol—by a pregnant

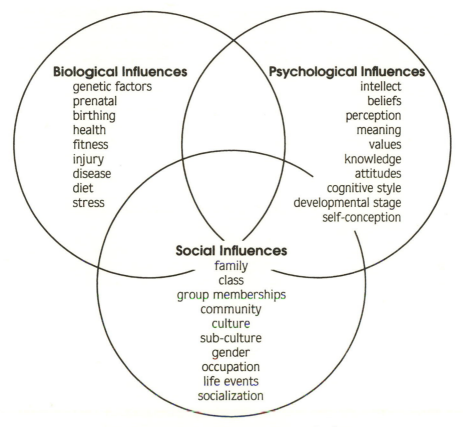

Figure 1.1. Influences on Behavior in Three Action Systems

woman can have damaging effects on fetal brain development and result in serious impairments of the baby that will last a lifetime. Less evident, but also affecting prenatal development, are issues such as prenatal care, nutrition, health, and stress of the mother. Diet, health, and fitness are additional biological factors that may affect behavior. Through these factors, social structure gets translated into the biological development of individuals: poor women are more likely than their more affluent counterparts to lack access to prenatal care, lack nutrition information, and experience stressors during pregnancy. It is also likely that factors affecting dietary choices and healthy lifestyles—information, motivation, and resources—are differentially distributed in social systems. Figure 1.2 illustrates how biological, psychological, and social factors may interact in a particular case.

With regard to the psychological, we accept the Meadian view that mind and

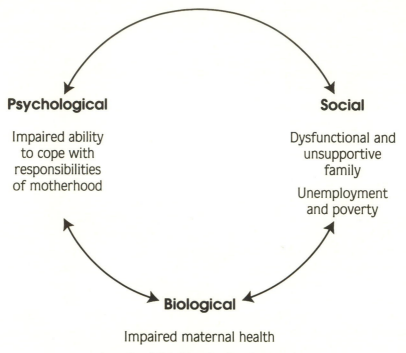

Figure 1.2. Substance Use and Pregnancy: An Illustration of the Interaction of Action Systems

self are social products acquired in the process of primary socialization in interaction with others, especially significant others. Glass (1992) recently reported
applying this perspective to the clinical treatment of individuals raised in alcoholic
homes. He noted that present problematic behavior can result from internalized
and troublesome cognitions, emotions, and behaviors derived from a person's
primary socialization. As a result of such socialization, people develop maladaptive strategies that are maintained and repeated in their daily lives. Glass derived
his theoretical perspective and intervention strategies from the work of symbolic
interactionists such as Cooley (1924), Mead (1934), Shibutani (1961), Thomas (see
Volkart, 1951), and Berger and Luckmann (1966).

We also note that while biological factors may set parameters, the possibilities
are called forth in a social setting. For example, there is ample evidence of a genetic
component to alcoholism; that is, certain individuals have a genetic intolerance to
alcohol. However, if such individuals never take a drink, they will not become
alcoholics. Family norms, religious prohibitions, and peer group behaviors are

critical factors in determining whether a person will use alcohol. Similarly, a child's rate of growth and development has social meaning for both adults and peers. For example, expectations of "early bloomers" often are heightened; they are given responsible roles by teachers and others, which, in turn, affect their peer group status (Newman and Newman, 1984:280). These factors influence children's definitions of self and their expectations of their own abilities.

Biologically determined features of an individual also have social meaning. Race, sex, size, and looks result in a variety of social responses that help to shape persons' thoughts about self as well as their actions. While most racial and ethnic differences are trivial, the norms of ethnic stratification within a society have broad implications for the life chances of members. The attention deficit hyperactive (ADHD) child or the learning disabled child may behave in ways that he or she cannot help. However, the reaction of the adult caretakers (parents, grandparents, teachers, etc.) of such children are crucial to the course taken by their disorders.

This biopsychosocial approach includes the following set of propositions. The first proposition is that behavior is voluntary. Humans are active constructors and participants in their everyday lives, they are not simply propelled, robotlike, by "forces." At various times, theorists have offered deterministic models of human behavior, proposing that biological, social, economic, or environmental forces determine human action. We reject these views and begin with the basic assumption that the actions taken by an individual are the result of a decision or choice from among available options.

The key here is "available options." A course of action can be followed, only if available; if its existence is known or, if known, the actor must have the necessary resources—skills and material resources—to follow through, and must define the course of action to be desirable, or associated with desirable outcomes.

The second proposition is that behavior is learned, particularly from its consequences; responses are acquired by an individual in interaction with the environment. As the actor interacts with the environment, certain responses come to be associated with preferred outcomes, or at least with the lesser of evils. Actions associated with preferred outcomes come to be preferred and, therefore, are those most likely to appear. In this context, it is important to note that "behavior" includes cognitive activity. Meanings, values, beliefs, knowledge, and attitudes are acquired or learned. Thus, actors' characteristic patterns represent their adaptation and accommodation to circumstances, as they define them.

The third proposition is that learned behaviors are chosen according to the actor's definitions of self and of the situation. Behavior does not "just happen." It takes place in context. Behavior is chosen by actors on the basis of their understanding of the context and of self-in-context. These understandings are derived, in part, from negotiation in interaction with others. The situation places constraints on this negotiation. Behavioral choices are influenced by the demands of the situation and actors' preferred outcomes. Humans reconstruct reality, internally.

Clinical Focus 1.1

The Cases of Allen and Barry

Biopsychosocial interplay is well exemplified by the cases of "Allen" and "Barry." Both are young white males who, serendipitously, showed up at a public mental health clinic at about the same time, less than a year prior to this writing. They have never met. Allen was 24 years old; Barry was 27. The two had similar medical histories during infancy and toddlerhood; had both been diagnosed with Attention Deficit Hyperactive Disorder (ADHD); had both revealed about the same degree of severe learning disabilities in childhood, disorders that generally are assumed to have a biological base; and both tested as having average intelligence.

At the time of intake, Allen had graduated from high school, had since been steadily employed, and had been putting himself through college. As a part-time student, he had successfully completed a two-year community college program, and was planning to transfer to a university where he would attend school full-time to obtain a BA degree while working part-time to support himself.

Barry, on the other hand, never completed high school. While in the ninth grade, he was dismissed from school as incorrigible and was placed in a residential facility, where he stayed until he was no longer legally required to attend school. Since that time, he had seldom held a job for long, and what jobs he had were low skill, and low paying. He has frequently been in trouble with the law, has served at least one jail term, and currently is on probation and awaiting trial. Most of Barry's problems have stemmed from his lack of social skills and extremely poor judgment in choosing associates.

It must be reemphasized that Allen and Barry's disorders are virtually identical. Over the years, both have been evaluated frequently by educational in-

(*continued*)

This internal representation acts as a guide for understanding reality and selecting behaviors in response to this understanding. People are also capable of planning ahead. They have the capacity, through language, to construct alternative realities internally and choose a course of action from among them.

The fourth proposition is that actors' social group memberships act as constraints and key shapers of all of the above. By social group membership, we mean macro-, meso-, and microgroups. Social organization is the most pervasive and universal tendency of human beings (perhaps so self-evident that it often is overlooked). As Durkheim (1895/1966) held, groups are sui generis, an entity, in themselves, that cannot be understood from analysis of individual members, no matter how thorough such analysis might be. As members of a group interact, they actively construct reality; they call forth and shape the roles they need, selectively

Clinical Focus 1.1 (*continued*)

stitutions, psychologists, and physicians, including psychiatrists. Their histories, provided at the time of intake, were obtained with their permission. The significant difference between these two young men lies in their family histories.

Allen was raised by his mother and father, who were supportive throughout his childhood and adolescence. In addition to providing a nurturing environment, encouragement, and help, his parents were Allen's advocates. They went so far as to bring a lawsuit against the local school system, which had refused to provide Allen with special educational services, even though the school system's test data showed that he more than met state criteria for the highest level of services for hyperactive and learning-disabled children. Despite the legal costs, the family persisted with the suit and won. Allen is independent, yet his family, including Allen, his parents, and two siblings, remains close-knit.

By contrast, Barry's father, who was physically abusive both to Barry and his mother, rejected him early. Barry's parents divorced when he was about 5 years old, and his father, a successful businessman, provided child support, but little else. He remarried, divorced, and remarried again. After divorcing Barry's mother, his father had little to do with Barry; in what contact there was, he gave Barry messages about his failures and inadequacies. Today, he generally refuses to have much to do with Barry or to help him in any way. Instead, he denigrates Barry as worthless and no good. Barry's mother, who tried to be protective, admittedly never understood his problem, and was unable, as a single parent, to cope with Barry, despite the fact that she was financially comfortable.

The similarity of the disorders shared by these two young men is remarkable, as is the difference in their socialization experiences and in their life courses. While biological and psychological factors may establish possible outcomes, social factors interact to affect the course of personal development.

approve and disapprove ideas and actions, create and shape relationships among members, and establish and enforce rules of thought and conduct. The social arrangements, on the sociocultural, as well as the interpersonal level, structure what options are available and influence the value assigned to various available options.

The basic and obvious fact is that all humans are born into an ongoing and established social order. Within that social order are widely shared definitions of what is good, desirable, and proper. As we grow and develop and live our lives, we interact with others who represent their conceptions of the social order to us. We are taught the language of our group. We are also provided with material about ourselves from which we construct conceptions of self. We learn from observation of others, from their overt socialization messages, and from their reactions, how to define situations, what to value, what outcomes to prefer, and how to conduct ourselves in various everyday life situations to obtain preferred outcomes. The established norms and values of the larger society provide the background within which specific membership groups—family, peers, etc.—teach us specific definitions of self and of context, as well as specific norms, values, and role performances. Though a seemingly infinite number of constructions can be placed on situations, and an infinite range of behaviors is possible, it is through their cultures, the norms and values of their social groups, and definitions of social reality that people have learned to channel their behavior into a finite range of options.

A metaphor may help tie all this together. For most of us in America, getting our drivers' license is a major rite of passage. By the time we reach adolescence, we have already learned the meaning of many significant symbols—the stop sign, traffic lights, etc. We have come to value driving, both for its instrumental value and the symbolic meaning that having a license (being a driver) has within our sociocultural context.

Agents of society (parents, older siblings, drivers' ed teachers, etc.) who already know them, undertake to teach us the skills and rules of the road. Eventually, we take our place as fully socialized drivers. Though each of us will develop individual differences and idiosyncracies as we learn and practice, the range of our differences will be limited. As we venture out, each of us will apply our skill and operate our vehicles on the basis of the way we were taught. Though each of us is operating our vehicle independently as an individual, the actions of others, the road, and the traffic signals and rules established by agents of the larger society act as constraints and shape our choices and actions. We have chosen our destination, but must enter the stream of traffic and, more or less, conform to traffic conditions, to the highway, and to the traffic rules to arrive safely at the chosen destination. Though we act independently—adjusting our speed, steering, changing lanes, etc.—the road and local conditions channel our behavior. Thus, our operation of our own cars falls into prestructured and reasonably predictable patterns. Our experience also allows predictions about everyone else's actions. Each time we drive, we bet our lives on the prediction that others know their roles; that oncoming traffic will stay on its side of the road and will not cross the double yellow line; that others will not enter a traffic-controlled intersection when we have the right-of-way or the green light, and so on. Whether or not we obey the posted speed limit, we are mindful that agents of social control—state troopers—are lurking just around the next bend, and perhaps, we choose our actions accordingly. This metaphor of driving is descriptive of all social behavior.

In sum, behaviors are learned within a social context and chosen as deemed appropriate for self in the specific situation. As a result of learnings, the larger sociocultural setting and the specific group memberships establish that certain responses to a situation have a greater probability than others. But it is not deterministic: Actors have the capacity to renegotiate their social reality, constantly, as they interact. When a person's usual response to a situation is not working, that person has the capacity to seek alternative strategies and adapt to the situation.

Interaction of Levels

Clinical work may take place at any location on the continuum, but events on one level have implications for events at other levels; the levels are interrelated. Collins (1988:3–7) demonstrated recognition of this fact when he stated that "microsociology overflows its boundaries into macrosociology ...," and that "... microtheory finds it less easy to ignore macro theory than vice versa." That is, individual or small-group behaviors, attitudes, beliefs, definitions of self, and context, preferences, life chances, and available range of choices are, to a large extent, structured by prevailing social, political, and economic structures, practices, events, and policies, mass media content, and sociocultural norms and role definitions. Thus, Collins stated, "... when we examine an individual, or situation, or thought process, in however micro detail, we tend to encounter elements which lead outward toward the wider society."

Similarly, mesolevel structures and processes may mediate between the macro- and microlevels. The networks and organizations (mesolevel) that people belong to and identify with may transmit and interpret the normative order (macrolevel) to the individuals and groups (microlevel). These mesolevel structures may also provide prescriptions and orientations in their own right. Thus, a person's job, occupational group, professional association or union, church, school, community, class, etc., are all sources of influence on the individual's consciousness and social interactions.

Recognition of the interplay of levels is critical for sociologically informed clinical work. The client system is likely to be affected by broad social changes on the macrolevel, by various cultural and subcultural memberships, by peer networks and primary group memberships, and by the unique socialization and definitions of individuals. The interplay of levels was the focus of a report by Stanley-Stevens, Yeatts, and Thibodeaux (1993), who noted that societal changes in the workplace, and in the family, are accompanied by a need for increased productivity, a trend for businesses to address the needs of workers and their families, more women in the workforce, and conflicting demands of work and family. The authors described the responses of over 300 employees at an electronics plant who worked in self-managed teams. To implement the change from more traditional to self-managed work teams, the company "trains employees in listening skills, communication, and cooperation—all important interpersonal skills which can have positive impacts on family life." Stanley-Stevens et al. found strong support for the hypothesis that skills learned at work "spilled over" into positive benefits for employees' families, in addition to increasing productivity and commitment among workers, and recommended their approach for clinical sociologists consulting with industries. Their report exemplifies the interaction of levels from societal trends (macrolevel), to the company (mesolevel), to individual employees and their families (microlevel).

Whether clinical work is with an individual, a family, or a larger group, it is important to the assessment of a case and the planning and delivery of an intervention that the clinical sociologist pay attention to the interplay among levels. Assessment data should inform intervention planning and delivery; full understanding of a case cannot be obtained by attention to the client only. Interventions should be culturally and individually acceptable, and workable for clients within their social context. Interventions in large systems should be examined for their impact on the groups and individuals that comprise these systems.

Nathan Church (1991:126) discussed the effects of macrolevel social change on clinical sociological work. Church noted that other clinical disciplines typically do not attend to macrolevel issues. As an example, he cited eating disorders, almost unknown in the 1950s, which were to become fairly common in the 1970s. Church stated:

> The sociological understanding of this symptom of social change is essential to the development of effective clinical interventions. To simply accept the existence of newly emerging clinical problems on the micro level, as do most disciplines that pursue interventions on this level, is to render even a basic understanding of the etiological process of the problem on various levels impossible. It is even possible for clinicians to exacerbate emerging problems by reifying them through labeling and the development of techniques of intervention without first coming to grips with the location or generation of the problem within dynamic social structures.

Changes in the world economy and America's place in it, as well as the changing nature of employment and the disappearance of low-skill jobs—macrolevel processes—have a direct effect on individuals, families, and communities as well as schools and churches and neighborhoods. Other economic changes often require both mothers and fathers to be employed outside the home. Norms have changed regarding child-bearing, marriage, and marital responsibility and divorce. These macrolevel processes have accelerated the number of single-parent households and "latchkey" children. They come down to the specific conflict situation, role relationships, and childrearing in a client family. The self conceptions and behavioral choices of client children and youth—drug and alcohol use, gang membership, sexual precocity, delinquency—are potentially related to macrolevel processes that affect families, neighborhoods, communities, and classes.

Church reminded clinical sociologists of what Mills' (1959) called the sociological imagination, "a vivid awareness of the relationship between personal behavior and the societal context in which it is framed" (Church, 1991:126). Church emphasized the importance for clinical sociologists of analysis across macro-, meso-, and micro-levels, and of a high degree of awareness and commitment to such analysis. The importance of analysis across levels cannot be understated. Where the primary unit of analysis is the individual (which often occurs even in work with groups), understanding is limited to the attitudes, motives, or other internal states of individuals.

On Theory and Practice

One of the things that makes the practice of clinical sociology sociological is its dependence on sociological theory. In this section, we consider the relationship between theory and practice.

The goal of any scientific discipline is the construction of theory. By the term, *theory*, we mean a set of general statements that attempt to explain a phenomenon. These statements usually are abstract; they are not bound to time or place. Theory serves several important functions. First, a good theory describes the reality it addresses. Second, it provides a taxonomy, or classification system, that directs attention to the important elements and concepts of the phenomenon to be considered. Third, a good theory provides statements about the relationships among those elements or concepts. Fourth, it provides an explanation of events that should help us understand how things happen the way they do. Such understanding should provide a guide to further action.

Research is the usual guide to action. Predictions about specific consequences of certain conditions can be derived from the propositions of a useful theory. These predictions, or hypotheses, are tested, and whether supported or not, contribute to the body of the theory. Another guide to further action is the application of theory to practice. As clinicians, we hold that the ultimate test of the value of a theory is its application in practice.

As Johnson (1986:58) stated, the role of theory "... is to provide models of social behavior that will facilitate the identification of human and organizational problems and suggest possible strategies for solution." Theory directs a clinician's attention to the features of a case that are important to investigate. Theory also can provide a framework for understanding the dynamics of a situation, including those features that prompt and maintain its problematic aspects. Such understanding is necessary if a problem is to be eliminated. Theory is especially critical in planning and carrying out interventions. Understanding the relationship between certain conditions and their consequences not only suggests what to change, but may point the way to change strategies. As clinicians wander into the *terra incognita* of a case, a theory can provide a sort of map of the territory. Anderson and Rouse (1988:137) elaborated on this point:

> Sociological theories offer basic models of social behavior which can influence counseling *goals* and provide a *rationale* for selection and use of particular techniques. Theories serve to clarify and open to critical evaluation the *assumptions* about social reality

implicit in practice. Theories make available to practitioners conceptual frameworks for *understanding* how, or why, certain interventions lead to, or fail to produce, desired changes. Theories also help to *organize* various techniques and exercises into a consistent, integrated approach. [Emphases in the original.]

Practice can also feed back to theory construction. The materials, insights, and results obtained in clinical experience can illuminate theory and offer tangible evidence for the validity and further development of theory. Albion Small (1896/1985:37) felt this strongly when he argued:

> The most impressive lesson which I have learned in the vast sociological laboratory which the city of Chicago constitutes is that action, not speculation, is the supreme teacher. If men will be the most productive scholars in any department of the social sciences, let them gain time and material by cooperating in the social work of their community.

Miller (1985) suggested conflict mediation as a role for clinical sociologists. Conflict theory has a long tradition in sociology, and an understanding of this theoretical base certainly can inform mediation work. However, clinical practice in mediation can provide feedback to theory with insights and details of conflict and conflict resolution that can test and add detail to theory.

Stoecker and Beckwith's (1992) work with community-based development organizations in Toledo, Ohio, valuable in its own right, offers insights and direction for theories of community organization, social movements, and social change. Anderson and Rouse (1988) developed techniques of intervention with battered women and battering men based on a combination of symbolic interaction and critical theory. Their formulations and application suggest strong compatibility between these two perspectives.

In sum, research, theory, and practice together offer the possibility of positive social change. At the same time, the inclusion of practice into the research–theory process offers the possibility of further development of our understanding of social life. Cox (1993:2) expressed the opinion that:

> ... our traditional role of creating knowledge can be enchanted to the extent that we play an active role as citizens in our communities and societies. Through such involvement, we test the limits of our theory-based understanding and discover unanticipated questions for research

On Scientific Sociology and Practice

The scientific method of sociology, as well the application of sociological theory, is relevant to clinical work. The distinction between clinical work and scientific work is the difference between *ideographic* and *nomothetic* models of explanation. Science, including the social sciences, uses the nomothetic model. This model "seeks to discover those considerations that are most important in explaining general classes of actions or events." The objective is "to provide the greatest amount of explanation with the fewest number of causal variables to uncover general patterns of cause and effect" (Babbie, 1983:56). The ideographic model addresses the unique case.

Work with a single case cannot be considered scientific, in the sense of developi⸱ ᶾ empirical generalizations about populations. But, the *scientific method* should guide us, as sociologists, as we work with a case. This involves the careful collection of data, theory development, and the formulation and testing of hypotheses. Durkheim's rules (1895/1966) are relevant: avoid preconceived notions; find and build on the facts to construct your understanding of a case; establish valid links between antecedent conditions and consequences; conduct careful measurement to determine if hypothesized interventions do, indeed, lead to proposed outcomes.

While work with unique cases is not exactly the same as scientific investigation, the techniques and mind-set should transfer. In addition, the findings of scientific investigation should help to illuminate the further understanding of cases. Thus, findings of studies of the differential effects of stressful life events on men and women (Conger, Lorenz, Elder, Simons, & Ge, 1993) may inform the understanding of intrafamily conflict, and of illness and intervention strategies.

The Structure of Intervention

Clinical sociology, like other clinical disciplines, has a structuring formula: Professionals, in some way, make their professional presence and availability known. Individuals or groups make contact to seek help with problems they believe to be within the scope of a professional's expertise: A couple may be experiencing severe marital discord; the staff of an agency may be severely discontented, leading to internal conflict and reduced effectiveness; a school and a family may be unable to cope with "an impossible child"; a community may be beset with drug and gang activity and want to take back its neighborhoods; and on and on. If a professional and client agree to work together, they form a relationship and begin to move through a process, the goal of which is problem solving and change.

Definition of the identity of the client may vary. We find it useful to distinguish between the terms *client* and *client system*. The client may be the one who brings the problem to the attention of the clinical sociologist (and may be the one who ultimately pays the bills). The client system refers to those coactors who participate in the problem, they may be the ones who define it as a problem, and may be involved in planning or participating in the intervention. They may be the ones to change or to be affected by change.

Although the structuring formula seems simple and straightforward, it may not be. The decision to seek professional help involves a commitment of resources—time, energy, and often, money. This is weighed against the costs of failing to seek professional help. Thus, the initial contact is the result of a subjective cost–benefit analysis by the prospective client or members of the client system. This analysis is ongoing; whether the relationship goes beyond the initial contact, and whether it continues, at any point in the process, involves the continuing estimation of whether the payoffs outweigh the costs. These calculations are influenced by estimates of the professional's skill and expertise, the nature of the relationship with the professional(s), the willingness of parties to work toward problem solution and change, and their estimate of the likelihood of reaching the goal, as well as its value for them. Several variables are at work.

Clinical sociologists are change agents. Ultimately, their work involves behavior change on the part of one or more members of the client system. Thus, one variable that affects the structure is who wants change and who is the target for change. Another, closely related variable is the degree of voluntary participation on the part of the target for change. Also involved in these issues affecting the structure are questions of why help is being sought, why now, and why help is being sought from the specific helper.

At one extreme, clients may have made their own choice whether, from whom, and when to seek help. They may have recognized the existence of a problem that it is beyond their present ability to solve, and may feel that they can benefit from professional help. At the other extreme, their presence may involve what they perceive to be coercion by more powerful agents. For example, individuals or families may be compelled by courts or social service agencies to seek professional services or suffer aversive consequences. Or, the upper management of a company or agency may impose professional intervention on a work unit in order to achieve some of management's objectives. The degree of their voluntary participation will affect the willingness of various actors to continue with and cooperate in the change process. It also will affect their evaluation of and response to the intervention agent.

The issue may be, "Who owns what problem?" Suppose the target for change is an adolescent boy who has been dismissed from school, has been involved in the juvenile justice system, has been a trial and an embarrassment to his mother, and has been court ordered to "treatment." The clinical worker is supposed to "fix" him. The parent, the school personnel, and the juvenile probation worker define the youth's behavior as "the problem" and want change—not necessarily in their own, but in this troublesome boy's behavior. From the youth's perspective, the problem may be that he is being hassled by these adults. His behavior may be highly adaptive, given the nature of the family, the community, the school, and the other youth in his area. His motivation to participate in any intervention may be quite low.

In the above example, powerful authority agents want change. The reverse could also be true. The solution of a problem facing community residents who ask for professional help may be blocked by powerful authorities who do not want change. The members of the community may own the problem but need change by others for its amelioration.

The structure of intervention, then, is found in the development of a working relationship between one or more professional workers and one or more members of the client system, and is affected by several variables, some of which have been mentioned here. The process of the work and its outcomes are based upon the nature of the relationship that emerges. Even where there is trust, confidence, cooperation, and willingness, the task will be difficult. Where there is suspicion and hostility it will be impossible.

The Process of Intervention

A "case" does not begin when clients first make contact. The problematic situation they bring to the clinical sociologist has developed over time. Some process within their social systems has reached a stage at which they have determined—or had determined for them—a need for professional intervention. They seek help because they feel a need for change. Something is "wrong," and they have been unable to correct it with their own resources. At the time of initial contact, clients enter into a new social structure, one that includes the clinical sociologist, for the purpose of alleviating the problem. They are "stuck" and need to develop creative options for behavior.

This is not to imply that intervention by clinical sociologists is confined only to dysfunctional situations. Clinical sociologists can have a positive role in intervention when things are going well but a person, family, group, or organization needs a "tune up," feedback about how to be better, perform better, or feel better. For example, a group or organization may want to reorganize for growth and greater effectiveness, may want help in setting up a format or approach to diversity, or simply, may want help in planning for the future or incorporating technological or personnel changes.

Intervention, the actual "work" of clinical sociology, is a dynamic social process. The clinical sociologist interacts and negotiates working relationships with members of the client system with the objective of bringing about behavior change that will benefit the client. The actual intervention plan results from negotiation within the context of the client–clinician relationship. The relative effectiveness of the intervention depends upon the quality of the relationships that are established.

From the clinician's point of view, clients need to be open and cooperative in providing information, be prepared to work for change, and be willing to enter into a working partnership. Therefore, clients must have confidence in and trust the clinical sociologist. They must feel safe in being open. They must feel valued, and believe that their unique circumstances are understood and respected. Clients must feel they have a stake in and stand to benefit from the relationship and recommended activities. A model of status inequality—professionals (high status) dictating to clients (low status)—in most instances, will fail. To be effective, working relationships must be democratic in character, and clients' autonomy, ability to problem-solve, and to make choices must be respected.

As a clinical sociologist, you will bring the knowledge and skills of scientific sociology to the client–clinician relationship. Sociological theory, methods, and research findings will be your point of departure. Scientific work and clinical work stand in a dialectical relationship. The empirical generalizations of science are based on patterns within populations of events. Each case is unique—a rare event. There can be no science of the unique case, but the scientific methods of sociology guide the intervention process, which involves careful investigation of the case, formulation of an understanding of the case, which is theory construction, and the development and testing of clinical hypotheses.

Intervention proceeds through four functional stages: *assessment, program planning, program implementation, and program evaluation.* The stages are not necessarily discrete, nor do they usually move in an orderly progression.

The assessment stage involves an investigation of the case in order to come to an understanding of the problematic situation and devise an operational definition of the problem. It is important to focus on the questions raised in the preceding section early in the assessment: What is the presenting problem? Is this an appropriate case for a clinical sociologist? Who is the client? Why is the client seeking help, and why now? What has happened to prompt help-seeking at this time?

The term *presenting problem* refers to the clients' statement of the problem as they see it, and is framed in their own words. It is important to pay careful attention to the clients' statement, and accept it as their formulation and understanding of "what's wrong." It indicates their definition of the situation. This is the subjective reality with which they have been living. It is also their point of departure: their interaction with a problematic situation stems from their understanding of it. Later, you may need to help clients reframe their problems to achieve behavior change.

It is important that the clients believe you have attended to and understood them. Their future motivation for work may depend on whether they think you correctly understood and are helping them address the problem. Finally, it will be useful to compare the clients' formulation of the problem with that of other members of the client system to determine the degree of consensus on "what's wrong." Lack of a shared definition may contribute to a problem or its maintenance.

A second key question that must be addressed during the early stages of assessment is whether or not to take the case. The issues are these: (1) Is this case within the scope of your expertise? (2) Can you work effectively with this client? and (3) Is there any reason why you do not want to take this case?

After completing the initial stage, the clinician must gather detailed data in order to develop an understanding of the case. Assessment is a case study. Depending on the nature of the case and of the client system, data gathering may involve obtaining structured or unstructured interviews, focus groups, survey questionnaires, psychometric data, educational records, archival data, and medical data. It will also involve identifying the key role-occupants in the case.

The goal of assessment is the construction of a formulation, a theory of the case, and an operational definition of what is to be changed. When the formulation is prepared, it should be presented to the client for further review and discussion, critique, and revision. When substantial agreement on the formulation and the objectives has been reached, clinician and client will be ready for the next stage of the intervention process.

The second functional stage in the process involves planning the various steps to take in order to achieve the objectives. This is a negotiation process. The plan should be fairly detailed, stipulating who will do what and when. Clients and clinician negotiate a contract, real or implied, for the work to be done.

The program plan should include statements of objectives. Objectives should be stated in observable, measurable terms. Well-formed objectives should have the following parts:

1. Verb and subject—state the condition to be met, for example:
   To reduce delinquency
   To improve study habits
   To provide case management
   To reduce caloric intake
2. Rate or amount: state how much.
3. Time frame: state when the objective is to be achieved.

Generally, two types of objectives are recognized: process objectives, and outcome objectives. Process objectives are statements about the program operation or services to be delivered, which, it is presumed, will lead to the desired results, in other words, who will do what with whom, and when. Outcome objectives are statements about the immediate and long-term results of the intervention. Examples of well-formed process objectives are:

1. To provide supervised recreational activities for 2 hours after school, from October 1 until the end of the school year, for 50 middle-school youth living in the housing project.
2. To provide 30 hours of training as youth recreational counselors, between September 1 and 30, to 12 college students for work with middle-school youth from the housing project.

An example of an outcome objective may be:
To reduce delinquency of project youth by 25% within one year after termination. The more concrete the statement of the objective, the easier it is to measure.

Program implementation is the third step in the process. The agreed upon steps are carried out according to the plan. The fourth functional stage is program evaluation. Evaluation measures the performance of the stated objectives, both process and outcome, to determine whether the plan is being carried out as prescribed, and whether or not it appears to be working. Like all the steps in the process, program evaluation is conducted jointly by the clinician and the client. Clients are in the best position to determine whether their needs are being met.

For the purpose of discussion, the functional stages have been presented here as discrete steps in a sequence. However, this is not the way they should, or do occur in practice. It is important that program evaluation and measurement be built into the program plan. Evaluation should be ongoing, and should carefully follow the progress of the program's implementation. The program should be monitored continually, to see whether it appears to be going according to plan, and whether it seems to be moving toward the objective. By the same token, both assessment and planning are ongoing. The evaluation data may reveal a need for additional assessment, or for modification of the plan, calling for changes in the program.

The functional stages in a case are the application of the scientific method to clinical intervention. Data are gathered, leading to theory construction and the formation of hypotheses, which are tested against actual outcomes. Like all theory, the case formulation is treated as tentative, rather than final and sacrosanct. Data either support or fail to support hypotheses. Results may lead to reformulation and new hypotheses or confirm the validity of the approach.

Ethical Guidelines for Practice

In addition to expertise in a substantive area, professions are characterized by codes of ethics. These codes derive from sets of values. In a later chapter, we will consider the value structure of clinical sociology in detail. Here, we conclude this general overview of the field with some attention to ethical issues. Bruhn (1991) defined ethics broadly when he stated:

> Ethics is the study of what constitutes good and bad human conduct, including related actions and values. Ethics is concerned with questions of right and wrong, of duty and obligation, of moral responsibility.

The most basic ethical requirement in all helping relationships is *Do no harm*. This must be the first criterion for decision making when ethical issues come before us, and the first criterion by which all acts are judged. Only then can we judge whether acts have positive value. The Sociological Practice Association (SPA) (1987), in publishing ethical standards, called for "competence, objectivity, and concern for the best interests of clients, colleagues, and society in general." One important set of principles involves professional expertise and accountability. The ethical requirement is, first, to have and maintain professional competence—*not* to go beyond the scope of professional competence. This means not to accept cases beyond our scope and/or to develop collaborative arrangements with other professionals as referral sources, or to contribute expertise when needed in a specific case.

As ethical professionals, clinical sociologists must be accountable, they must accept legal and moral responsibility for their actions. Accountability also indicates willingness to conduct careful process and outcome measures of interventions to assess the quality of work.

A second major ethical requirement is to respect people's autonomy and their right of self-determination. This means that clinicians should refrain from imposing their values on clients, that they should affirm the clients' dignity and their ability to make decisions and choices. This implies a specific type of relationship between clinician and client, a partnership among equals. As Hepworth and Larsen (1986:65) stated:

> The type of relationship that affirms self determination and fosters growth, is a partnership wherein practitioner and client ... are joined in a mutual effort to search for solutions to problems....

Partnership implies that clients have access to all pertinent information, that they participate in decision making at all stages of the intervention process, and that they give their informed consent to all steps taken. It also implies that clinicians approach clients with an attitude of respect for their uniqueness, and with cultural sensitivity. Thus, the Sociological Practice Association (SPA) requires that "the clinical or applied sociologist is committed to avoid any act or suggestion that would support or advance racism, sexism, or ageism."

Ethical practice also implies that clinicians respect the welfare of students, clients, and research subjects. Clinicians must avoid any action that may appear to be exploitative or a violation of trust. Occasionally revealed incidents of sex between practitioners and clients constitute one example of such exploitation. More commonly, clinicians become exploitative when they use clients to meet their own ends, whatever these might be. Ethical practice requires respect for all clients' legal and civil rights.

Confidentiality is another major aspect of ethical practice. According to the code of the SPA:

> Safeguarding information about an individual or group that has been obtained by the clinical or applied sociologist in the course of teaching, practice, or research is a primary obligation of the sociologist.

Readers should note the phrasing—*primary obligation*. Violations of clients' confidentiality are violations of trust. All possible care should be taken to protect clients' confidentiality. Security must be maintained on all notes and other data, provision made for adequate privacy during all conversations, interviews, etc., and care taken not to discuss cases in inappropriate settings. Confidentiality also implies withholding clients' identities, and even the fact that they are clients.

It may be useful or necessary for professionals to share information with other professionals or organizations. Ethical (and sometimes legal) practice requires that such information be exchanged only with clients' informed consent, including written permission from the client for such information exchange.

Confidentiality, while extremely important, is not absolute. When clients may be a danger to themselves or others, it is the clinician's duty to take preventive measures including the violation of confidentiality. Hepworth and Larsen (1986: 69) advised:

> ... the client's right to confidentiality may be less compelling than the rights of other people who could be severely harmed or damaged by actions planned by the client and confided to the practitioner. For example, if a client plans to commit kidnapping, injury, or murder, the practitioner is obligated to disclose these intentions to the intended victim and to law enforcement officials so that timely preventative action can be implemented.

Courts may subpoena clinicians to testify, and to provide material from records. Ethical practice requires clinicians to reassure clients that confidentiality will be maintained, but to clarify the limits of confidentiality.

An issue that should be addressed in one of the early sessions with a client is the matter of fees. Clients should be told what the charges are, the expected timeline for paying these charges, and the estimated total time and cost of the services. If this discussion is held at the onset of the encounter, it should decrease the likelihood that the client will terminate the services because of cost. If the client states that the services cannot be afforded, the clinician should be prepared to refer the client to other competent helpers.

Clinicians should be fully cognizant of their limitations and biases, be willing to discuss these with the client, and refer the client at any time it is perceived that expected outcomes are being compromised. A possible alternative to referral, is consultation with other clinicians. Sometimes, clinicians are reluctant to consult with peers, fearing that this appears to be an admission of a lack of professional knowledge. Problems often are complex, and may span the competencies of several disciplines. Being up front with the client about soliciting other opinions should elicit more respect and confidence from the client than trying to mislead the client into believing that one is "the" expert. In ethical practice, both client and clinician are themselves, and not playing games.

Summary

In this chapter, we have tried to provide a broad overview of the subdiscipline of clinical sociology. It is the application of sociology— the sociological perspective, theories, methods, and research findings—to active intervention. Clinical sociologists are active change agents. Collectively, clinical sociologists conduct their work at all points on the social spectrum, from macrosocial to microsocial, while maintaining an awareness of the interplay of levels. As clinical sociologists apply their skills and knowledge to unique cases, they are guided by the scientific methods of sociology through an intervention process. The intervention process consists of four stages—assessment, program planning, program implementation, and program evaluation—which are seen, not as a linear progression, but as functional activities. In the process, clinicians work to develop and maintain a partnership with clients, in which they demonstrate respect for clients' uniqueness, ability to solve problems, and to make decisions. Work with clients is guided by standards of ethical practice that require all practitioners to protect and act in the clients' best interests.

References

Abbott, M.L., & Blake, G.F. (1988). An intervention model for homeless youth. *Clinical Sociology Review*, *6*, 148–158.

Ackerman, N.W. (1958). *The psychodynamics of family life*. New York: Basic Books.

Anderson, C., & Rouse, L. (1988). Intervention in cases of woman battering: An application of interactionism and critical theory. *Clinical Sociology Review*, *6*, 134–147.

Babbie, E. (1983). *The practice of social research*, 3rd ed. Belmont, CA: Wadsworth.

Berger, P.L., & Luckmann, T. (1966). *The social construction of reality, a treatise in the sociology of knowledge*. Garden City, NY: Doubleday.

Billson, J.M., & Disch, E. (1991). Empowering women: A clinical sociology model for working with women in groups. In H.M. Rebach & J.G. Bruhn, (Eds.), *The handbook of clinical sociology* (pp. 323–344). New York: Plenum.

Brabant, S. (1993). Successful facilitation of a children's support group when conditions are less than optimal. *Clinical Sociology Review*, *11*, 49–60.

Bruhn, J.G. (1987). The clinical sociologist as a health broker. *Clinical Sociology Review*, *5*, 168–180.

Bruhn, J.G. (1991). Ethics in clinical sociology. In H.M. Rebach & J.G. Bruhn (Eds.), *The handbook of clinical sociology* (pp. 99–123). New York: Plenum.

Bryan, M.E. (1992). Intervention among children of substance abusers and school success. *Clinical Sociology Review*, *10*, 118–125.

Bulmer, M. (1984). *The Chicago school of sociology*. Chicago: University of Chicago Press.

Church, N. (1991). The effects of social change on clinical practice. In H.M. Rebach & J.G. Bruhn (Eds.), *The handbook of clinical sociology* (pp. 125–142). New York: Plenum.

Clark, E.J. (1990). Contemporary clinical sociology: Definitions and directions. *Clinical Sociology Review*, *8*, 100–115.

Collins, R. (1988). *Theoretical sociology*. San Diego, CA: Harcourt Brace Jovanovich.

Conger, R.D., Lorenz, F.O., Elder, G.H. Jr., Simons, R.L. & Ge, X. (1993). Husband and wife differences in response to undesirable life events. *Journal of Health and Social Behavior*, *34*, 71–88.

Cooley, C.H. (1924). *Social organization*. New York: Scribner.

Cox, H. (1994). Presidential Address, Society for Applied Sociology: The sociologist as activist. *The Journal of Applied Sociology*, *10*, 1–24.

Cuthbertson-Johnson, B.A., & Gagan, R.J. (1993). The subjective dimension of a bipolar family education/support group: A sociology of emotions approach. *Clinical Sociology Review*, *11*, 61–75.

Dunham, H.W. (1964). Anomie and mental disorder. In M.B. Clinard (Ed.), *Anomie and deviant behavior* (pp. 128–157). New York: Free Press.

Dunham, H.W. (1982). Clinical Sociology: Its nature and function. *Clinical Sociology Review, 1*, 23–33.

Durkheim, E. (1966). *The rules of sociological method.* (G.E.G. Catlin, Ed.). New York: Free Press. (Original published in 1893)

Eisenstadt, S.N., & Helle, H.J. (Eds.) (1985). *Macro-sociological theory: Perspectives on sociology theory,* Vol. 1. Newbury Park, CA: Sage.

Fein, M. (1988). Resocialization: A neglected paradigm. *Clinical Sociology Review, 6*, 88–100.

Fein, M. (1990a). *Role change: A resocialization perspective.* New York: Praeger.

Fein, M. (1990b). Dysfunctional role maintenance. *Clinical Sociology Review, 8*, 87–99.

Fein, M. (1991). Personality disorders or role negotiation problems? *Clinical Sociology Review, 9*, 37–47.

Ferguson, T., Ferguson, J., & Luby, E.D. (1992). Integrating psychodynamic, cognitive, and interpersonal therapies: A biophysical role theory. *Clinical Sociology Review, 10*, 37–49.

Freedman, J.A. (1982). Clinical sociology: What it is and what it isn't—a perspective. *Clinical Sociology Review, 1*, 34–49.

Fritz, J.M. (1991). The emergence of American clinical sociology. In H.M. Rebach & J.G. Bruhn (Eds.), *The handbook of clinical sociology* (pp. 17–30). New York: Plenum.

Gardner, H. (Ed.) (1979). *Clinical Sociology Newsletter, 1*, 2.

Glass, J.E. (1992). An alternative understanding of the cognitive, emotional, and behavioral characteristics of individuals raised in alcoholic homes: A clinical theory of the individual. *Clinical Sociology Review, 10*, 107–117.

Gouldner, A. (1956). Explorations in applied social science. *Social Problems, 3*, 169–181.

Gordon, L. (1986). The sociological expert witness in a case of collective interracial violence. *Clinical Sociology Review, 4*, 107–122.

Hall, C.M. (1991). Clinical sociology and religion. *Clinical Sociology Review, 9*, 48–58.

Hepworth, D.H. & Larsen, J.A. (1986). *Direct social work practice: Theory and skills.* Chicago: Dorsey.

Hochschild, A.R. (1979). Emotion work, feeling rules, and social structure; *American Journal of Sociology, 85*, 551–575.

Huber, J. (Ed.) (1991) *Macro–micro linkages in sociology.* Newbury Park, CA: Sage.

Johnson, D.P. (1986). Using sociology to analyze human and organizational problems: A humanist perspective to link theory and practice. *Clinical Sociology Review, 4*, 57–70.

Kammeyer, K.C.W., Ritzer, G., & Yetman, N.R. (1994). *Sociology: Experiencing changing societies* (6th ed.). Boston: Allyn & Bacon.

Knorr-Cetina, K., & Cicourel, A.V. (Eds.) (1981). *Advances in social theory and methodology: Toward an integration of micro- and macro-sociologies.* Boston: Routledge & Kegan Paul.

Lee, A. McC. (1955). The clinical study of society. *American Sociological Review, 20*, 648–653.

Lennard, H.L., & Bernstein, A. (1969). *Patterns in human interaction* San Francisco: Jossey-Bass.

Lorion, R.P., & Ross, J.G. (1992). Programs for change: A realistic look at the nation's potential for preventing substance involvement among high-risk youth. *Journal of Community Psychology,* OSAP Special Issue, 3–9.

Lundman, R.J. (1993). *Prevention and control of juvenile delinquency.* New York: Oxford University Press.

May, D., & Kelly, M.P. (1992). Understanding paranoia: Towards a social explanation. *Clinical Sociology Review, 10*, 50–70.

Mead, G.H. (1934). *Mind, self and society.* Chicago: University of Chicago Press.

Miller, J.S. (1985). Sociologists as mediators: Clinical sociology in action. *Clinical Sociology Review, 3*, 158–164.

Mills, C.W. (1959). *The sociological imagination*. New York: Oxford University Press.

McDonagh, E.C. (1944). An approach to clinical sociology. *Sociology and Social Research, 27*, 376–383. (Reprinted in *Clinical Sociology Review*, 1986, *4*, 14–18).

Newman, B.M., & Newman, P.R. (1984). *Development through life: A psychosocial approach.* Homewood, IL: Dorsey.

Rebach, H.M., & Bruhn, J.G., (Eds.) (1991a). *The handbook of clinical sociology*. New York: Plenum.

Rebach, H.M., & Bruhn, J.G., (Eds.) (1991b). Clinical sociology: Defining the field. In H.M. Rebach & J.G. Bruhn, (Eds.). *The handbook of clinical sociology* (pp. 3–15) New York: Plenum.

Rebach, H.M., & Johnstone, M. (1992, May). *Group treatment for the dually diagnosed.* Paper presented at the 1991 Maryland Conference on Social Work Practice in Public Mental Health, Marriotsville, Maryland.

Rosenberg, M. (1990). The self concept: Social product and social force. In M. Rosenberg & R.H. Turner (Eds.). *Social psychology: Sociological perspectives.* New Brunswick, NJ: Transaction.

Shibutani, T. (1961). *Society and personality*. Englewood Cliffs, NJ: Prentice-Hall.

Small, A. (1896). Scholarship and social agitation. *The American Journal of Sociology, 1*, 564–582. (Reprinted in *Clinical Sociology Review*, 1985, *3*, 25–38.)

Sociological Practice Association (1987). *Ethical standards of sociological practitioners.*

Stanley-Stevens, L., Yeatts, D.E., & Thibodeaux, M. (1993). The transfer of work experiences into family life: An introductory study of workers in self-managed teams. *Clinical Sociology Review, 11*, 76–92.

Stephenson, K. (1994). Diversity: A managerial paradox. *Clinical Sociology Review, 12*, 175–188.

Stoecker, R., & Beckwith, D. (1992). Advancing Toledo's neighborhood movement through participatory research: Integrating activist and academic approaches. *Clinical Sociology Review, 10*, 198–213.

Straus, R. (1982). Clinical sociology on the one-to-one level: A social behavioral approach to counseling. *Clinical Sociology Review, 1*, 59–74.

Straus, R. (1984). Changing the definition of the situation: Toward a theory of sociological intervention. *Clinical Sociology Review, 2*, 51–63.

Swan, L.A. (1984). *The practice of clinical sociology and sociotherapy.* Cambridge, MA: Schenkman.

Swan, L.A. (1988). Grounded encounter therapy: Its characteristics and process. *Clinical Sociology Review, 6*, 76–87.

Thoresen, J.H. (1993). The sociologist as expert witness. *Clinical Sociology Review, 11*, 109–122.

Thornton, W.E., & Voigt, L. (1988). The roles and ethics of the practicing criminologist. *Clinical Sociology Review, 6*, 113–133.

Van der Merwe, H.W., & Odendaal, A. (1991). Constructive conflict intervention in South Africa: Some lessons. *Clinical Sociology Review, 9*, 71–86.

Volkart, E.H. (Ed.) (1951). *Social behavior and personality.* New York: Social Science Research Council.

Watts, W.D. (1989). Reducing adolescent drug abuse: Sociological strategies for community practice. *Clinical Sociology Review, 7*, 152–171.

Watts, W.D., & Wright, N.B. (1991). Drug abuse prevention: Clinical sociology in the community. In H.M. Rebach & J.G. Bruhn (Eds.), *The handbook of clinical sociology* (pp. 363–381). New York: Plenum.

Watzlawick, P., Beavin, J.H., & Jackson, D.D. (1967). *Pragmatics of human communication.* New York: Norton.

Watzlawick, P. (1990). *Munchhausen's pigtail or psychotherapy and "reality."* New York: Norton.

Wirth, L. (1931). Sociology and clinical procedure. *The American Journal of Sociology, 37*, 49–66. (Reprinted in *Clinical Sociology Review*, (1982) *1*, 7–22.)

Wolf, S., & Bruhn, J.G. (1992). *The power of clan: The influence of human relationships on heart disease.* New Brunswick, NJ: Transaction.

Recommended Readings

Anderson, C., & Rouse, L. (1988). Intervention in cases of woman battering: An application of interactionism and critical theory. *Clinical Sociology Review*, *6*, 134–147.

This excellent article illustrates the application of sociology to the real clinical problems of domestic violence. The authors emphasize social psychological and sociocultural causes rather than psychological causes. More important, the authors demonstrate the fit between theory and practice. In particular, they show the compatibility of symbolic interaction and critical theory and their combined application to understanding and intervention in cases of domestic violence.

Fein, M. (1990). *Role Change: A Resocialization Perspective*. New York: Praeger.

The author described clinical work with individuals that locates individual problems as problems with social roles and relationships. Role problems may arise from primary socialization or roles may become dysfunctional over time. The intervention process involves social support, socialization, and resocialization with the emphasis on resocialization. However, the author noted that resocialization may be difficult for clients and identified factors may act as barriers to change. The author also described the skills and qualities needed by clinicians to be effective. This book has a strong base in sociological theory and illustrates the relationship between theory and practice.

Johnson, D.P. (1986). Using sociology to analyze human and organizational problems: A humanist perspective to link theory and practice. *Clinical Sociology Review*, *4*, 57–70.

This article represents a basic statement of the relationship between sociological theory and sociological practice. The author stated that theories provide models of social behavior that help identify and solve human and organizational problems. Theories indicate what are the typical and important patterns in social life. Four theoretical traditions were reviewed: *Symbolic interaction*, *functionalism (systems theory)*, *exchange theory*, and *critical theory*. For each, the author gave a brief overview of the theory, suggested the kinds of problems that they might apply to, and how they might lead to developing steps to problem solution.

Stoecker, R., & Beckwith, D. (1992). Advancing Toledo's neighborhood movement through participatory research: Integrating activist and academic approaches. *Clinical Sociology Review*, *10*, 198–213.

This article describes community organization work by clinical sociologists and has two important additional features. First, the authors, one an academic researcher, the other a community organizer, discuss the integration of their roles as researchers and activists and how they were able to enact these roles to bring about social change. Second, the article describes a powerful approach called Participatory Action Research (PAR). As applied in this report, PAR involved community members in all phases of community development. Community members are allowed control via PAR over all phases of research, and structural change is emphasized.

Watzlawick, P. (1990). *Munchhausen's Pigtail or Psychotherapy and "Reality."* New York: Norton.

Watzlawick takes issue with conventional psychotherapy oriented to examining an individual's past and changing the individual. He suggested that personal problems are rooted in troubled relationships and that intervention should focus on troubled relationships. The author suggested observation and analysis of interaction patterns in relationships and the way interactants negotiate and construct their joint reality. Change involves assisting actors in redefining situations, not in terms of what is "true," but in pragmatic terms—what works for the individuals involved.

Approaches to Problem Solving

Introduction

Problem solving is the essence of professional practice. Professionals often are unable to explain how they approach problem solving or how they learned problem solving. Many professionals solve problems without being able to describe what they do; therefore, they cannot teach problem solving to others. Problem solving requires more than acquired skills and techniques; it requires a frame of reference, acquired through experience, and a style for dealing with situations for which there are no well-established responses. Schön (1983) noted that it is interesting that professionals who are unique, creative problem solvers often are considered less rigorous than others who more strictly frame a problem and its solution. Personal style and "know-how" contribute to spontaneity in problem solving. Schön challenged professionals to be more reflective when "setting" or "framing" a problem and considering solutions, and not to allow themselves to be locked into technical expertise.

Problems seem to call for solutions. Usually, clients consult with and pay experts to solve their problems. Too often, professionals, especially beginners, react to the urgency projected by clients and prematurely offer solutions. There are dangers in this approach. To ignore study of the problem and consideration of the various alternative strategies and their consequences may result in ill-conceived solutions that create more problems than they solve. In addition, it usually is more important for clients to develop problem-solving skills than to get past particular problems. Providing a solution to a specific problem may be helpful in the short run. Teaching the client problem solving strategies will have lasting effects.

Problems which clients seek professional help for usually are reactive. They deal with situations that have created disruptions in a client's way of life. Many problems can be prevented. Perhaps one of the greatest challenges to clinical sociologists is to change clients' perceptions and expectations about solutions to problems by teaching them problem-solving strategies and encouraging them to take greater responsibility for solving their own problems. This is consistent with a view of clients as autonomous and capable of decision making.

The purpose of this chapter is to explore approaches to problem solving that might be useful to clinical sociologists. First, we will discuss problem solving in general, then we will discuss four approaches to problem solving: the social systems approach, the ecological approach, the life cycle approach, and the clinical approach.

Definition of Problem Solving

Problem solving is a process of thinking and acting that involves changing a person, social entity, or social situation from an undesired to a desired state (Gelfand, 1988). In the process of problem definition, a situation and its boundaries frame the context of the problem. Options for solutions are guided by the way problems have been defined, which, in turn, is influenced by the practitioner's experience and theoretical approach. Schön (1983) wrote that professional practice has as much to do with finding a problem as with solving it. Theory helps frame the practitioner's role and provides the practitioner with a repertoire of facts and tasks and a larger social context for tackling a problem. As Schön noted, only when the objectives are fixed and clear is there a problem that can be solved.

The Creative Problem Solver

When a practitioner adopts a particular theory from which to work, a potential drawback may be that all problems are seen from the same theoretical perspective. For this reason, several authors have stressed the importance of creativity in problem solving. Gelfand (1988) suggested producing a number of alternative problem definitions, developing a broad definition of the problem, and breaking the problem into workable components. Alternative solutions can then be generated using strategies that can encompass more than one theoretical approach. Flood and Jackson (1991) suggested that the problem solver examine the interactions among all elements that make up a situation and consider how the elements relate and the effects of their relationship. They pointed out that most problems involve other people and organizations and therefore are problems of "open systems," which are continually affected by, and affect other systems. Thus, careful definition of the boundaries of a problem is essential before solutions can be explored (Wilber, 1979).

Problem solvers also need to be aware of change, uncertainty, and uniqueness in defining problems and in applying experience in developing strategies for solutions. Each case is unique and exists in its own time and place. What may have worked once, may not be applicable to a situation that seems similar to previous cases.

The Problem-Solving Process

As we noted in Chapter 1, the first step in problem solving is assessment, the accurate determination of the problems and needs of the clients. The second step is the determination of the objectives of the intervention and the formulation of a plan for reaching them. The third step is the implementation of the intervention strategies designed to resolve the problem and meet the need. The last step is the evaluation of the intervention to determine if the objectives have been met.

Problem solving does not follow a smooth step-by-step progression. It is a process in which the steps often merge, blend, overlap, or fold back on themselves. The process is circular rather than linear. Additional complexity occurs because clients' needs do not exist separately. As primary needs are presented, other, equally important and related needs also may have to be addressed. Attention to one problem may solve only that problem. Other problems may continue to exist. Indeed, the solution to one problem may create or exacerbate others. Thus, problem solving should not be viewed as an end in itself. The solution of most of the problems brought to clinicians does not promise clear sailing and rosy futures. Social life is more complex than that; the amelioration of a particular problem situation has far-reaching implications as it interacts with other facets of the client's situation.

A variety of perspectives can be used in problem solving. We turn now to a consideration of some of them.

The Social Systems Approach

A systems approach is a framework, a way of looking at social structures, rather than a specific theory of human behavior (Chess & Norlin, 1988). Historically, sociologists have had differing opinions about which level should receive primary attention. Macrosociologists view the total society as the prime focus, and the behavior of the system and its components as a product of the total system's needs and goals. In other words, the whole determines the actions of its parts (Lenski & Lenski, 1987). At the opposite pole are social behaviorists who advocate focusing on the individual. In their view, the acts of individuals cluster into patterns, and the social system is constructed from these patterns; that is, the whole is the sum of its parts. The systems approach takes the former view.

Systems Concepts

The most basic concept is *system*. Hall and Fagen (1956) defined *system* as: "a set of objects together with relationships between the objects and between their attributes." Systems exist within environments, which allows us to characterize systems either as open or as closed. *Open systems* interact with their environments— they exchange material, energy, and information with their environments; *closed systems* do not. For our purposes, we will consider only open systems.

Open systems have the properties of *wholeness* (Hall & Fagen, 1956) and *nonsummativity*. Wholeness refers to the property that, "Every part of a system is so related to its fellow parts that a change in one part will cause a change in all of them and in the total system" (Watzlawick, Beavin, & Jackson, 1967:123). That is, the parts of a system are functionally interrelated and the system functions as a coherent whole, not as individual parts. As such, the system is more than the sum of its parts—it is nonsummative—and cannot be understood by even the most careful and thorough analysis of its individual parts. The system must be understood as a whole in terms of its organization. For elements to function as a system, they must be connected and in communication with each other. They stand in relationship with each other and exchange activity, information, and material. The key to understanding systems is to understand the nature of the interaction and relationship among the parts and how they function.

Dubos (1968) pointed out that it is tempting to dissect a system in the belief that one can learn about it by examining its individual parts. Yet, he noted, most of the pressing problems of humanity involve situations in which systems must be studied as wholes in all the complexity of their interactions. We believe that both the system as a whole and its individual parts must be taken into consideration.

Open systems also have the property of *equifinality* with regard to system outcomes. This concept refers to independence from initial states. It means that different conditions can bring about similar outcomes, and that similar initial conditions can produce different outcomes. The process of the system—the interaction of the parts—is the most important consideration in understanding the nature of the system at any given point in time. Open systems also can be characterized as having a *hierarchical order*. Within an open system, it may be useful to notice subsystems, subsubsystems, etc.

Open systems are characterized by *boundaries*—which demarcate the system from its environment. Open systems also are characterized by their attempts to maintain stability or *steady state* through *adaptation*. Adaptation refers to the system's "ability to react to the environment in a way favorable to continued operation of the system" (Hall & Fagen, 1956). The condition of steady state, or stability, refers to a system's continued existence or functioning. Systems never exist in a condition of complete change or complete stability. Steady state occurs when the whole system is in balance. It is a way of describing the health of a system. The system in a steady state is changing and acting, but maintaining a viable relationship with its components and its environment. Its functioning is adequate to ensure its continued existence (Anderson & Carter, 1990). Open systems are systems with *feedback*; that is, the output of a system is fed back into the system to affect subsequent output.

Open systems receive inputs of information, material, and activity, which are processed by the system for the maintenance of a steady state, and act on the environment with an output of information, material, and activity. The effects of the output are fed back as part of subsequent input. Resources that meet the needs of the system's functioning can be considered one type of input. Outputs reflect activities that assure a continued flow of these resources. Another type of input, of things that threaten the stability of the system, can be considered potentially harmful. These inputs must be processed by the system and must be met with an output of adaptive responses that act on the environment to avert the threat. If the threat is not rebuffed effectively, the stability of the system may be disrupted and the system fails to survive.

Social Systems

Social systems can be understood in terms of these systems concepts. And, social systems can be conceptualized as existing at all levels, from microsocial to macrosocial. Depending on the level of analysis, a social system's elements may be persons, facilities, organizations, communities, social institutions, societies, or cultures. At whatever level, elements interact and mutually influence each other's behavior. The elements are functionally interrelated, which means that the action of any element affects all the others and the system as a whole. At the macro-sociological level, for example, changes in political structures affect activity in economic structures, which also affect broad changes and adaptations throughout other major social institutions and throughout the society as a whole. Weber's (1992) classic analysis of the effects of changes brought on by the rise of Protestantism reflects the functional interrelationships of macrosocial structures. This religious change could be thought of as having created a certain imbalance that stimulated adaptations by other social institutions resulting in large scale qualitative changes throughout society.

Action (energy) and the organization of action are the prime characteristics of social systems. All social systems have an exchange of activity among persons or groups of persons. The interplay of people in a marriage, in a family, or on the job involves the sending and receiving of activity and/or information, both within a system and between the system and its environment. A system's capacity to act is its power to maintain itself and change (adapt). Its energy derives from many sources including the physical stamina of its members, common values and loyalties among the members, and external resources. When this energy reinforces and strengthens a system, it is said to be synergistic; that is, individuals and the group or organization interact smoothly and efficiently to reach common goals (Anderson & Carter, 1990).

A viable system must not only have energy, the energy must be organized to fulfill the goals of the system. Organization refers to the ordering of the energies of the component parts that result in a whole. Systems differ in the degree of formality of their organization. Disorganization results when a system is not sufficiently organized and its components do not relate or interact efficiently enough to sustain the system's energy.

Consider a family as a social system. Figure 2.1 represents the system graphically. A family exists in a social as well as in a physical environment. The family is an open system in that it obtains inputs of information, material, and activity (energy) from the environment for the maintenance of its stability. These resources are used (processed) within the family, and members engage in activity (output to the environment) to try to maintain the flow of resources. The behavior of every individual within the family is related to and dependent upon the behavior of all the others. Each member influences and is influenced by the others. Changes

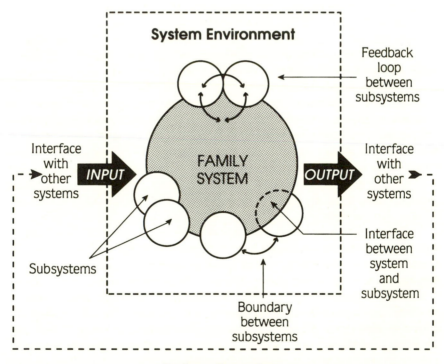

System Boundary

Figure 2.1. The Social System Model

in any one member or in the relationship between any two members, bring about changes in all the others and in the family as a whole.

A family is also composed of subsystems. The relationship between the parents is one such subsystem, the relationship among the siblings is another. The relationship of the parents to one of the children, is yet another subsystem, and still another is, for example, the relationship between the father and one of the children. As Martin and O'Connor (1989) observed, a family of five can have 25 subsystems in addition to the core system of all five members. The number of subsystems increases geometrically with family size. If family arrangements are the problem, the clinician needs to understand the family system in its totality as well as its subsystems.

> The analysis of a family is not the sum of the analysis of its individual members. There are characteristics of the system, that is, interactional patterns, that transcend the qualities of individual members.... (Watzlawick et al., 1967:134)

> Inputs (actions of family members or of the environment) introduced into the family system are acted upon and modified by the system. The nature of the system and its feedback mechanisms must be considered as well as the nature of the input (equifinality). Some families can absorb large reverses and even turn them into rallying points; others seem unable to handle the most insignificant crises. (Watzlawick et al., 1967:139)

Families also attempt to cope with threats to the stability of the family group. Members may be bound together by strong ties, both instrumental and socioemotional. Stability refers to the maintenance of the family unit, its movement toward goals, and its continuing to meet the needs of individual family members as well as the family system as a whole. A stressful life event, such as the death or departure of a parent, or the severe illness of one of the income earners, calls forth attempts to adapt and to maintain the boundaries of the family. These attempts may have varying degrees of success or may result in chaos and dissolution.

Application of the Systems Approach

Systemic thinking refers to the process of using the mind to recognize, conceive, and form the coherence of wholeness; to seek the complete picture. The system consists of elements capable of being understood, which cohere to one another. Systemic thinking seeks coherence (Anderson & Carter, 1990).

The systems framework avoids the usual linear cause–effect approach to problem identification by calling attention to the interplay of many factors and system levels as well as to feedback loops. Phenomena are labeled "problems" when they threaten the stable functioning of the social system. Thus, solutions may involve changing actions, the nature of relationships, perceptions, beliefs, norms, or expectations. The systems approach also calls attention to the fact that solutions create new problems, calling for renewed efforts at adaptation, and that stability maintaining mechanisms may exist that will work against change and for maintenance of the present system, no matter how maladaptive it may seem to the clinician. This is expected of a human system, which is characterized by two general assumptions: (1) the state or conditions of a system, at any one point in time, is a function of the interaction between it and the environment in which it operates; and (2) change and conflict are always evident in a system (Longres, 1990).

The systems approach offers general principles applicable to problem solving in social systems. The first principle is to identify, accurately, the system of interest. Thus, we define the concept *focal system*, which is simply the system of interest or study, the one the investigator is focusing on. Depending on the problems, the system of interest may be a department within a county agency, in which case, relations among workers and between workers and the supervisor are subsystems. The environment includes other departments that interact with this department at the same system level. Agency management may be a suprasystem, a system level above. County government and its policy and fiscal apparatus may be considered the next step above. The public to be served is also part of the environment. Inputs to this system may be support services from other departments, policy guidelines from management, resources, legitimization and mission statements from county government, or demands from the public for services. Outputs may include the services, reports, and accountability.

On the other hand, the entire agency may be the focal system, in which case, the various departments, as elements of the system, are subsystems. Or, the problem may dictate that the county itself is the focal system, with the environment represented by the rest of the state, including other counties, state government, and perhaps other state and federal agencies. In this case, county government, agencies, and residents are subsystems.

The focal system will probably be defined by the clients. Assessment should identify the condition in the focal system that is dysfunctional or disruptive to the functioning of the system. In problem analysis, it is important to consider whether the needs and problems of client systems are a product of the transactions between them and the individuals and groups that make up the environment of the system. It is also important to identify the factors in the system, as well as in the environment that contribute to the dysfunction. Consideration needs to be given to the identification of resources available within and outside the system that will help to solve the problem.

A second principle is to avoid confusion of levels. Careful definition of the focal system helps avoid confusion of levels. That is, it helps avoid dealing with system, suprasystem, and subsystem problems as though all the problems were of the same class and at the same level of complexity. The confusion of levels may result in a misidentification of the problem and direct attention away from the most appropriate locus of intervention.

Third, systems thinking directs us away from simple linear thinking and helps us to look for complex interrelationships and processes; this includes feedback loops. For example, while rigid authoritarian rules may be a response to rule breaking, they also may cause it. Deviance from the rules may lead to vigorous enforcement, which in turn may lead to an acceleration of deviance, further increasing enforcement. The two may stand in a dialectical relationship. This is not to say that removing authority will solve the problem of rule-breaking; we are calling attention to the interactive, rather than the linear nature of problems. The clinician, as the outside observer, needs to recognize and perhaps address the nonlinear aspect. Watzlawick et al. (1967:54) pointed out that what is cause and what is effect depends on the "punctuation of the sequence of events." Actors on different sides of an issue are likely to punctuate events from their own perspectives. Workers may find management harsh and intractable, whereas management finds workers stubborn and unyielding. For the clinician, system thinking points to the relationship, the interaction—how the acts of each element prompt the subsequent interaction within the system.

Fourth, the systems approach calls attention to the fact that social systems tend toward a steady state, even though it may be dysfunctional for some or all parts of the system. The system may have adapted to the disruptive element and developed a stable pattern of functioning that includes it. For example, families with an alcoholic member often develop stable patterns that take the member's alcoholism into account. They use modifications in role relationships and role performance to adapt to the disruptive effects of the alcoholic member.

The tendency to steady state of social systems also calls attention to the assessment of systems' needs and how they are or are not met. Parsons' (1951) formulation of the basic functions, or "functional requisites," that must be fulfilled in any social system is useful here. His four function model included:

1. Latent pattern maintenance—the tendency of social systems to have and to maintain existing patterns and boundaries.
2. Integration—the tendency of social systems to try to keep their parts together.
3. Goal attainment—the tendency of social systems to define and attempt to achieve certain objectives.
4. Adaptation—the tendency of social systems to change to counter threats to their steady states.

As a clinician assesses a social system, understanding the existing structures and relationships that maintain the pattern of the present system is essential. Many social systems engage in boundary maintenance. The tightness of boundaries helps to define the "we" and "they" and, therefore, helps to control membership, communication, and adaptation to the larger environment. Systems that do not maintain boundaries may be weakly organized and have difficulties dealing with

---

Clinical Focus 2.1

Application of the Social Systems Approach

The social systems approach can be illustrated by a report by Bobo, Gilchrist, Cvetkovich, Trimble, and Schinke, (1988) describing alcohol and drug prevention programming for Native American youth. Substance abuse clearly threatens the stable functioning of Native American communities. Efforts by majority-culture agencies, using approaches that have worked with majority culture youth, have not been particularly successful with Native youth. These authors and others (e.g., Beauvais & LaBoueff, 1985; May, 1982) noted the resistance of Native American communities to programs sponsored or imposed by majority-culture agencies. "Programs lacking indigenous support or poorly reflecting ethnic group values fail to achieve their objectives and offend or alienate service recipients" (Bobo et al., 1988:263). In this case, we can define the community as the focal system. Analysis of the system must include the key subsystems and the network of interacting structures. Thus, Na-tive American youth, the target group, represent one such subsystem. Other components of the system include the schools and school administration, community agencies and their directors, parents of the youth, tribal elders and other "influentials," and, more generally, community members at large.

System assessment led to creation of an advisory board composed exclusively of Native Americans from tribes and agencies within tribes. The members of the advisory board created program materials that were culturally syntonic, sensitive to ethnic norms, and that would be presented by indigenous community people. Following board approval of the program materials, board members began negotiations with potential intervention communities. They identified tribal people with access to youth. These included social service personnel, tribal council members, educators, and tribal elders. These gate-keepers and legiti-

(continued)

---

outsiders. Systems with rigid and carefully maintained boundaries may have histories of conflict with other systems or problems incorporating innovation. Conflict or dysfunction in a system is likely to yield a mixture of positive and negative results.

Finally, the tendency to maintain a steady state may result in forces that resist or work against change. While a particular situation may be dysfunctional for some elements of a social system, and even for the system as a whole, it may be functional for certain other elements. The history of race relations in America is an example. While discrimination and racism have not been functional for the targets or the society, segments of the society have benefited greatly, and thus resist change. In many social systems, the present pattern is beneficial in that it is predictable to the members, who have made their own accommodations. Change

---

Clinical Focus 2.1 (*continued*)

mizers evaluated the program, suggested revisions, and eventually validated the proposed program as culturally acceptable. The next step was for gate-keepers to turn to community people for fine-tuning of the program, and to establish a base of support for the program.

Systemic problems were identified by the authors: "The biggest hurdle between community approval ... and actual implementation was selection of the intervention site. Intratribal politics and agency jurisdictional issues often resulted in intense, time consuming debate about where the classes should take place."

Though the authors did not specifically identify their work as based on a systems approach, their method clearly exemplifies such an approach. Majority-culture agencies and programs, brought in from the outside directly to the target group, failed to recognize the systemic nature of the community. More careful analysis of the system identified key actors and structures including the various stake-holders and legitimizers. The community was seen in its wholeness, and

the authors developed an understanding of the community. They identified the structures and relationships within the community of interest and worked through that network to encourage development and implementation of the intervention program.

For this brief review, we have purposely avoided consideration of the "environment" of the focal system. Systems that affect the focal system directly include local, state, and federal agencies (e.g., education, social services, the U.S. Indian Health Service, etc.) that make policy and regulations, provide funding, and have power to influence events in the community. The environment, more broadly, includes the larger society and majority culture with its economic and political structures that impinge on Native American life. Beauvais and LaBoueff (1985) stated that failure to understand the social, cultural, and geopolitical realities of American Indian life leads to inappropriate and thus ineffective solutions to social problems including alcohol and drug abuse.

---

can threaten their predictive base; though things might not be as good as they could be, the very predictability of the system allows some level of functioning. Change may bring unpredictable results requiring the development of a new accommodation—a step into the unknown. Thus, elements of social systems may resist or work against change.

The Human Ecology Approach

A variation of the systems approach, the *human ecology approach*, makes use of most of the systems concepts. Human ecology derives from three main sources: plant and animal ecology, geography, and studies of the spatial distribution of social phenomena. The word *ecology* was first proposed by the German biologist, Ernst Haeckel, in 1869. Usually, ecology is defined as the study of the relationship of organisms or groups of organisms to their environment. Biologists and sociologists share an interest in the "web of life," in which living things are bound together in a system of interlinked and interdependent lives. The term, *human ecology*, was introduced in 1921 by two sociologists of the Chicago School, Park and Burgess. They were concerned with spatial relationships and the struggle for space, independence, and the division of labor. Of particular interest to social scientists is how an ecological system maintains its wholeness and viability when confronted by forces of change.

A key concept in ecology is the *ecosystem*, which is concerned with the "self nourishing" and "other nourishing" aspects of an interrelationship. When interaction or exchange between internal and external forces is impeded or altered, the stability or viability of the relationship is upset. Thus, social and biological systems attempt to maintain balance, or homeostasis, or a steady state. This is an ideal situation, which may be realized only temporarily when all aspects of the system are in balance. Due to the constant forces of change that act on systems, they usually are attempting to achieve balance between elements within systems as well as between systems and their environments. How social systems respond to insults and return to their "normal" or natural states following intervention—the process of adaptation—is of interest to clinical sociologists involved in problem solving. It is of particular interest to know what "normality" is for a client system, and assist in movement toward or restoration of a steady state when the system becomes dysfunctional or out of balance.

Characteristics of Ecological Systems

The ecological perspective draws attention to the concept of levels of organization as shown in Figure 2.2. The major levels of social organization, individual, group, social institution, community, and society are shown at the left in Figure 2.2. Each of these system levels indicates a different extent of and an increase in complexity. No level can completely explain the phenomena occurring at that level since all levels are interrelated. For example, an individual cannot be fully understood by analysis of the individual alone; individuals are influenced by all other levels. The right side of Figure 2.2 indicates the key components of any system. All of these components are involved in the individual and collective functioning of the various levels of organization.

It is well known that problem solvers or intervention agents usually work at only one level of an organization, such as the individual or group level. Since each level explains only part of a system, responses at a higher level of organization (e.g., community) cannot be predicted from the behavior of a lower level (e.g.,

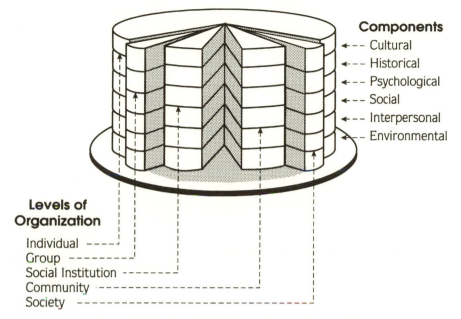

Figure 2.2. The Ecological Model: A "Layer Cake" Analogy

individual). Indeed, while one system level may be selected for intensive study, explanations based on information gathered at only one level cannot be expected to be sufficient.

Sanders (1994) pointed out that, for years, sociologists have attempted to understand gangs as social organizations. He stated that to understand the phenomena of gangs, we need to examine the situation(s) that precipitate gang violence. Gang activities and gang organization mutually define each other. Both exist in the larger context of certain types of communities. This larger context generates a set of experiences that are handled with resources, language, ideologies, and folklore, which are available to the individuals who live there. The gang is grounded in community realities. Instead of seeking to discover the source of delinquent values, we should attempt to determine how common values are grounded in the experience of community members.

Mexican American gangs are best understood in terms of the barrio and the family. The gang members have a highly romanticized definition of themselves in terms of the barrio, which they protect, and the Chicano culture and history of which they see themselves to be an integral part. The organization of the Mexican American gang is an extension of the barrio–family ideal of close ties and caring for those who live in the same neighborhood. The gang's primary orientation is sociability; violence, at any given time, is determined by the leadership. As Sanders noted, since most of the work done by police is reactive, unless gangs act criminally, the options of the police are limited.

Too often, we view the community or individual as the victim and the police as the problem solvers of gang violence. Our perspectives, analyses, and solutions to the problem of gang violence remain largely reactive and are focused on one level of organizational analysis. An ecological approach to understanding and intervention requires analysis of the various levels of social organization to learn how and why gangs attract and retain members, and what conditions are conducive to nonviolent as well as violent behavior. Not all gang behavior is negative. Therefore, it is necessary to examine different levels of gang culture to obtain a complete analysis.

Activities that are defined as problems are conceptualized as upsetting to the balance or steady state of the system. Problem solving, clinical intervention, places emphasis on restoring the balance of the entire system. The task of the problem solver is to learn how a system operates, especially what forces or conditions help it to function in the desired manner, and help to bring about this result. Indeed, it would be difficult to introduce an intervention or change in one segment of an ecological system without affecting all other parts of the system. The challenge is to learn what facilitates and what inhibits balance in the system, with the intention not of eliminating impediments, but of minimizing or controlling them, so that the system can be enhanced and function in the preferred way.

The Person–Environment Fit

Stern (1964) expressed the view that people are not randomly distributed among various environments. Their choice appears to be based on the congruence between personal needs and "environmental press," conditions that impede or facilitate expression of a need and its fulfillment. High levels of performance, satisfaction, and minimal stress indicate a match or "fit" of an individual to the environment. The lack of fit often results in decreased performance, dissatisfaction, and stress. This is not to suggest that everyone in an environment or situation is alike or behaves in the same way, but that most behavior is compatible with the setting in which it occurs. When we see someone acting inappropriately in a setting, we often make inferences about their actions, label them, and limit their freedom.

The processes that mediate the congruence between actions and the environment are of great importance to clinicians and other problem solvers. The study of a setting may provide answers to some critical questions. Why, for instance, do predictable, regular patterns of behavior occur within the boundaries of the setting? What experiences lead people to change their behaviors as they go from one setting to another? How is it possible for people to behave appropriately when they enter unfamiliar settings?

People behave in ways that are congruent with the immediate setting because they have learned to do so through trial and feedback. People are able to get positive reinforcement and avoid punishment by attending to environmental cues that signal what consequences will follow a given act. Observation of models and responses to behavior in specific social settings also helps people to choose or refrain from choosing certain behaviors. The social settings themselves provide clues that help people determine what is and what is not acceptable behavior. For example, behavior that is acceptable at a football game is not acceptable in a classroom.

As people experience a variety of environments and the behaviors that occur in them, they develop preferences for particular responses to particular settings. They may also limit or restrict themselves to settings that best fit their personalities and needs. Behavior congruence is learned. It can readily be observed by watching adults model and teach children how to behave in new environments.

Application of the Ecological Approach

People enter settings that are likely to promote or enhance their goals and try to avoid settings that do not. They obtain satisfaction from the settings they occupy and actively seek to remain in those settings. When disruption occurs, some take steps to eliminate the disruption. People tend to maintain stability and familiarity in those environments that meet their needs. They shape their settings to attract others who fit them. This permits them to provide continuity and to control change in settings that best meet their collective needs. Thus, when assessing a problem and considering options for reaching solutions with clients, it is important to determine the fit between the person and the environment.

Various levels of organization, as shown in Figure 2.2, are flexible social units that change and adapt in response to a dynamic environment. Van Valen (1973) proposed the Red Queen Paradox as a way of conceptualizing the dynamic aspect of adaptation. In Lewis Carroll's *Alice Through the Looking Glass*, the Red Queen tells Alice that, even though they are running at top speed, they should not expect to get anywhere. Inhabitants of Looking Glass Land are obliged to run as fast as they can just to stay where they are. To get anywhere, they would have to run ever so much faster. Social units face the same dilemma. The Red Queen Paradox suggests that social units must not only cope with current change, they must continue to refine their coping skills in order to survive. Thus, adaptation and the maintenance of a steady state involve coping, and not only with present circumstances. Generally, coping skills must be enhanced over time.

Like the systems approach, the ecological approach calls attention to the interplay of system levels. This approach also draws attention to the complex interactions, or systemic relationships, of the component parts of a social system that make it function as a coordinated whole. Ecological problem solving requires consideration of the whole and of its parts.

Several other principles emerge from the ecological approach. Since individuals and social groupings have established histories of adaptation, it is useful to identify the factors that enable adaptation and/or threaten equilibrium. A longitudinal or historical perspective often is valuable in identifying causal relationships to problems. Comparisons between the same or similar levels of social organization in similar environments and time periods also can be enlightening. These comparisons can be useful in identifying anomalies or traces of the past that have lingered despite a changed environment.

The concept of *niche* also can be useful. This place or function that an organism occupies within an ecosystem contributes to its survival and to the total system. The niche defines the role of the individual, group, or other social unit. It indicates what the unit is doing, not just what it is expected to do. Understanding the niche also places the social unit of study in an environmental context. For the clinician, understanding the niche requires an analysis of the conditions under which it exists, its "fit" in the environment, and how it relates to other components of a larger social system. In this way, the problem solver can identify niche isolation, niche overlap, or a fundamental niche.

Milgram (1977) discussed the importance of psychological maps for adaptation to living in large social systems, such as large cities. These maps are not only individual products, but are shaped by social and cultural factors. Psychological maps help to define cognitive and emotional boundaries that are critical in controlling overload. Milgram (1970) listed several responses to system overload that apply equally well to individuals, groups, organizations, and other social groupings.

1. Less time given to each input.
2. Disregard of low priority inputs.
3. Redrawing of boundaries in certain social transactions to shift the burden of the overloaded system to another party in the exchange.
4. Blocking off reception prior to entering a system.
5. Diminishing the intensity of inputs with filtering devices.
6. Creating specialized institutions to absorb inputs that would otherwise overwhelm the individual.

Application of the cognitive map concept to gain insight into the different perceptions held by members of cultural, age, or other subgroups is relevant to many current social issues. In many social systems, the violation of norms is covert and cannot easily be observed. The cognitive map can be applied to families, social institutions, and small communities to verify perceptions, clarify role behavior, identify the limits of social responsibility, and understand the norms of anonymity and noninvolvement. Milgram's approach could be used by the clinician to identify ecological supports. Milgram, Liberty, Toledo, and Wackenhut (1986) note that any social system requires a means of defense to protect its integrity. Clinical sociologists will be faced with many clients whose integrity has been violated or whose identity has been threatened.

The Life Cycle Approach

Introduction and Definition

The course of life unfolds, not as a steady stream, but in stages. Age, time, and circumstances are major considerations in the study of the life cycle. Researchers and theorists may classify time periods differently, may stress different kinds of events, or may believe that one influence is of greater significance than others. Most would agree, however, that over the course of a lifetime, individuals pass through various developmental stages and experience critical events that require coping and adaptation. Viewed another way, the study of the life cycle is the study of development, which begins at birth and ends with death.

Despite the uniqueness of individuals and the different cultures and environments in which they are reared, all persons have several aspects of life in common:

1. They have a limited life span.
2. They have similar biological needs.
3. Their lives go through a cycle of maturation, maturity, decline, and death.
4. They need to learn to adapt and become integrated persons.
5. They are dependent upon others to help provide an environment and society in which to live.
6. They must experience change. (Lidz, 1968)

Indeed, development means change. As lives move from one developmental stage to the next, people need to adapt to the changes, challenges, and demands of each stage, and to integrate the changes. Thus, in adolescence, people are faced, among other things, with rapid changes in their bodies that must be coped with and integrated into the self. Erikson (1963) observed that the way the challenges and demands of one stage are resolved sets the stage for the approach to and resolution of the challenges and demands of the next stage. Each individual meets developmental issues differently, and individuals often repeat the pattern of behavior with which they handle various life crises.

Developmental Theories and Concepts

Several theorists have addressed the life cycle. Freud noted five phases of psychosexual development between birth and maturity. Freud's stages were used,

Clinical Focus 2.2

Application of the Ecological Approach

Drug use and abuse is part of a very complex ecological system. Whether an individual will use or abuse a particular drug will depend on a host of factors, all of which relate to one another: (1) the social and economic system in which one lives; (2) the values and belief system of one's culture relevant to a drug; (3) the nature of the person's relationship to others who do or do not use drugs; (4) the availability of the drug; (5) the development of an attitude toward, or belief in, the effects of a drug; (6) a process for interpreting one's experiences with the drug; (7) the extent to which the person is successful in learning how to use the drug; (8) the interweaving of the drug experience with the individual's total life experiences and the importance of the drug experience relative to other life experiences. These are some of the factors that must be considered in determining the complexity of forces which result in a drug's use or abuse.

Consequently, in approaching an intervention aimed at reducing drug use or abuse it is first necessary to investigate those phenomena which will result in drug use or abuse. Developing conceptual ecological models for viewing phenomena is not difficult. The difficult task is operationalizing the model into specific measurable variables which makes possible the testing of the efficacy of the model (Fisher & Strantz, 1972).

Monroe (1966) points out that the classical ecological model ignores crucial interactional variables which bridge environmental conditions and human behavior. He notes that most studies of drug addiction have focused on either the addict or community and societal factors as they relate to drug use. Monroe says that these factors need to be addressed simultaneously to learn of the multiple "habitats" of drug users and abusers. The key to a decision to stop using drugs is an expectation of a better life without drugs. The primary factor in the decision to stop using drugs is an increase in the expected utility of not using drugs. This is a complex issue that involves the simultaneous consideration of an individual within a sociocultural framework.

in a broader sense, to draw attention to important aspects of child development and parent–child interaction. Harry Stack Sullivan (1953) and Erik Erikson (1963) formulated modifications of Freud's developmental theory. Sullivan postulated the importance of interpersonal transactions between parent and child and the child's development in a social system. Erikson superimposed critical psychosocial tasks upon Freud's psychosexual stages, stating that certain psychosocial tasks needed to be completed at each of eight stages to prepare an individual to move to the next stage. Erikson's formulations emphasized that "Every psychosocial crisis reflects some discrepancy between the developmental competencies of the person at the beginning of the stage and the societal pressures for more effective integrated functioning." Thus, "certain kinds of psychological work and certain kinds of social interaction appear to be necessary in order for a person to continue to grow at each life stage" (Newman & Newman, 1984:34).

Jean Piaget (1952) divided cognitive development into four major periods, which, in turn, were subdivided into stages and substages. He dealt, in detail, with the problems of logic, thought, and philosophy, stressing invention, creativity, and the ability of the person to grow. Piaget stressed the importance of the continuing interaction between the person and the environment. Lawrence Kohlberg (1981) applied Piaget's theory to the development of moral judgments. Kohlberg identified six stages, centering upon increasingly wider social systems in making moral judgments.

Robert Havighurst (1972) proposed a theory of development that was based on the concept of developmental tasks. He believed that development is achieved as a person learns and successfully completes each of a series of specific age-related tasks in six general categories. Abraham Maslow (1968) proposed a theory of basic needs and growth needs. Some individuals are growth motivated while others depend on their environment to meet their needs. Growth motivated individuals can, when their deficit needs are met, achieve greater individuality and self-actualization (Anderson & Carter, 1990; Lidz, 1968; Longres, 1990).

Across these theoretical approaches to the life cycle, two concepts stand out: transitions and individuality (Spierer, 1977). Lidz (1968) identified three major options as one moves along the life course: progression, fixation, or regression. The ability to cope successfully with challenge and change prevents stagnation and regression.

Life Cycle Transitions and Life Patterns

Transitions within a life cycle can be defined in three ways: (1) by time periods within the life span, (2) by role changes, or (3) by event (Spierer, 1977). Age may be an important factor in most transitions, but it is often difficult to find societal consensus about ages at which specific life transitions should occur. The age at first marriage, the age at first job, the age at which puberty begins, and the age for bearing the first child vary from group to group and vary over time. Changes in social norms change expectations about the time at which certain life transitions should occur. Societal responses to teenage marriages and motherhood, and opinions about what should be the legal age for purchasing alcoholic beverages are examples. Chronological age is only one aspect to consider in regard to life transitions. Psychological age, social age, and functional age all influence the ability of an individual to assume new role responsibilities and to cope with new life events. From the clinical point of view, how individuals, groups, or organizations coped with past life transitions, and how their experiences with life transitions compare with the experiences expected by critical others, is of particular interest.

Families also progress through stages of development and experience critical transitions. The most frequently used set of developmental stages of family life was developed by Duvall (1977), who identified eight stages. Success in one stage made for success in later stages. Hill (1970) emphasized three-generational aspects of the life cycle. His view is that each stage constitutes a complex distinction of generational roles among family members.

Most family development research has focused on descriptions of the family within specific stages, but information on the developmental processes still is scarce. Researchers differ in their views regarding whether equilibrium or structural change is more characteristic of families over time. The concept of "ease of role transition," from stage to stage, was created to account for variability among families (Mederer & Hill, 1983). However, the recognition of particular stages allows one to concentrate on the changes and adaptations in role relations, reciprocities, and role conflicts at different periods in a family's development.

Stages of group development also have been recognized by various researchers and theorists (Bales, 1950; Tuckman, 1965; Tuckman & Jensen, 1977). In general, these formulations recognize that newly formed groups have a "natural history." They must complete certain developmental tasks as they move toward accomplishing the work of the group. Developing groups need to arrive at a stable structure of roles and relationships as they progress toward task performance and accomplishment. Knowledge of the various stages, and assessment of the particular stage in which a group is involved, fosters understanding of the challenges facing the group and of their developmental trajectory.

In focusing on life cycle stages, we have noted some common themes. One theme is that development and change must be undergone and integrated in some way. Another is that tasks or challenges are confronted at various stages of development. The accomplishment of these tasks or resolution of these challenges is summative in that coping at one stage is influenced by resolutions arrived at in the previous stage. Underlying these themes is the idea that individuals, families, and groups maintain both continuity and change.

Continuity and Change

Although the main theme of the life cycle approach is change, it emphasizes the continuity of life as well. Individuals and social groupings develop and change over time, face, and attempt to cope with new challenges in each of the various stages of development. Their course is molded by their resolution of the challenges and conflicts at each stage. There is continuity in their movement, and they maintain their identity.

These themes are reflected in the work of Levinson (1978) who used biographical interviews with 40 North American men, aged 35 to 45, to study life periods and transitions. Within each of these periods or "seasons of a man's life"—childhood, adolescence, early, middle, and later adulthood—Levinson noted stable periods of development that overlapped transitional periods. In the transitional periods, the men evaluated their positions in life and explored new options. Levinson's major aim was the study of the midlife crisis. The resolution of this crisis involves struggles in unifying four polarities: young/old, destruction/creation, masculine/feminine, attachment/separation. Continued development is shaped by the way individuals integrate these polarities.

Fiske and Chiriboga (1990) used detailed case studies and quantitative data to trace stability and change in 216 middle-class adults as they negotiated late adolescence, young adulthood, early middle age, and later middle age. Over a period of 12 years, they explored the role of stress on personal functioning, gender differences in aging, and the effects of self-concept, goals, and values in achieving life satisfaction among their sample. Though stress disrupted continuity, it also served as a catalyst for change. The impact of stress was greater when the sources of continuity were weaker. The key sources of continuity tended to begin to wane during the middle and later years.

Continuity was also evident in a 40-year longitudinal study of 142 persons. Maas and Kuypers (1974) found the life-styles and personalities of older people to be remarkably similar to their lifestyles and personalities as young adults. They found considerable evidence for regularity in people's progression from one life stage to the next, as well as evidence that people actively participated in shaping and reacting to their environments. As social and technological change causes dramatic shifts in the way we live, we witness a greater blurring of life periods. For example, there now are grandparents in their early forties and parents in their sixties and seventies who are waiting for their children to marry.

Transitions produce anxiety. Coping strategies are ways to reduce stress and make transitions less painful. David Hamburg observed patients and parents of patients with severe injuries and illnesses, and developed a general model of coping that consists of *tasks* and *strategies* (Spierer, 1977). Tasks are the requirements for adaptation while strategies are the way to accomplish the tasks. Hamburg identified four tasks that persons under stress need to accomplish: contain the distress within tolerable limits, maintain self-esteem, preserve interpersonal relationships, and meet the conditions of a new environment. Multiple strategies are used to accomplish these tasks: form intermediate goals that are achievable, mobilize existing and new sources of social support, and reminisce about happy experiences.

Similarities in coping strategies among patients or their parents led Hamburg to further specify elements of effective coping:

- Regulate the timing and dosage of the acceptance of adversity; recognize that it is a gradual process.
- Deal with one crisis at a time.
- Seek information from various sources on what is needed to adapt.
- Develop realistic expectations for progress.
- Formulate attainable goals.
- Rehearse behavior patterns in safe situations.
- Test behavior in actual situations.
- Evaluate the reaction to this behavior.
- Try more than one approach.
- Make a commitment and prepare a contingency plan as a buffer.

Individuals, families, groups, and organizations can learn tasks and strategies to help them cope more effectively. Social support is one important resource for coping (Bruhn & Philips, 1987; Horman, 1989). Life's transitions are less stressful when they are seen as new options and support is provided by an encouraging network of people.

Application of the Life Cycle Approach

The life cycle approach to problem solving offers several unique perspectives. It shows how and why a client or client system is experiencing problems. It provides both a current and a retrospective view of periods of stability and change, used and needed resources, and their effectiveness in maintaining stability and coping with change. The life cycle approach also can be used to contrast the life cycle under review with others in order to determine appropriateness, timeliness, and the fit of life events and transitions. The life cycle approach allows problem solvers and their clients to take stock of the clients' life situations and explore specific future paths. This approach also can provide clients with the motivation and optimism to assume greater responsibility for events and situations within their control.

The so-called Watermelon Model (Spierer, 1977), shown in Figure 2.3, provides a framework for integrating knowledge about the human life cycle. The horizontal lines represent processes, and the vertical lines represent critical stages. The third dimension, time, indicates the dynamic aspects of the system. A slice of the melon represents a slice of life at a particular point in time. It represents all of the experiences that influenced an individual's life up to that time. This model can be useful to clinicians in problem solving; it provides a holistic way to examine the strengths and weaknesses of an individual, family, or other social unit in a historical perspective. Successes, achievements, and coping styles can be assessed longitudinally to provide the problem solver with factors that may be good predictors of future behavior. The model is flexible, adaptable to different cultures,

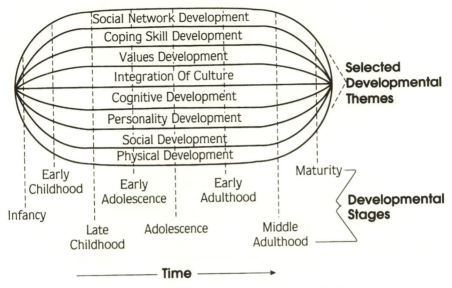

Figure 2.3. The Watermelon Model of the Human Life Cycle

and additive in its perspective. It emphasizes a life history approach, which focuses on patterns that may have contributed to problems.

Organizations also have life cycles, much like individuals. Members are socialized to acquire the elements of the organizational culture. The way in which leaders deal with an organization's crisis creates norms, values, and procedures for members of the organization. Schein (1992) suggested that organizational leaders manage a culture and must develop new insights into the realities of the world and themselves, high levels of motivation to survive learning and change, emotional strength to manage their own and others' anxiety in the face of change, new skills for analyzing change, the ability to involve others and elicit their participation, and the ability to learn a new organizational culture. Schein pointed out that leaders of organizations must become marginal in their own culture if they are to be able to recognize maladaptive behavior. They need to learn new ways of thinking as a prelude to unfreezing and changing their organization. Unfreezing forces can come from the outside or inside by taking advantage of technology, subcultures within the organization, or planned change by leaders. The inability of organizations to adapt to change is at the root of most organizational problems. In Schein's view, in order to prevent stagnation and decline, organizations and their leaders must become perpetual learners.

Clinical Focus 2.3

Application of the Life Cycle Approach

The most common application of the life cycle approach is with individuals. Here, however, we would like to offer an alternative—the application to group work with early adolescents, say of ages 11 to 14. Experience has shown that prevention efforts with this age group are more effective than with older youth. Research evidence also suggests that the later youth become involved in substance use or sexual experimentation, the less likely these are to become problematic. Group work with early adolescents, as an intervention, is based on the developmental aspects of this life cycle stage.

Erikson (1963) originally defined all of adolescence as one life cycle stage. However, Newman and Newman (1984) argued persuasively for considering early and later adolescence as two steps. In early adolescence, youth are experiencing rapid physical changes of growth and sexual maturation accompanied by changes in their body image that affect their self-concept. They experience cog-

nitive changes with the onset of formal operational thinking. This allows them to think about things not thought of before: they can anticipate the consequences of their actions, be aware of different role demands and role conflicts, be objective about problem solving, and have insight into their own cognitive activity.

At the same time, they are going through emotional changes. Their emotions show marked intensity and fluctuation, which can cause anxiety. They can be quite impulsive, which may result in problem behaviors. And they are influenced strongly by their peer group. Understanding their need for membership in the peer group, and the influence of their peers is essential to understanding youth at this age.

Youth, in this stage of their development, are starting to assert their independence from adults and are trying to establish their identity. But the process of self-evaluation takes place in the context of a peer group that youth can iden-

(continued)

The Clinical Approach

Introduction and Definition

The clinical approach, which has been associated with physicians and patients, is a way of evaluating disease, illness, and distress in persons who have sought professional help. It involves three broad perspectives:

1. An assessment of the person as a whole. (See Figure 2.4)
2. An assessment of the functioning and state of the components of the body.

Clinical Focus 2.3 (*continued*)

tify with. Early adolescents seek groups that give meaning to their identity, and draw their identity from peer group membership. The price of acceptance by their peers is their willingness to be influenced by group norms. Thus, early adolescents learn and test their realities and themselves in a group context. This makes group work, as intervention and prevention programming, particularly effective with this age group.

Bryan (1992) described just such an intervention. She worked with 116 male and female sixth to ninth grade students who were the children of substance abusers; 95% were African American, 75% were male. All were at high risk for substance abuse and other problem behaviors. They met weekly, away from school, in groups consisting of about seven youths and an adult facilitator. The emphasis was on peer interaction in a primary-type group setting.

Bryan, who called her approach socialization-resocialization, noted that most socialization takes place in primary

groups. The intervention included structured support group counseling about alcohol and other drugs, along with less structured group sessions. It focused on resisting peer pressure, the identification and communication of feelings, and resources for coping with family addiction problems. Program attendance was found to improve school attendance and grades significantly, which was the objective of the program, and which was seen as a protective factor against adolescent substance abuse.

As demonstrated by Bryan's intervention, the group setting fits well with the needs and developmental tasks of early adolescents. The peer group setting allows youth to explore alternatives and test realities with peers, with gentle guidance from the adult facilitator. If the group develops a positive peer culture, that is, if the individuals within the group commit to prosocial behavior, the peer pressure within the group can prevent, or at least, sufficiently delay the onset of problem behaviors.

---

3. An assessment of how the person interacts with the external environment.

The clinical approach can be applied, beyond the individual patient, to increasingly complex levels of organization, such as families, communities, and so on. Usually, the clinical approach attempts to uncover the reasons for asynchrony in the system, which creates unpleasant symptoms, dysfunction, or breakdown.

Leigh and Reiser (1992) suggested a format for organizing information from a client or patient. They pointed out that disease is a concept that implies biological dysfunction, while illness refers to the biological dysfunction in a social and cultural context. The Patient Evaluation Grid (PEG) in Table 2.1 displays the intersection of data from three dimensions similar to our biopsychosocial notion, mentioned in Chapter 1.

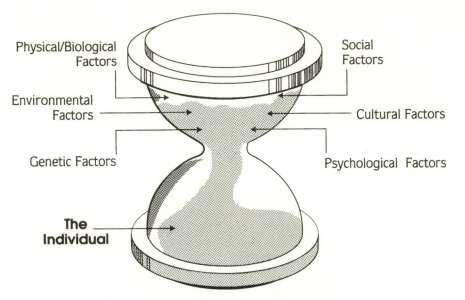

Figure 2.4. The Clinical Model: An Hourglass Analogy

The three dimensions, biological, personal, and environmental, along with three time periods, current, recent, and background, create a nine-compartment grid. Each of these compartments can be conceptualized as part of a total system, known as "the patient."

The biological dimension covers the person's physical state. The personal dimension includes qualities, personality characteristics, habits, events, and behavior. The environmental dimension concerns the physical and social environment. The inclusion of the time dimension permits analysis of stability and change, and of factors that may be resistant to change. The PEG emphasizes a comprehensive assessment and allows the problem solver to assign priorities to management plans.

The clinical approach is not limited to medicine, nor does it necessitate a narrow, disease-centered focus. How the clinical approach is used depends on the orientation, training, and motivation of the user. The model provided by the PEG could be applied to a family, group, organization, or community. It calls attention to the interplay of different action systems and their operation over time.

Application of the Clinical Approach

How a client adjusts to or copes with a problem is the product of the problem, the characteristics of the client, and the environmental factors that affect the client.

Table 2.1. Patient Evaluation Grid (PEG)

Dimensions	Contexts		
	Current	Recent	Background
Biological	• Physical exam unremarkable • On no medications • No abnormal lab values	• Onset of symptoms began with the diagnosis and impending surgery of only daughter's aneurysm • Daughter is divorced and sole support of two young children	• History of generally good health • Periodic episodes of headaches with situations of stress • Family members in good health
Personal	• Depression, unable to eat, sleep, loss of energy, feeling stressed, angry, worried	• Crying spells, loss of appetite, weight loss, difficulty sleeping, loss of energy, migraine headaches, bleeding ulcers	• Personal habits: compulsive, neat, orderly, punctual, stresses importance of responsibility and loyalty, works hard, perfectionist
Environmental	• Patient lives with husband • Married 25 years • Husband and wife both employed professionals	• Left to care for daughter and her children upon hearing daughter's diagnosis • Husband alone at home and not too self-sufficient	• Lived in same community and worked at same job for past 20 years • Happy marriage • Middle class

Different problems place varying limitations on a client's functioning. The clinician is faced with three major tasks. First, an attempt must be made to solve the problem. If a problem cannot be solved, the client should be helped to cope with its chronicity. Second, the problem must be prevented from recurring, and its solution from interfering with the client's functioning. Third, the problem and its management must only minimally disrupt the client's social systems. The clinical approach acknowledges that no problem exists by itself, and that all problems and their solutions are interrelated in an interacting system that involves individuals and their environments.

The clinical approach calls attention to the relationship between a client and a clinician. Veatch (1991) viewed the physician–patient relationship as a partnership of two persons of different backgrounds, coming together while retaining substantial autonomy. We propose that this model generalizes beyond the medical setting, and applies to clinical sociologists.

The clinical approach, in the practice of medicine, involves careful and

Table 2.2. Illustration of Use of Patient Evaluation Grid (PEG)

Dimensions	Treatment Plans		
	Diagnosis	Short term	Long term
Biological	• Depression	• Medication for ulcer • Antidepressant and headache medication and short-term therapy	• Wean from medication • Supportive therapy
Personal	• Stress related to daughter's health and outcome of surgery • Future income and care of two grandchildren • Worry about husband back home	• Obtain part-time assistance in caring for two grandchildren	• Depending on outcome of surgery relocate daughter closer to parents • Involve daughter in self-help group
Environmental	• Change in geographical environment and routine • Away from job	• Mobilization of relatives and friends to assist husband • Obtain leave of absence from work	• Encourage involvement with support network

thorough investigation of a case, leading to a diagnosis. Typically, "diagnosis" refers to attaching the correct label to a problem or disorder. This is particularly important in medicine because correct assignment to a diagnostic category usually points the way to specific therapeutic routines derived from the knowledge base of the field. The treatment is monitored carefully to determine its effectiveness and to be alert to harmful effects and other problems.

The technique of rigorous investigation leading to problem definition easily transfers to nonmedical problem solving for clinical sociologists and other non-medical problem solvers. Planning and following up intervention strategies on the basis of what is learned during the investigation also transfer. The two techniques for problem solving differentiate at the stage of the assignment to diagnostic category and the prescription and application of the treatment program. Prescribed treatment programs do not exist for most problems dealt with by clinical sociolo-gists. Like the medical practitioner, the clinical sociologist has a knowledge base to draw upon; however, solving the problems with which clinical sociologists are confronted involves developing creative strategies to apply to unique sets of circumstances.

Clinical Focus 2.4

Application of the Clinical Approach

The clinical approach is perhaps most commonly associated with individuals, although it can be applied to families, organizations, communities, and even countries. The clinical approach is framed around a problem and its prevention, or its partial or full solution through intervention. It is rare that there is only a single problem with a single solution. Therefore, a clinician can combine parts of the other three approaches we discussed in diagnosing, intervening, and rehabilitating clients. The clinical approach usually involves more than one meeting with a helper and many involve more than one kind of helper.

There are voluminous applications of the clinical approach. In general, the clinical approach is one in which a problem is assessed and possibly categorized, and compared to "standards or definitions" of normality to assist the clinician in deciding what to do or not to do to "correct" the problem and return the client to "normalcy." It is beneficial to the clinician to know as much as possible about a client to assist in the diagnosis—treatment or intervention process. Thus, it is assumed that the client will cooperate with the clinician, be truthful, and motivated to resolve his or her problem.

The brunt of responsibility is often put on the clinician, but without the desire and persistence of the client, not much can be done. Researchers often study why some clinical relationships succeed and others fail. Generalizations often cloud the complex and changing aspects of clinical relationships. Wolf (1965) notes that too often clinicians direct all of their efforts toward deciding on an intervention, feeling they are responsible for "doing something" to solve the problem rather than learning about the problem and its broader impact to frame a solution. Indeed, a clinical relationship in which the client learns about him or herself and applies this knowledge proactively can help to prevent the same or related problems from recurring. Some problems solve themselves with time, some become worse, others are solved, in part or totally, perhaps never to reoccur in the same way. The presence and personality of the clinician is a factor itself in helping to resolve problems. Clinical sociologists need to accept the fact that there are some unsolvable problems and some solvable ones that they cannot attribute to their interventions. Sometimes the clinical sociologist him or herself is the best intervention.

A Decision Tree of the Process of Problem Solving

The various approaches to problem solving share some essential features. All are oriented toward change. All emphasize careful problem assessment. All suggest a multifactor approach to understanding problems, and to framing their solutions. And all suggest the follow-up and evaluation of positive, negative, intended, and unintended effects. The decision tree in Figure 2.5 offers a practical guide to the identification of key processes in problem solving.

In its elemental form, the decision tree consists of five components: problem assessment, intervention plan, intervention, outcome, and follow-up. These components can be summarized in four basic questions:

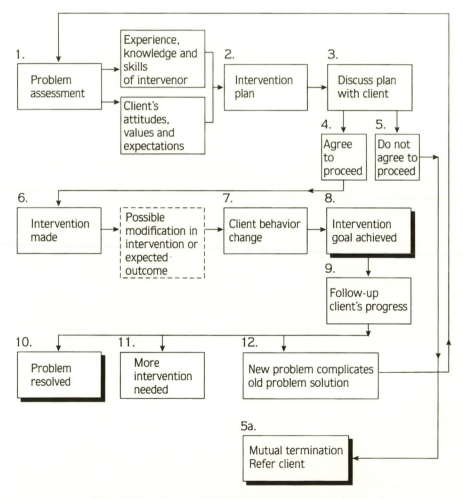

Figure 2.5. A Decision Tree of the Process of Problem Solving

1. What is the presenting problem?
2. Of several options, what is the intervention of choice?
3. Under what conditions can the intervention be most effective?
4. Was the intervention effective?

Several assumptions are associated with this decision tree: first, that the client and the clinician have already established rapport and a working alliance; second, that the effectiveness of the techniques and methods cannot be detailed in the model; and third, that one of three endpoints or outcomes will be reached—the goal will be achieved, the client will be referred, or an unresolved or new problem will emerge and the problem solving will recycle. Other outcomes are possible. The client may drop out at any time in the process, or behavioral changes may not be sustained following the intervention, in which case, the intervention must be considered unsuccessful.

This decision tree helps to remind problem solvers that the process of problem solving has some degree of order, which can affect its outcome. It also serves to remind the user to involve the client at all steps in problem solving, and to monitor the client and the process. The tree should be useful, irrespective of theoretical orientation.

Conclusion

All practitioners develop methods of thinking and working toward change that are embodied in the client systems they work with, their relationship to them, and their techniques for helping with change. Experience helps practitioners mold the models and approaches that they find most useful. Although we emphasize the uniqueness of each situation or case, new situations often are reminiscent of earlier ones and may benefit from a practitioner's experience, calling upon his or her knowledge of what worked well in similar situations, in the past, and might work again. Four problem solving approaches, presented in Table 2.3, have been discussed in this chapter. No one approach is superior to another, and most can be used in working with individuals, families, groups, and organizations. The approaches are analytic; they emphasize interrelationships and boundaries. All are characterized by a need for feedback and an attempt to maintain balance, or equilibrium, or steady state. The life cycle model provides a set of expectations about the future that is based on past events. It has a directional focus and a temporal frame of reference. The clinical model tends to take a here-and-now approach. The social system and ecological models are applicable to human relations in small or large units. These approaches have the advantage of avoiding simple cause and effect thinking, being useful for identifying loci of intervention, and helping to identify stable and changing aspects of the system.

Table 2.3. Assumptions and Interventions in Four Approaches to Problem Solving

Model	Assumptions	Possible interventions for solutions	Usual level of intervention
Social system	• Stability • Change constant and unique	• Unfreezing of beliefs and behavior • Control and guide input and output	• Individual • Family • Organization • Community • Society
Ecologic	• Equilibrium/homeostasis • Interrelatedness	• Confront stresses, strains and tensions • Removal of blockages to collaboration	• Organization • Community • Society
Life cycle	• Continuity • Change	• Build on positive resources and networks	• Individual • Family • Organization
Clinical	• Health • Function adquate	• Change in self (habits, lifestyle) • Removal and amelioration of symptoms	• Individual • Family • Group

In problem solving, all professionals, regardless of the model they use, must deal with the reality that change occurs while they are attempting to observe and cope with it. Thus, in a way, all models are removed from the concreteness of events. Intervention programs do not fall neatly into the models clinicians use. Each clinician's approach combines experience, skill, risk taking, and know-how.

Problem solving has three main aspects (1) drawing upon clinical know-how, (2) choosing preferable courses of action, and (3) translating professional knowledge and ethics into effective solutions or options. Clinical know how refers to understanding and explaining problematic events. This includes using an assessment, choosing the best approach to working with a difficult client, or choosing an intervention on the basis of clinical effectiveness. Choosing the preferable course of action sometimes requires considering the risk–benefit ratios of atypical courses of action. Examples include withholding information from a client, or choosing not to use scarce treatment resources. Such decisions represent the ethical and value-related aspects of problem solving. Determining whether to pursue an intervention, sometimes requires considering values as well as data. Indeed, value conflicts between clients, family members, and clinicians may need to be resolved before any intervention is feasible. The pragmatics of problem solving involve the translation of professional knowledge and ethics into effective solutions or options.

The three components of problem solving are present in every problem situation. They may occur simultaneously or separately, but each requires a somewhat different approach, and the situation may require that greater emphasis be placed on one or another aspect. For example, some problems may mainly demand clinical know-how, others place equally important demands on the clinician's judgment in deciding on alternative courses of action, and still others, principally demand the translation of professional knowledge into ethical decision making. Every problem has a theme, which may emphasize different aspects and permutations of the problem situation. All problem solving requires equal consideration of the professional facts and data, and of the unique characteristics of the client.

Summary

All practitioners develop approaches to thinking and working with change that are embodied in the client systems they work with, their relationships to them, and their methods of helping with change. Practitioners encounter resistance, readiness to change, adaptation, adjustment, integration, disintegration, growth, and deterioration. Experience helps to mold the models and approaches practitioners find most useful. New situations or cases are never completely new; practitioners face each new situation knowing what worked well previously, and suspecting what might work again.

Four problem-solving approaches have been discussed here (see Table 2.3). No one approach is superior to another; most can be used in working with different configurations (e.g., families, groups, organizations, communities). Most approaches are analytic; they emphasize interrelationships and various boundary configurations. Feedback is important in all approaches, and all attempts to maintain some semblance of balance, equilibrium, or steady state. The life cycle model provides a set of expectations about the future that are based on the history of performance. It has a directional focus and a temporal frame of reference. The clinical model tends to be a here-and-now approach. The social system and ecological models are applicable to human relationships in small or large units. These approaches have the advantages of: (1) avoiding simple cause-and-effect thinking; (2) being useful in identifying points of intervention; and (3) helping to identify stable versus changing aspects of the system.

All interventionists must deal with the reality that, irrespective of the problem-solving model they use, change occurs while they attempt to observe and cope with it. All models, in a way, are removed from the concreteness of events; interventions do not fall neatly into models. In the final analysis, each practitioner's approach combines personal experience, skill, risk taking, and know-how.

References

Anderson, R.E., & Carter, I. (1990). *Human behavior in the social environment: A social systems approach* (4th ed.). New York: Aldine De Gruyter.

Bales, R.F. (1950). *Interaction process analysis: A method for the study of small groups.* Cambridge, MA: Addison-Wesley.

Beauvais, F., & LaBoueff, S. (1985). Drug and alcohol abuse intervention in American Indian communities. *The International Journal of the Addictions, 20,* 139–171.

Bobo, J.K., Gilchrist, L.D., Cvetkovich, G.T., Trimble, J.E., & Schinke, S.P. (1988). Cross-cultural service delivery to minority communities. *Journal of Community Psychology, 16,* 263–272.

Bruhn, J.G. (1977). Effects of chronic illness on the family. *Journal of Family Practice, 4,* 1057–1060.

Bruhn, J.G., & Philips, B.U. (1987). A developmental basis for social support. *Journal of Behavioral Medicine, 10,* 213–229.

Bryan, M.E. (1992). Intervention among children of substance abusers and school success. *Clinical Sociology Review, 10,* 118–125.

Chess, W.A., & Norlin, J.M. (1988). *Human behavior and the social environment: A social systems model.* Boston: Allyn & Bacon.

Dubos, R. (1968). *So human an animal.* New York: Scribner.

Duvall, E.M. (1977). *Marriage and family development* (5th ed.). Philadelphia: Lippincott.

Erikson, E.H. (1963). *Childhood and society* (2nd ed.). New York: Norton.

Fisher, G., & Strantz, I. (1972). An ecosystems approach to the study of dangerous drug use and abuse with special reference to the marijuana issue. *American Journal of Public Health, 62,* 1407–1414.

Fiske, M., & Chiriboga, D.A. (1990). *Change and continuity in adult life.* San Francisco: Jossey-Bass.

Flood, R. L., & Jackson, M.C. (1991). *Creative problem-solving.* New York: Wiley.

Gelfand, B. (1988). *The creative practitioner: Creative theory and method for the helping services.* New York: Haworth.

Hall, A.D., & Fagen, R.E. (1956) Definition of a system. In *Yearbook of the Society for General Systems Research, 1,* 18–28.

Havinghurst, R. (1972). *Developmental tasks and education* (3rd ed.). New York: David McKay.

Hill, R. (1970). *Family development in three generations.* Cambridge, MA: Schenkman.

Horman, S. (1989). The role of social support on health throughout the life cycle. *Health Education, 20,* 18–21.

Kohlberg, L. (1981). *The philosophy of moral development: Moral stages and the idea of justice.* San Francisco: Harper & Row.

Leigh, H., & Reiser, M.F. (1992). *The patient: biological, psychological, and social dimensions of medical practice* (3rd ed.). New York: Plenum.

Lenski, G., & Lenski, J. (1987). *Human societies: An introduction to macrosociology* (5th ed.). New York: McGraw-Hill.

Levinson, D.J., with Darrow, C.N., Klein, E.B., Levinson, M.H., & McGee, B. (1978). *The seasons of a man's life.* New York: Knopf.

Lidz, T. (1968). *The person: His development throughout the life cycle.* New York: Basic Books.

Longres, J.F. (1990). *Human behavior in the social environment.* Itasca, IL: Peacock.

Maas, H.S., & Kuypers, J.A. (1974). *From thirty to seventy.* San Francisco: Jossey-Bass.

Martin, P.Y., & O'Connor, G.G. (1989). *The social environment: Open systems applications.* New York: Haworth.

Maslow, A.H. (1968). *Toward a psychology of being* (2nd ed.). Boston: Beacon Press.

May, P.A. (1982). Substance abuse and American Indians: Prevalence and susceptibility. *The International Journal of the Addictions, 17,* 1185–1209.

Mederer, H., & Hill, R. (1983). Critical transitions over the family span: Theory and research. In H.I.

McCibbin, M.B. Sussman, & J.M. Patterson (Eds.), *Social stress and the family: Advances and developments in family stress theory and research* (pp 39–60). New York: Haworth.

Milgram, S. (1970). The experience of living in cities: A psychological analysis. *Science, 167*, 1461–1468.

Milgram, S. (1977). *The individual in a social world.* Reading, MA: Addison-Wesley.

Milgram, S. Liberty, J.H., Toledo, R., & Wackenhut, J. (1986). Response to intrusion into waiting lines. *Journal of Personality and Social Psychology, 51*, 683–689.

Monroe, J.J. (1966). *Rehabilitating the narcotic addict.* Washington, DC: Vocational Rehabilitation Administration, U.S. Government Printing Office, 343–357.

Newman, B.M., & Newman, P.R. (1984). *Development through life: A psychosocial approach.* Homewood, IL: Dorsey Press.

Parsons, T. (1951). *The social system.* New York: Free Press.

Piaget, J. (1952). *The origins of intelligence in children.* New York: International Universities Press.

Sanders, W.B. (1994). *Gangbangs and drive-bys: Grounded culture and juvenile gang violence.* New York: Aldine De Gruyter.

Schein, E.H. (1992). *Organizational culture and leadership* (2nd ed.). San Francisco: Jossey-Bass.

Schön, D.A. (1983). *The reflective practitioner.* New York: Basic Books.

Spierer, H. (1977). *Major transitions in the human life cycle. A summary of a conference on the significance of the biomedical and the social sciences in understanding the aging process.* New York: Academy for Educational Development.

Stern, G.G. (1964). B=f(P,E). *Journal of Personality Assessment, 28*, 161–168.

Sullivan, H.S. (1953). *The interpersonal theory of psychiatry.* New York: Norton.

Tuckman, B.W. (1965). Developmental sequence in small groups. *Psychological Bulletin, 63*, 384–399.

Tuckman, B.W., & Jensen, M.C. (1977). Stages of small group development revisited. *Group and Organization Studies, 2*, 419–426.

Van Valen, L.M. (1973). A new evolutionary law. *Evolutionary Theory, 1*, 1–30.

Veatch, R.M. (1991). *The patient-physician relation: The patient as a partner, Part 2.* Bloomington: Indiana University Press.

Watzlawick, P., Beavin, J.H., & Jackson, D.D. (1967). *Pragmatics of human communication.* New York: Norton.

Weber, M. (1992). *The Protestant ethic and the spirit of capitalism* (T. Parsons, trans.). New York: Routledge.

Wilber, K. (1979). *No boundary.* Boston: New Science Library.

Wolf, S. (1965). *The stomach.* New York: Oxford University Press.

Recommended Readings

Brown, F.H. (Ed.). (1991). *Reweaving the family tapestry: A multigenerational approach to families.* New York: Norton.

This book provides a basic multigenerational framework for working with families. This model, applicable with individuals, couples, and families, stresses the complexity of themes in the fabric of family life and the process of reweaving them into the tapestry that makes for a more satisfying life for clients. The multigenerational model is a three-stage model in which the client moves from defining and working on presenting issues to exploring multigenerational themes, and finally to initiating differentiating steps in the family of origin. Each chapter centers on a case study to illustrate the model.

Carroll, G.G. (Ed.). (1989). *Ecological models of organizations*. Cambridge, MA: Ballinger.

Organizational ecology brings into a single model both institutional and ecologic variables. Environment, for example, is definable as a complement of institutions, an ideology, a body of rules, or as an attribute of client populations. Another aspect of organizational ecology is longitudinal analysis of the shifting capacity of the environment, the founding and death of organizations, and the competition among units. A less explicitly stated feature of organizational ecology is its acknowledgement of microlevel factors and the importance of niche.

Hannon, M.T., & Freeman, J. (1989). *Organizational ecology*. Cambridge, MA: Harvard University Press.

An ecology of organizations seeks to understand how social conditions affect the rates at which new organizations and new organizational forms arise, the rates at which organizations change forms, and the rates at which organizations and forms die out. In addition to focusing on the effects of social, economic, and political systems on these rates, an ecology of organizations emphasizes the dynamics that take place within organizational populations.

Kets de Vries, M.F.R., & Associates (1991). *Organizations on the couch: Clinical perspectives on organization behavior and change*. San Francisco: Jossey-Bass.

This book shows how the psychoanalytic perspective can be applied to the analysis and change of unhealthy, but deeply rooted behavior patterns in organizations, such as addiction to power, the undermining of personal responsibility, and the development of strategies that are based more on fantasy than reality. Case examples from a wide range of public and private sector organizations are used to show how studying the irrational side of organizational life can improve managers' ability to diagnose organizational problems and introduce common sense into organizational systems.

Kimberly, J.R., Miles, R.H., & Associates (1980). *The organizational life cycle*. San Francisco: Jossey-Bass.

The 13 chapters in this volume are grouped into three parts—organizational creation, organizational transformation, and organizational decline. One chapter in each section focuses on the organizational level of analysis, one concentrates on the ecological level of analysis, and one empirical study in an organizational setting illustrates the kinds of understandings about organizational phenomena that can emerge from a life cycle perspective.

Lowenthal, M.F., Thurner, M., Chiriboga, D., & Associates (1975). *Four stages of life*. San Francisco: Jossey-Bass.

This is a study of 216 men and women at four life stages: high school seniors, young newlyweds, middle-aged parents, and an older group about to retire. A major objective of the study was to delineate parameters and identify concepts useful for the study of adaptation to changes across the adult life course. A single-minded family centeredness was a dominant theme. Parenthood was the main transition seen by the young; work, education, and marriage were viewed largely as a means to that end. Underlying the general theme of family-centeredness at four life stages was a marked lack of role diversity among women and, among both sexes, boredom with occupational roles. The authors suggest that future studies utilize a cross-sequential design rather than a life-stage sampling approach in order to distinguish developmental from transitional issues.

Seligman, M.E.P. (1991). *Learned optimism*. New York: Knopf.

The author explores the ways in which we learn to be predominantly optimistic or pessimistic in our individual thinking, behavior, and explanations of misfortune. Ultimate pessimism is learned helplessness, in which problems are externalized, responsibility is minimized, and pervasiveness is maximized. One's explanatory style has implications for success at work, school, and health. Explanatory style develops in childhood through parental analyses, criticisms heard, and early losses and traumas. Optimism or pessimism develops and is reinforced by experience and perceptions until it becomes a patterned way of thinking. Organizations also can develop explanatory styles that are predominantly optimistic or pessimistic, and reinforce them by selecting employees who reflect the chosen style.

3

Problem Solving on the Microlevel

The Individual as a Social Unit

Human life takes place in a social context. Billson (1994:118) noted the inseparability of society and self:

> The cross-fire debate over the relationship between the individual (with all his or her unique qualities) and society (with its capacity for blueprinting that uniqueness) confuses our attempts to understand human behavior. Some disciplines ... claim to focus on the individual, relegating cultural and societal forces to a nebulous "background."

Cultural and societal forces are *not* background and, as Billson further observed, "The attempt to separate individual from societal factors has been a thankless and largely fruitless task ..." engaged in primarily to maintain disciplinary boundaries.

At birth we enter an existing social system and are shaped through primary socialization. Membership in a family and other primary and secondary groups, location in a community, a culture, subculture, and a social class status contribute to and maintain present behavior and influence change and development. We actively participate in the process by assembling the materials of experience to construct a unique definition of self and of reality. The developmental possibilities are infinitely diverse, but the social context in which we develop imposes constraints and makes certain developmental paths more likely than others.

Contextual influences range from macrosocial to microsocial. The times, the individual's placement in history, and the social, political, and economic forces and movements present establish the influences on our life chances and our construction of reality. Consider, for example, an African American woman in her early thirties, college educated, living in San Francisco as compared to her grandmother, now in her early seventies, born in the early 1920s and raised on a farm near a small Southern town, educated to the 5th grade, eventually migrating to Baltimore as a young woman. For most Americans, even this sparse description is enough to conjure detailed scenarios of the different life courses of these two women. Social, political, and economic factors in the half-century between their births presented a different context for the granddaughter. Changes in race relations and opportunities for women, technological changes, economic changes, and correlated changes in norms and values present the granddaughter with a different world to adapt to, different materials from which to construct herself and her reality.

Macrolevel realities are mediated and interpreted within day-to-day social settings. Interactions with family members, at school, on the job, in the community, within a peer network, provide more specific materials for the person's self construction. Those we interact with have understandings and expectations that place a demand on us and call for creative adaptation. Throughout life, each of us works to develop an "acceptable" identity, cope effectively with situations, and meet our needs. We approach these tasks as "naive scientists," forming and testing hypotheses about how to be and how to act. The things that are perceived as "working" for us are incorporated into our repertoires. These hypotheses are tested in social settings. We judge ourselves and our actions against the reactions of others.

In this way, we develop fairly elaborate patterns or modules or sequences of behavior that involve thoughts, feelings, and actions with respect to self, others, objects, and situations. The total is our cognitive map of reality, our basis for patterning behavior and our program for adapting to situations and settings. Consider the commonplace activity of going to the supermarket. If analyzed carefully in detail, the event involves planning, negotiating the aisles to find and identify the products sought, interacting with the various role-players—the market's employees and the other shoppers—completing the financial transactions, and leaving with the packages. The sequence involves a complex interplay of thoughts, feelings, and actions, involving awareness of a host of norms and role performances, and it is usually all performed more or less automatically. Like most of our behavior sequences or modules, this one has been built up over time as we observe models, and interact with other members of our culture. Our own trial-and-feedback experience also enters in as we try certain behaviors, observe what happens, and keep the bits that work—however we define "working."

As clinical sociologists, we conceptualize the individual as a social unit. We agree with Dunham (1982:23–24) who considered "... the analysis of one human personality as a social unit with respect to the ingression into the psychic of various types of social experiences that emerge from the person's involvement with ecological structure, historical events, interpersonal relations, and cultural patterns." Who we are and how we act is conditioned on the social settings and relationships that we had to learn to respond to. Whatever the makeup of the private part of one's personality, the reality is that the typical patterns of behavior—both the adaptive and the problematic—are available for the reaction and judgment of others. These reactions, actual and anticipated, shape behavior.

What is more, the individual is always acutely aware of and frames behaviors with the real or imagined judgment of others in mind.

The structuring formula for clinical sociology consists of the professional sought by potential clients because the clients are faced with problems that they cannot solve with their own resources. The person enters into a new social relationship with the clinician to seek a remedy to the problem. We turn now to consideration of clinical sociology on the micro level.

Microlevel Intervention

It is not possible in a chapter such as this to include the full range of microlevel problems and interventions, but there are general considerations that guide clinical sociological work at this level. Our approach will be to discuss these in terms of the four intervention stages: assessment, program planning, program implementation, and program evaluation.

Assessment with Individuals

Assessment begins the study of a unique case. The purpose is to determine the physical, personal, familial, and sociocultural bases of the problem and the relative importance attached to each. Assessment is a research task. The assembled data will lead to (1) an operational definition of the problem; (2) a formulation or theory of the factors that contribute to the presence of a problem and/or maintain it; (3) a clinical hypothesis about what approach(es) to take toward problem solving; and (4) evaluation procedures to test the hypotheses.

The assessment stage should begin with whether to take the case. The issue turns on several questions. The first is whether the case is within the clinician's range of skills and qualifications or those of the practice organization. For example, cases requiring medication or other forms of medical supervision are beyond the scope of clinical sociologists unless they are working in conjunction with physicians. Similarly, cases that require special expertise in educational techniques for handicapped persons should be considered only if you have such expertise or are part of a team that includes specialists in these areas.

Another question to ask yourself is: Do you want this case? Taking a case is a commitment of your time, energy, and skills. Ethical practice requires that clients get the best service you can give, and that requires your whole-hearted attention. Practical matters are relevant here: Do you have the time, energy, and resources to devote to this case? This needs to be assessed in terms of the other demands upon you.

Your interests are also relevant. Most clinicians, if they can be honest with themselves, are more interested in some kinds of cases than others. Or, after the three hundred and tenth case of truancy over the past 2 years, your reaction to the present case might be, "Oh no, not another truancy case." If you are not interested you may not be able to give this case the attention it deserves.

Work with clients requires the ability to apply your best dispassionate judgment. Your values and personal issues may be involved in deciding to take a case. If the nature of the clients or the issues involved in the case engage critical values or would cause intense values-conflict, this may not be an appropriate case for you. In addition to the distress you may experience, your communication with clients may be adversely affected or you may unduly and inappropriately influence clients' decision making. For example, in domestic violence cases, the issue, of course, is to put an end to the violence. But, if the issues engage your own unresolved experiences or you are revolted by these clients and feel that they deserve only the harshest punishment, your own feelings can be a barrier to effective work. Your revulsion may interfere with your ability to communicate effectively and to influence positive change. Or, an intense personal commitment to either the pro-choice or anti-abortion movements may make you an inappropriate counselor for clients struggling to decide whether or not to terminate a pregnancy. No practitioner can be value free. Our own experiences and our values, as they evolve, can be a resource in our work. But when they are a potentially negative influence in a particular case, it may be best to acknowledge this fact and turn the case over to others.

This brief survey of preliminary assessment issues calls attention to a question often neglected: Should you become involved with this client and problem? Many clinical workers, especially beginners, seem to feel an obligation to take all cases that come to them. We are often prompted to take up this line of work out of strong concern for people's suffering. But we have to learn—sometimes the hard way—that we cannot always be effective with all cases that come to our attention. We need to be able to say, "I can't help you," and do so without guilt. Recognize

Table 3.1. Quick Reference: Questions to Help You Decide Whether to Take a Case

1. Is this case within your expertise?
2. Does this case create a values conflict for you?
3. Do clients or problem cause you an intense reaction?
4. Are you interested in this case?
5. Do you have the time, energy, and resources necessary?
6. Are there going to be distractions or competing demands on you?
7. Does this case invoke unresolved personal issues?
8. Are there conflicts of interest between this and other cases or clients?
9. Will you be able to help?

also, that deciding to take a particular case may mean not taking other cases that may have greater need or that we can work with more effectively.

Most of the time you should be able to assess fairly quickly whether or not this is a case you can or will take. If you decide not to take the case, this should be revealed early. Your obligation is to assist the prospective client in identifying resources that will be helpful and to help them with the referral. The focus changes. The goal becomes finding the best referral or a range of options and assisting the client in gaining timely access to the services needed. Sometimes the correct referral is a major contribution to helping clients solve their problems. To fulfill, completely, your responsibility to clients being referred requires making sure they can use the referral. Sometimes this involves nothing more than making a telephone call and helping the client set up an appointment. Sometimes it may involve assessing barriers and working with the client to overcome them. It is also useful to follow up to make sure that the referral was appropriate, that they got there, and can work effectively.

Once the decision is made to take the case, we move on to a more detailed assessment. You must work with the client and any other significant role-occupants to assemble as much relevant data as possible so that you and the client can come to a shared understanding of the problem and can begin, jointly, to plan steps to alleviate the problem. The task, citing Dunham (1982:24) again, is "... the examination and analysis of an individual social unit, the personality." And the objective "... is to arrive at a judgment, supported by evidence, concerning the nature and influence of the environmental factors—physical, social, and cultural— that contribute to explanation of the organization and behavior of the personality under examination."

It may help the discussion to have a case in mind. So let us introduce "Tony," age 14. No confidentiality has been compromised. Tony is not a "real" person but a composite of the many children and youth that one of us (HR) has worked with over the years. Some details have simply been made up for our purpose here. Follow the story in the Clinical Application boxes in this chapter. Note the problem with "textbook examples." Our need to be brief and to illustrate points may make it all seem neat, simple, and tidy. It never is.

The discussion of assessment can be divided, for analytic purposes, into process, structure, and content. "Process" refers to techniques that can be used, by "structure" we mean the form, and "content" refers to the types of information sought. We will address each of these in turn.

Process: Techniques Useful in Assessment

BASIC PROCESS: INTERACTION WITH CLIENTS. The most basic element of the process of work with clients, not only during the assessment but throughout, is the interaction and the relationship that you offer. The course of the substantive

---

Clinical Focus 3.1

The Case of Tony

Tony is a 14-year-old white male, the son of Fran and Bill. He has an older brother, Sam, aged 17. Tony has been referred by the guidance counselor at the Middle School where Tony is in the 8th grade.

Brief Background

Tony's parents separated when he was 4 years old and eventually divorced. Fran became the custodial parent. About 2 years later Fran remarried and she and husband, Warren, have a child, Andrea, now age 6. Tony and Sam lived with Fran in a distant city. About 3 years ago, when Tony was about to enter the 5th grade, Fran contacted Bill insisting that he take custody of the two boys. She stated she could no longer cope with them or control them. In addition, the boys' behavior, problems with school, and with juvenile authorities had been a source of conflict between Fran and Warren.

Bill, who also had remarried—wife, Doris—accepted custody. Bill and Doris vowed to "get these boys straightened out." Sam and Tony moved to the town where their father lived, about 3 hours travel from where they had been living, and were enrolled in the local schools. Tony went to 5th grade, Sam to the 8th grade, both at the middle school.

Presenting Problem

The initial meeting was attended by Bill, Sam, and Tony. Bill announced that Tony was the problem. In particular, Tony did not want to go to school and did everything he could to avoid going to school. When he did go to school, he was in constant trouble and had three suspensions of from 1 to 3 days. He is also a discipline problem at home. That is, at home he rarely does what he is told to do, including homework, and "does not listen to anyone." Overall, Tony was described as lazy, irresponsible, impulsive, always wanting his own way, and doing whatever he wanted without thinking about the consequences of his actions for himself or for others.

---

work of problem solving depends on the formation of a positive working relationship with clients. "Forming positive relationships with clients is as much art as science. It involves coming to the encounter with certain mind sets, a few techniques, the ability to 'read people,' and the flexibility to adapt interaction in response to others behaviors." (Rebach, 1991:81)

The process of all clinical work is the dynamic interaction between you and the client. The clinical work of problem solving, the activities and techniques used, depend for their success on the quality of the relationship that develops between you and the client. For you to conduct a successful assessment and continue work beyond that requires that clients trust and are willing to work cooperatively with you. During the assessment, your task is to develop as much information as possible. For clients to be willing to offer information, they must trust you, feel that they are safe in disclosing to you, and feel that their information is safe with you.

From the assessment you must come to know and understand the person. You must not only understand *about*, you must also understand *with*. The former, understanding about, is the expert's, the outside observer's understanding of events and conditions in an analytic sense. The latter, *understanding with*, is an empathic understanding—of being able to understand what the world looks and feels like to the client. It is akin to Weber's *Verstehen*; you have it when you can put yourself in the person's role, when you can accurately and consistently predict how the person will respond to situations. It helps if the client can risk being open and honest with you.

The relationship with clients, like all social relationships, emerges from interaction. Your behaviors will affect their response. In a very real sense, the relationship you get is the one you asked for by the way you communicate with the particular individual. You will need to develop skills of tuning in, active listening, and effective interviewing. More important, you will need to learn to adapt your communication in context. The conditions you present depend on how you view clients and how you define the client–clinician relationship.

The client comes to you because of a problem. But the person is more than a problem, more than a "case." The person is not a static entity to be categorized in terms of "pathology." At the outset, it is important to focus on the uniqueness and complexity of each person who comes to you. Differences in cultural and ethnic background, age, gender, class, all affect how individuals construct experience and how they interact and form relationships. Their own experiences add to their uniqueness and complexity. Each individual will also have a personal style: Some are more concrete, while others are more comfortable with abstractions; Some are more open, others are more guarded; some are more inner directed, others are more external or other directed; some are quick to grasp ideas and skills, others are slower; some are more and some are less reflective and insightful. You need to be alert to differences and adapt your communication to these differences.

Of all possible approaches to relationships with clients, we suggest the "client-centered" approach (Rogers, 1951) as most consistent with humanistic values and with effectiveness. This approach is not unique to clinical sociology but is useful for all clinical disciplines. It involves showing genuine concern, acceptance, warmth, nonjudgmental respect for the person, honesty, and empathy. The relationship is a partnership between status equals; it is nondirective, noncontrolling. (The fact is, you cannot *make* anyone do or be anything anyway and if you attempt to do so, your efforts will only bring antipathy and resistance.)

Though you will eventually focus on a problem, you must see the client as someone who has strengths and resources that must be acknowledged and learned about. The person also has a history, is a member of various social systems, and has roles and interacts within them. The person is striving to be effective and solve problems, is striving for positive social relationships within social contexts, and is striving to maintain dignity, a positive definition of self, and to have some control over life. The person also has a range of feelings, values, expectations, and goals.

The relationship of status equality requires respect for the person's individuality and autonomy. The person should be viewed as capable of self-determination, of acting in his or her own best interest, and of making choices. The person is also capable of learning and growing and of solving problems. Respect also involves refraining from moralizing, judging, criticizing, or blaming. Avoid lecturing, advice giving, arguing, analysis, interpretations, threats, and warnings (Hepworth & Larsen, 1986:86). The goal is a partnership over a "shared concern" (Lane, 1990:124) where you and the client take agreed upon roles in problem solving.

As you begin with a person, some consideration of initial interactions is useful. Anticipate some anxiety, and attempt to reduce ambiguity by outlining the procedures. Explain your role, the sequence of events, and any agency or organizational requirements that you must meet. It may also be useful to address any strong feelings that are evident at the moment. Authority relations are an example. Some people may be overly deferent to those they perceive to be authority figures while others may be resentful. Youths like Tony, nonvoluntary clients, are often hostile and sullen. Addressing these feelings directly and negotiating a place to start is essential if the interaction is to proceed productively.

The task of assessment is to assemble as much relevant data as possible. One obvious source of data is the interview with the client. A place to start is with the presenting problem. Listen carefully to clients' statements of the problem. This is their construction of their reality. In their statement of the problem, they will reveal their theoretical formulations about what is wrong, their theory of causation, their theory of its effects, and the list of coactors who are significantly involved and the nature of their involvement. Listen also to the form as well as the content of their recitation. Make careful note of illogic, fuzzy thinking, and ill-formed statements. That is, jot them down or file them in memory for later follow-up for clarification.

As an example of the latter, consider the client who arrives at your office, on time, well groomed, is employed, has a family, and announces, "I can't do anything right." As a matter of content, the client is stating a perception about self, perhaps a perception of interactions with others, and/or perceptions about handling specific recent or earlier life events. The statement may reveal fuzzy thinking and is not well formed. As an example of fuzzy thinking, first it is illogical, not consistent with observable facts: The client managed to find you and arrive on time (got here maybe using public transport or drove, found a place to park, etc.). In addition, this client is functioning as an employee (has not been fired) and a family member. It is likely that the client is doing (and is capable of doing) some things "right." The statement of allness—which reflects the client's deletion or selective failure to recognize areas of effectiveness and selective emphasis of the negative— adds to the fuzzy thinking. It will be important to discover if such deletion is a characteristic pattern. The statement is also incomplete. What is it that this client cannot do right? When? Where? And, importantly, what does "right" mean and whose standards is this client applying? These will become issues for later follow-up and further investigation.

Taking a life-history is a useful method to expand understanding of the problem behavior. The objective is to learn about the client's primary socialization experiences and the family culture. It should begin with the family of origin and work through the life-cycle stages. The life-cycle stages (Newman and Newman, 1984) provide a handy framework for the life history. A technique found useful is to begin by developing a "genogram" with the client. Figure 3.1 provides an abbreviated example. It starts by locating the client, then spouses, children, siblings, parents, and grandparents and trying to elicit whatever is known about the family history and relationships.

From the family background, the life history proceeds through the early stages: prenatal, infancy, and toddlerhood. Many people will have heard family stories about themselves and their families from those years. Most people will have their own memories from the school years, adolescence, and beyond. Key issues are family relations, peer relations, school memories, academic performance, parental expectations, religious and moral teachings, health and mental health, developmental problems, rate of development, romantic and sexual experiences including possible instances of abuse, drug and alcohol use, and so on. Having the interviewee focus on specific developmental periods helps to keep the history organized and aids clients' recall.

Several possible additional sources of information should also be considered. These include interviews with significant others, direct observation, the use of questionnaires and rating scales, and the use of archived data.

INTERVIEWS WITH SIGNIFICANT OTHERS. Family members, friends, co-workers and supervisors, teachers and other school staff, and various members of a person's social network may provide useful information on the nature of the client and the problem. Their feelings, attitudes, and reactions may figure into the definition of the problem and may provide alternative views of the client's life-space. As the labeling theory suggests, "deviance" may be the product of ob-servers who have the power to label and stigmatize the person and make their labels stick. These persons may also be a resource as potential providers of social support for the client's efforts to change. They may also play a role in maintaining the problem and may eventually have to change their ways of interacting with the client to facilitate change. You must be sure to get the client's written permission to talk to these persons.

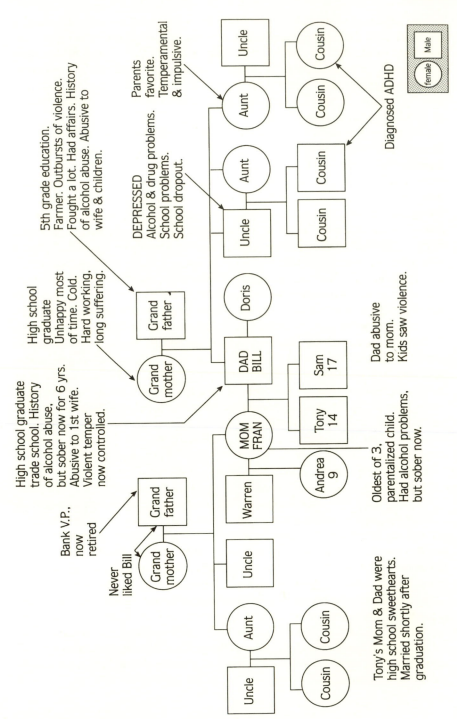

Figure 3.1. Example of Genogram of Tony's Family

DIRECT OBSERVATIONS.   Observation of behavior in relevant settings (e.g., at school, on the job, at home, etc.), provides information about the pattern of the person's typical performance and interactions. This will also permit an assessment of the client's environment. Be aware that actors in the setting may be influenced by the presence of an outside observer and may attempt to modify their actions and may even be successful at it for a short time. However, the norms and culture of most settings will make it difficult for them to radically alter their habitual patterns and keep it up for a long time, so plan to stay long enough or return often enough to get a reasonably good set of observations of the context. Here again, it may be necessary to obtain the client's written permission. Note, however, that even with written permission, obtaining cooperation may still be difficult.

QUESTIONNAIRES AND RATING SCALES.   Parents, teachers, coworkers and supervisors, partners and spouses, and even the individual client may be able to provide their perceptions using standardized instruments as a way of providing data. A checklist such as the SCL-90R (Derogatis, 1983) or the Social Readjustment Rating Scale (Holmes & Rahe, 1967) may be useful sources of information on symptoms or recent life-event stressors. There exist a variety of questionnaires and checklists for both parents and teachers to provide information on children and youth (Achenbach & Edelbrock, 1983, 1986; Barkley & Edelbrock, 1987; Conners, 1973). Hollon and Kendall (1980) constructed a useful questionnaire, the Automatic Thoughts Questionnaire, to assess the frequency of various troubling cognitions. The Social Performance Survey Schedule (Lowe & Cautela, 1978) is another useful questionnaire that may be filled out by the person and by others who know the person. It presents a list of behaviors; respondents check how often the behaviors occur. It is also possible to construct questionnaires for specific cases. Asking clients to keep records of specific behaviors—eating, worrying, panicking, smoking, etc.—can be helpful, especially if they are provided with guidance and a format on what to record and how. Unstructured journals or diaries kept by clients can also be a useful source of information.

ARCHIVED DATA.   In today's corporate world, most people have a paper trail. School records, psychological reports, work records, educational test results, medical records, court and police records are sources of useful data on clients and their problems as well as their strengths and resources. It is also necessary to secure written permission to have access to these materials.

Structure of the Assessment

Assessment should include detailed description of the problem behavior and variations of it. Along with analysis of problem behaviors, an analysis of their antecedent conditions and consequences should follow. Figure 3.2 provides a graphic summary of this framework.

The term *antecedent conditions* refers to those things that precede in-

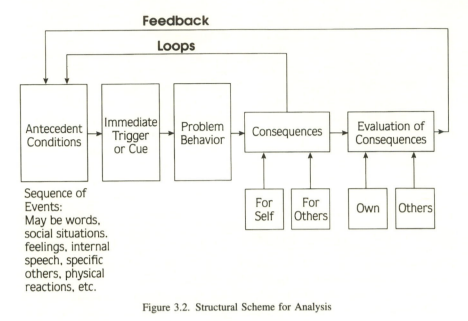

Figure 3.2. Structural Scheme for Analysis

stances of the problem behaviors. It includes those things that bring them on, make them worse, or make them better. Sequences of events or stressors may lead up to a specific cue or trigger for the occurrence of problem behaviors or exacerbation of behaviors to the point of becoming a problem. These antecedent conditions may be some combination of events or circumstances, social contacts or social situations, role relationships or settings, thoughts, feelings, internal self-speech, or physical reactions. The question might be phrased: Who does what under what conditions? It is also important to know what makes things worse and what seems associated with an easing of the problem. The latter may prove especially useful in providing direction for problem solution.

Assessment should also examine the consequences, both manifest and latent, that follow from the problem behaviors. What events or reactions, and by whom, keep these behaviors in place and/or work against alternative behaviors appearing? Problem behaviors emerge, generally, as actors try to adapt and achieve goals within a context. But the factors that have shaped the behaviors may be separate and distinct from those that maintain them. Thus, a hyperactive child may have a teacher who understands the disorder and can work with the child. On the other hand a less patient and knowledgeable teacher may define the child as "bad" and place demands that the child cannot meet. The latter response may have the effect of accelerating problem behaviors.

Clinical Focus 3.2

Tony Continued

The presenting problem with Tony, a 14-year-old in the 8th grade, is "school refusal." That is, he does everything he can to avoid going to school. In addition to the effect this can have on his future, it is an immediate problem for his parents. Thus, the problem behavior is Tony's avoidance of school. He has had four suspensions in the first half of the school year. Tony has also learned how to get himself suspended. One technique that worked for a while was to curse out a teacher. When that stopped working, he found other methods. When asked why he did not want to go to school, Tony's typical reply—the worst thing he could say about anything—was, "'cause it's stupid … the teachers are all stupid."

Consultation with Tony's teachers revealed that, in classes or situations where students worked on group projects, Tony was well behaved, contributed to the group effort, got along well with the teacher and the other students, and clearly showed intelligence. However, when he had to do work on his own, he quickly stopped working and withdrew into himself. When pressed by a teacher, he got sullen, argumentative, and defiant, eventually becoming abusive toward the teacher, which would lead to ejection from the classroom and being sent to the principal. Abusive language from Tony accelerated when he got to the principal's office. This sequence led to further avoidance of school.

The payoff for his frequent truancy and suspensions was successful avoidance of what was, for him, a frustrating and aversive situation. He stated that, unlike the other students, the work was too hard for him. He also noted that since he was the only one who could not do it, he feared appearing stupid and receiving ridicule from classmates—something to be avoided at all costs. The sequence of antecedent conditions appeared to be:

reading task ⟶ feelings of inadequacy ⟶ frustration ⟶ anger ⟶ abuse toward authority figures ⟶ disciplinary action ⟶ suspension ⟶ successful avoidance.

An illustration can be found in Clinical Focus 3.2. Note how Tony's response to his task engaged his sense of personal worth from his internal estimate of his peers' evaluation. The problem itself arises as behavior that deviates from the norms and expectations of the school and the larger social system and impacts on Tony's family as well.

Content of the Assessment

The assessment is a search for information that will provide an understanding of the client and the problem and point the way to program planning and implementation. We turn now to consideration of the types of information to be sought. This is not meant to be a step-by-step guide nor is it meant to indicate the order in which topics are to be addressed. Experience has taught that information does not come in neat little packages with topic headings. It comes in bits and pieces that must be organized and integrated. We offer questions that may eventually help you organize your material. Thus, what follows is meant to suggest the kinds of things you need to know so that you will be able to plan a program for problem solving.

Clients' statements of presenting problems are statements of why they are seeking help. It is important to know what they have done previously to address the problem and why they are seeking your help now. They may have tried to solve the problem on their own. Usually their attempts at problem resolution are consistent with their personal theory of the problem, its causes, and its consequences. They may have sought professional help before. If previous attempts had worked to their satisfaction, they would probably not be seeking your help. Explore what they have tried and what the results of their efforts have been. What effect have previous efforts had on the client and what have been the effects on others in the clients' social system? Such information will be useful in planning the intervention.

Also explore why they are seeking help at this time. Have they reached an impasse or is there some crisis that made previous adaptation no longer workable? Or, are they satisfying the demands of others such as spouses, partners, or parents? Are they prompted by involvement with agents of formal social control such as school, court, or juvenile court personnel? It is not uncommon for nonvoluntary clients to state that they do not know why they have to come and that they have no problem. The answer to the question, Why are they here and why now? may significantly affect clients' motivation, their response to you, how you establish a relationship with them, and the nature of the intervention program.

The assessment is organized around the presenting problem and it represents the point of departure. Find out what ideas the client has about the problem. Find out feelings and actions as well. Find out what relationships are involved. Find out all you can about the client's intentions and subjective reality. Does the client have a metaphor or visual representation of the problem. Knowledge of these elements will help you enter the client's model of reality and provide a basis for more effective communication.

One objective is the development of a clear operational definition of the problem itself. This is often difficult because clients present problems in global or vague general terms. For example, one frequently heard complaint is "I worry a lot." Another is, "I can't get anything done." In Tony's case, the problem might have been stated as, "Tony resents authority. At home he never does what he is told to do and at school he is always rebelling." Or it might simply be, "He won't go to school." None of these statements tell what he does. A clear statement of problem behaviors is required. Since problem solution involves behavior change, the problem must be recast in terms of observable behaviors by specific role-occupants.

It is important to reach for specificity and to make connections. The task is to determine the sequence of observable events leading up to specific behaviors that are defined as problematic and the consequences that follow. In Tony's case we learn initially that he behaves poorly in school and tries, often successfully, to avoid having to go to school. The use of various approaches also revealed a repeated sequence of related behaviors. Tony functions well in group work but problems arise when he has to work quietly on individual tasks—what the teachers called "seat work." He has trouble following written directions, usually finds written material too difficult, has difficulty staying on a task, and does not stay in his seat. He often bothers other students or gets out of his seat and wanders around the classroom. Since these behaviors are disruptive, teachers try to get Tony to comply with their instructions. This prompts some retort from Tony and the conflict escalates. Eventually Tony gets ejected from the classroom and sent to the school disciplinarian. There, Tony becomes more abusive and eventually gets sent home. Suspension from school causes problems for Tony's parents who attempt to impose additional discipline leading to further conflict.

A useful approach is to cast problem behaviors in terms of excesses and deficits: too much of some behaviors and/or not enough of some preferred behaviors. It may be that merely the existence of the behavior is the problem: vandalism, theft, truancy, spousal abuse, thoughts of suicide, are examples. It may be the frequency or intensity of behavior: eating is a common action but nonstop binging can be problematic. Occasional and moderate use of alcohol is acceptable for many people, but excessive use may be problematic. Most people worry about things like finances, their health, their significant others, and many people get the jitters before a test or some other important task or event. When these worries and anxieties accelerate beyond a certain level, they can become problematic also.

Investigation of the problem should include identification of key actors in addition to the client. Members of the client's social system are the social context in which the client acts. They may be the ones defining the client's behavior as deviant, the ones demanding change, and they may also influence the client's present behavior. Their actions, judgments, and experiences with the client are a rich source of information on the problem. The list should include those persons who are involved in the problem behaviors and those who are in a position to influence the change process.

You need to know their positions in the systems they represent and the constraints that these systems impose on them in their interaction with the client. What are their expectations? What are their attitudes toward and reactions to the client? What power relations are involved and how do these actors and the client react to power relations? You will also need to know as much as possible about their involvement and interaction with the client. Specifically, do they do anything to trigger or maintain the problem behaviors? Can they be a resource in helping the client to change? Are they willing and able to change their interaction with the client?

While the problem behavior may be detrimental to some, there may be other members of the client system that derive some benefit. Change by one or more members may upset the steady state of some relationships. The members of a role-set may have a long history with an individual and have formed stable definitions and stable patterns of relating to and interacting with that person. Change by that individual may be resisted by other members of the role-set because they are unaware of the need or do not want to change because they benefit in some way from keeping the situation as is. For example, more adequate role-performance by one or more members of the client system may mean loss of power by others. Redefinition of a child from "bad" to learning disabled with a hyperactive disorder may be seen by school staff as pointing up their inadequacies and may require extra effort and additional expense by the school system to meet this child's needs. Thus, in examining consequences, it is necessary to be alert for both manifest and latent consequences and for whom the consequences exist. Consequences maintain problem behaviors and/or work against change.

Carefully investigate the problem. Problems are often couched in the terms of deviance from some norm or standard within a context. It helps in defining the problem to know the norms that the client deviates from. Whose norms are they? What roles do the "norm makers" occupy? What is their relationship to the client? What gives them the right to insist that the client conform? Are there special circumstances that bring a deviant label to this client but not others behaving in a similar manner? The label given to the client (or the way the client labels self) influence how others understand and act toward the client. The way the client labels self also influences actions and understanding of self and the problem.

It is often helpful, in clarifying the problem, to find out when the problem first arose. Details of the circumstances surrounding the first recognized episode include the following:

What were the conditions at the time?
Where did it happen?
When did it happen?
Who was present? What were their roles? How did they react?
Were there specific life event stressors prior to the first instance or present at the time of the first instance?

It may be that the problem behaviors existed earlier and were not identified as such until they began to interfere with certain activities or came to the attention of specific agents in specific contexts. This may be the answer to the "Why now?" question. Be alert for earlier instances of the behaviors. For example, it is common with children such as Tony that hyperactivity does not come to attention until the child starts school, or even later as the child advances to a grade where the tasks or expectations they face make difficulties evident.

In addition to the first episode, similar details of specific episodes, especially vivid episodes, can help you clarify what the problem behaviors are and many of the issues of antecedents and consequences. Details such as time, place, who was present, and who did what should be determined.

The sequence of events leading up to instances of problem behavior, the antecedent conditions, are important. This may help you to determine why the problem exists. Starting with the problem itself, track it back. What is the immediate precursor or trigger? It could be a setting, a person, a group, a relationship, a context. It could also be a thought or a feeling, an action or a physical state. Then, what precedes this triggering event? And, what precedes that, and so on as far back in the sequence as it is possible to reach.

The use of the genogram to obtain intergenerational information can possibly reveal genetic and/or family culture elements that contribute to the client's present behavior. Family, primary socialization, and developmental influences can be obtained from the life history. As you work through the life cycle stages there are some general things to be alert for.

- *Family circumstances at each stage*: These include economic circumstances, health of members, the quality of relationships among members including power relationships, the nature of role performances, living arrangements, family solidarity, and clients' thoughts and feelings about the family at each stage.
- *Developmental mileposts and tasks*: At each life cycle stage there are developmental tasks: Such things as when a child began to walk, talk. How did toilet training go? Did the child separate easily when he or she started school? What was the process of physical maturation and growth—early bloomer or late bloomer? When did puberty take place and what was the reaction to it?
- *Socialization messages received*: What overt messages about self did/does the client receive? What moral prescriptions were given? How was gender-role socialization accomplished? What religious or spiritual training was given? What messages were given about the client's nature and worth? What were expectations for performance? How were they communicated? What feedback was given regarding meeting expectations? In general, what brought rewards and punishments? Who were key models and how did they act?

There are also issues specific to the various stages that might be useful to know. Several life cycle stages involve schooling and the school years. The following lists items that help the clinician understand the client:

- *How far did the client go in school*? What were the aspirations and what was the reality? What were scholastic activities, general trends in academic performance, disciplinary problems, relations with school staff and teachers,

Clinical Focus 3.3

Tony Continued

Interviews with Tony's father and stepmother revealed that Bill and Fran married when Fran became pregnant with their first child, Sam. Both Bill and Fran had been heavy users of alcohol with occasional use of marijuana and cocaine. They continued to drink heavily after Sam's birth. Bill said, however, that Tony was a wanted and planned for child but that he continued to drink heavily while Fran was pregnant with Tony. Fran occasionally joined him while pregnant though she generally abstained during pregnancy. After Tony's birth, Fran returned to regular alcohol use that involved daily use. Bill also revealed that his relationship with Fran was stormy, involving frequent conflict, arguments, and physical fighting and abusiveness that continued to accelerate. Their marriage ended after Fran called the police following a particularly violent confrontation. Both Fran and Bill started alcohol treatment after their break-up. Bill asserts that he has been clean and sober for 8 years.

Bill reported that Tony was a cranky baby who cried a lot and was not easily pacified. At age 3 months he had serious ear infections which were difficult to treat. This condition recurred frequently until Tony was about age 7. Tony walked and talked on time but was difficult to toilet train.

Fran was a stay-at-home mother until Tony entered first grade. Before their separation Bill held two jobs which kept him away from home a lot. He reported that much of the conflict between him and Fran stemmed from her frustrations and complaints about the children and her inability to cope with them and control them. On his first day of kindergarten, Tony cried and screamed and had to be taken home. The first few weeks of that year, Fran stayed at school in Tony's classroom where he could see her.

Tony's early school years were difficult for Tony, and for Fran as a single mom with 2 boys. Both Tony and Sam were frequently disciplinary problems both at home and at school. Bill's visits were sporadic and he was generally uninvolved with the

(continued)

peer relations, reactions of peers and teachers, attitudes toward school and academic achievement, expectations of parents for academic achievement, interests, and career preparation if any.

• *The transition to adulthood is another important stage.* Issues include the following: sexual relations; love relationships; attitude and orientation to marriage; careers and occupations, plans, aspirations and realities; relations with family of origin; the timing of transitional steps (e.g., age and circumstances of getting a driver's license, jobs, sex, etc.)

Specific issues to learn about include substance use—drugs and alcohol—

Clinical Focus 3.3 (*continued*)

boys though he paid support more or less regularly. When Tony was about 6 Fran met and later married Warren. They had Andrea about 2 years later. When the boys came to live with their father and Doris, Tony was in the 5th grade. He did well in 5th and 6th grades but his progress declined in the 7th grade. There were no behavior problems until this year in 8th grade.

Tony, interviewed alone, described coming to live with his father 3 years earlier. He was unhappy about it at first, having to leave his friends behind and coming to a new school where he did not know anyone. He said meeting people was hard for him. Asked about school today, he called it "stupid" and said the work was too hard. He said he only had one friend at school and that most of the other kids did not like him. At some point he was asked to read aloud from a daily newspaper and later from a third-grade reader. He strongly resisted at first, denigrating the task as "stupid"; he held that, of course, he could read, everybody can read, he just does not want to. When he eventually agreed to do it, he opened the 3rd-grade reader. He appeared to have great difficulty with the 3rd-grade material. He could read some of the words but also filled in with words not in the text. He seemed to be composing sentences based on the pictures that accompanied the text and on the few words he was able to read. Thus, one hyposthesis was to raise questions about Tony's ability to read as one problem.

Tony was referred to the school psychologist who conducted educational and psychological testing. Educational test data revealed that Tony's reading level was about 4th grade and also revealed a possible learning disability. He usually could not follow the written directions and if the task was a reading task, he was usually unable to do the task. Discussion with Tony revealed that he had developed some strategies to cover his reading deficit and how hard he worked not to appear stupid to his classmates.

Tony was also referred to a pediatric neurologist whose examination and review of observations and teacher and parent reports confirmed a diagnosis of Attention Deficit/Hyperactivity Disorder and learning disability.

including age at onset, extent of use and substances used, and pattern of use in family of origin. It is also important to ask, specifically, about physical and sexual abuse. Evidence for the prevalence of both substance use and physical and sexual abuse suggest that significant portions of the population have one or both in their history. An individual's adaptation, social behavior, and thoughts about self and others, and present circumstances may be significantly grounded in these experiences even though they are not identified as the specific presenting problem.

In Clinical Focus 3.3, we present an abbreviated version of Tony's assessment that illustrates the integration of the various sources of data. Assessment with a child like Tony involves interviews with parents, with Tony, meetings with teachers, the use of teacher report forms, and direct observation.

Assessment with Families

Families as Social Systems

Analysis of family functioning requires an active awareness of meso- and macrosociological realities. Social changes have occurred on many levels. On the macrolevel, political and economic trends have consequences for families. For example, such trends as the shift toward political conservatism and its effect on structures of the welfare state, demographic shifts such as the growth of the aging population and the growth of immigrant groups, and the emergence of religious fundamentalism as a social and political force, all affect families and the mesolevel structures that families are involved with. Competition in a world economy, the shift toward a postindustrial economy, and downsizing of corporations affect families' economic outlook. While these features are not, typically, the targets for change when working with families, they set the context for family adaptation and functioning.

The forms of marriage and family contained within a society are related to other aspects of social organization and culture. Major influences on family forms include the economic system, the political system, the kinship system, religious system, and stratification system. The most evident recent social change is an expansion of the definition of what constitutes a "family." Many Americans now live in families that differ from the monogamous and nuclear family forms. These include single-parent families, binuclear families ("a group of parents and children who used to live together but now live separately due to divorce or separation"; Stover and Hope (1993:11), cohabiting couples, foster families, blended families (one or more parents bringing children from former relationships with them), gay and lesbian families, families in communes, migrant families, dual career families, joint custody families, commuter marriages, and so on. The variations seem quite extensive. The various forms of marriage and family have unique cultures, norms, and expectations which may differ from the normative definition of a legally married couple and their own minor children of a short generation ago.

Clinical sociological intervention with families is also intervention at the microlevel. Having briefly reviewed assessment with an individual, we turn now to families. Families sometimes seek professional help because collectively they recognize a problem in family functioning that they have not been able to solve with their own resources. More often, a family member such as Tony is seen as having a problem that disrupts family functioning and provides an entry to family intervention. Thus, Minuchin (1974) and others (e.g., Ackerman, 1958; Haley, 1963; Jackson, 1965) have long urged an approach to individuals' problems that considers their family and social contexts.

> ... when a family labels one of its members "the patient," the identified patient's symptoms can be assumed to be a system-maintaining or a system-maintained device. The symptom may be an expression of a family dysfunction. Or it may have arisen in the individual family member because of his particular life circumstances and then been supported by the family system. In either case, the family's consensus that one member is the problem indicates that on some level the symptom is being reinforced by the system. (Minuchin, 1974:110)

A family is a social system. Attention must be given both to interaction among its members and with its external environment. To deal only with the interaction among members is to ignore the influence of vital transactions with external systems. Likewise, to focus on a family's external interactions ignores its internal milieu. Families as social systems link individuals with the larger society and serve members in many ways. For example, one important function is socializing the young by teaching language, skills, knowledge, and roles that they are expected to display, know, and perform.

As a social system, family members are functionally interdependent; each member and the whole is affected by actions of each member. The way that members enact their roles is shaped by and emerges from interactions among members. Role performance is shaped by the needs of the group and its members. Needs are those things required for the maintenance of boundaries and a steady state. Steady state, with regard to families, refers to the maintenance and continuation of the family as an identifiable unit. The members individually and collectively are affected by both the external environment and by each other. Failure to cope with the combination of external and internal pressures that results in family dissolution is the failure to meet needs and maintain a steady state. Families are disrupted when internal and external conflicts and pressures driving members apart exceed the pressure keeping them together. That is, the social system of the family is unable to process potentially disruptive forces to maintain its integrity. Family dissolution occurs when the disruptive forces are such that the family is unable to adapt.

In general, family dissolution is not the norm. When it does happen, clinical experience suggests that it usually comes after repeated struggles to adapt and stay together. Clinically, the usual issue is not whether the family unit adapts, but what form the adaptation takes. Over time, families develop patterns, relationships, norms, and shared understandings that, at any given moment, represent their present adaptation to their internal world and their external world. Assessment involves analysis of the present system and its development.

Issues for Assessment

As with individuals, a reasonable place to begin the process of assessment with families is to determine the presenting problem. In general, the needs and problems of families are a function of their transactions with each other and the environment. Early in the assessment basic demographic information can be obtained: Age, sex, income, education, and socioeconomic status. It is also helpful to find out why this client system is seeking help and why now. Have there been recent critical events or contact with outside agencies that have directed this family for services?

The goal of the assessment is to identify the condition within the family system that is seen as disruptive and to clarify how it disrupts; to identify factors within the system and the environment contributing to dysfunction. The major question to be kept in mind for later program planning is, What will help this family to adapt and to function more effectively?

The nature of the problem often depends on who you talk to, so be sure that each family member has an ample opportunity to express their views. This is not always easy. Families keep secrets. Individual members may have hidden agendas. Family members may have learned that certain topics are not "safe," and may bring reprisals once they have left the session. Some member or members of a family may have a stake in maintaining the status quo and may resist or sabotage efforts to change. It is useful to determine the extent of consensus over problem definition. While these are problems for assessment, note that they are also clinical issues that may need to be addressed if positive change is to occur. The clinician's efforts at establishing a climate of trust and safety are very important in this regard.

Very often, families attribute the problem to the deviant behavior or perverse nature of a particular member. "If only he or she would be/act different," they say, "everything would be OK." This is rarely the case. Sometimes parents, influenced by their experience with medical problems, define the child's behavior as the problem and send the child to a clinician with the attitude, "Here's my kid. Fix him." The family systems approach offers a set of alternative hypotheses. The most general of these is that systemic problems require systemic solutions. The individual's behavior is seen as a manifestation of a systemic problem; that something about the relationships and family functioning shaped the identified member(s) and that family needs for maintaining a steady state require the blaming of the identified member(s). Successful assessment and intervention may require the clinician to provide some level of instruction to the family members on the systems point of view. Here again, sensitivity to the family members and the establishment of good rapport are necessary; for example, no parent wants to hear that he or she "caused" the deviant performance of one of the children. Thus, the task is to foster understanding without placing blame.

As our general model specified, study of the antecedents and consequences of the problem is also necessary. How does the problem manifest itself? Under what conditions does the problem appear, accelerate, or diminish? What triggers instances of problem-related behaviors? Who are the coactors in transactions that are manifestations of the problem? What effect do their actions have on the rest of the family? And how does the problem and its manifestations affect transactions with the outside world?

As assessment begins, it is important to determine the boundaries of the family; who is in and who is out. Sometimes the determination is as simple as who resides in a household together. Thus, one family cluster involves a husband and wife and their minor children. But many other configurations exist. For example, the addition of an aging and ailing grandparent to the household may affect the relationship between parents and children. Or, consider the case of a young single mother who lives with her parents, the grandmother taking care of the children while the mother works. Often, in such situations, the mother has difficulty establishing parental authority over her children because the grandmother enacts a mother role over her daughter and her grandchildren. Sometimes the children treat the mother more as a sibling than as a parent.

The system can grow even more complex and involve parents, stepparents, siblings, half-siblings and/or stepsiblings, housemates, and unrelated individuals who live together sometimes, apart at other times, or do not live together at all but are regularly involved with each other. Thus the determination of the definition of the client system may be a necessary early step in assessment.

Whatever the makeup of the family cluster, the life cycle approach reminds us that some attention must also be given to the family's stage of development (Stover and Hope, 1993:349). In general, family stages of development are dependent on the presence or absence of children and their ages. Clearly, the issues and relationships of a young man and woman with an infant are different from a family group such as a blended family with three teenagers. Couples who have recently entered the postparental stage may be trying to cope with role-loss and relations with their now-adult offspring. An understanding of the family makeup and the demands of the various stages of development will help clinicians understand the family context.

Explorations of the adult family members' socialization for family roles is another important step in the assessment. An interesting feature of our modern society is that we educate and train people very carefully for many of their roles yet generally neglect training for familial and parental roles. Socialization for familial and parental roles is most often based on the models that the adults had and the way they themselves were parented. This is one explanation for the common finding that abuse tends to run in families. Clinical experience suggests that individuals often choose as mates persons similar to their own family of origin, sometimes, over and over again.

Assessment should include determination of relations with extended family members. In our highly mobile society, nuclear family units are often at some distance from extended family members and contact is sporadic either by choice or by necessity. But close extended family relations can be a resource as social support and a buffer in coping with life-event stressors. Extended family members can be helpful in providing child care, may be able to provide material assistance in an emergency, and may help simply by offering emotional support and advice in times of family conflict or difficulty. On the other hand, relations with extended family members may be part of the problem. In any event, it pays to include this in the analysis of a family system.

In addition to contact with extended family, it is useful to determine the family's contact with other systems. These include employment, religious organizations, community and ethnic organizations, schools, and voluntary associations. Specific attention should be given to involvement with agents of social control such as courts and social services agencies. These organizations may be related to problem development and/or a source of resources for problem solving.

The primary focus of family systems analysis are the relationships among family members, the subsystems of the family. As Martin and O'Conner (1989) noted, a family of five can have 25 subsystems in addition to its core system of five members. These include every combination of mother, father, and three children. Alliances and coalitions form and change in families. Clinicians are concerned with family subsystems because they exist in all families and are sometimes denied, distorted, or conflicted in families with problems. The number of family subsystems increases geometrically with family size.

Family assessment requires an understanding of the concept of "wholeness" as discussed in Chapter 2. The system is more than the sum of its parts. The entire family "owns" the problem. The clinician needs to assess the family as a social structure, as a whole social system. Hepworth and Larson (1986) provide a detailed description of family assessment from the social systems perspective. Readers are encouraged to consult their chapter for an extended discussion. Here we provide an introduction. The key elements are the sets of family rules and the relationships within the family. Relationships involve the role structure, the distribution of power in the family, the communication patterns, the family's approach to problem solving, and the affectional structure.

FAMILY RULES. Families, like all social systems, are rule-governed. Rules evolve in the negotiation of family roles and expectations. They include rights, duties, behaviors, ways of relating, and ways of interacting. The rules are expressed as patterned and predictable organized responses to situations. For assessment, clinicians should go beyond content and observe regularity of patterns of action. For example, if we observe that every time John or Mary expresses an opinion about something, the other immediately disagrees and expresses the opposite opinion, we have learned something about the rules of their relationship.

There are both overt, published rules and implicit rules. The overt rules usually are explicit statements about what must be done, what may be done, and what is forbidden. They specify the expected actions in specific situations of various role-occupants. The overt rules for children are often the subject of child discipline. Examples in families specify things for children like bedtimes, household chores such as keeping their rooms clean or taking out the trash, use of the family car or telephone, doing homework, and having friends in the house.

Issues for assessment include finding out what these rules are, the consistency with which they are enforced, and the sanctions and consistency of sanctions for violation. The overt rules are often a source of parent–child conflict. As children develop, they may feel that certain rules, established when they were younger, should be changed or no longer apply. Assessment should attempt to determine whether rules are renegotiated and if so, how they are renegotiated. For example, early bedtimes are often considered appropriate for younger children while some families allow older adolescents to set their own bedtimes. Discovery of how such changes occur is useful in understanding family organization.

Discovery of the implicit rules is more difficult because they are usually outside the awareness of family members, but they are very important. As we observe repetitive patterns within a family we note that they are behaving "as though" a rule existed. A simple, everyday example may be seating arrangements at the family dinner table where, by unspoken agreement, each member has his or her seat. The observation that each time the family sits down to a meal the seating arrangement does not vary, even though it was never discussed or legislated, suggests that the rule exists.

Some issues for assessment of implicit rules include rules for gaining attention, rules for expressing sentiments, especially anger, and rules about togetherness and separateness. Do rules for children emphasize obedience or autonomy? Are the rules consistent, generally agreed upon, or a source of conflict? Learning about family rules is important to the assessment. Specifically, the rules governing family interaction patterns are among the important rules to observe for assessment.

As Hepworth and Larsen (1986:227) pointed out, one important dimension for assessment of family rules is their flexibility or rigidity. Extreme rigidity of rules may make adaptation to changing conditions or advances through life cycle stages extremely difficult and cause disruption within the family. On the other hand, extreme fluidity, to the extent that family members cannot be sure, from day-to-day what the rules are can also be disruptive.

FAMILY ROLE STRUCTURE.   Assessment should determine the family role structure including the roles within the family and roles that members play outside the family group. Since a family system is more than the sum of its parts, roles should be seen as parts that fit together a certain way. They are defined and enacted in a certain way to fulfill needed functions. Role relationships are based on reciprocity and functional interdependence and emerge through mutual adaptation. This is the case whether the emergent structure is positive or problematic. In order to maintain interaction, family members must achieve some congruence in the definition of members' roles.

Within the family there are, of course, the structural role relationships: husband/wife, parent/child, son or daughter, brother or sister, grandparent/

grandchild, aunt or uncle, etc. Assessment should attempt to discover how these roles are defined and how they are actually enacted within the family group; are expectations met; are there conflicts over role definitions. For example, the parent may define the teenager's role as obedient and conforming while an adolescent may be reaching for greater autonomy.

Clinicians should also be alert to cultural and subcultural variations in the definition of these roles. One interesting source of conflict within immigrant families may be between parents' definitions of their roles and adolescents' desires to assimilate and be more like their peers. Some immigrant families also face problems when the parents do not speak English while a child does. The English-speaking child gains exceptional power as the one who acts for the family in dealings with various outside systems such as schools, rental agents, social services, etc. Such a situation can place the parents in an embarrassing and status-diminishing position.

Roles outside the family impinge on family functioning. Assessment should determine the presence of actual or potential role-conflict. The typical example is conflict between the parent role and the worker role. Certainly, the continued well-being of the family is bound up with the stability of sources of income. Also, adults' personal identity and sense of self-worth are related to performance of their career roles. These may conflict with children's need for care, attention, and involvement with parents. While there are no easy answers here, helping families to improve their functioning may require helping them to develop strategies to deal with such conflicts.

Assessment also involves discovery of emergent roles. Like all social groups, families "create" the roles they need and the roles belong to the group, they are part of the system. One such role is "legitimizer." Who in the family must approve before a course of action is undertaken. Another role is "arbitrator." Is there someone in the family that mediates conflict among other members. A third role is "scapegoat." Is there someone in the family who is blamed when things are thought to be going wrong. A fourth role is that of the "parentalized child": Does one of the children take on a parental role with regard to siblings? These and other emergent roles are shaped up in the day-to-day interaction within the family as the family assigns a role to one of the members and behaves in a consistent manner toward that member and reinforces their performance. These roles are assigned to meet some sensed need of the system.

Inappropriate role assignment or role-reversals may take place in some problematic families. Thus, a child may be expected to perform the role of an absent or nonfunctioning parent and partner. A son may be assigned the role of his mother's male partner with responsibility for the mother's well-being. A daughter may be placed in a "housewife" role with responsibility for the well-being of the father and siblings. The parent comes to rely on the child for support and to meet some of the parent's needs. Depending on the situation, this kind of role assignment can be overwhelming or confusing for the child who is not equipped to handle the responsibilities thus assigned. Another consequence may be that the child placed in a spousal role comes to see self as parent's peer, which affects the distribution of family power and may create conflict between parent and child as the parent attempts to exercise parental control. There may be additional conflict when the parent attempts to form relationships with age-appropriate partners.

FAMILY POWER STRUCTURE.   One important set of relationships for assessment is the family power structure. Family power can be determined in terms of who influences whom about what and how. Assessment must reveal who has power, in what areas, and how do they use it. Those with power set the agenda. For example, Tony exercises a great deal of power in his family. The family is organized around dealing with Tony and his behavior. More generally, a member may govern the family by their symptoms and problem behaviors. This is systemic, however, since it takes others to respond appropriately for this usurpation of power to occur.

As with any hierarchically organized social system, families have "order givers," and "order takers." Typically, legitimate exercise of power is assumed by the adults who can be considered "the executive subsystem." In some family settings, the adults are in agreement and act in concert, support each other, and present a unified front as the order givers and generally get the response they want from children as order takers. Problems arise in this context when family members comply with socially unacceptable orders.

Dysfunctional patterns often emerge when the adult or adults abdicate their parental role or allow a child to seize power. Another pattern that may lead to dysfunction may occur when one adult forms a coalition with a child to thwart or undermine the authority of another adult. A grandmother who joins with a granddaughter to overrule the mother's discipline is an example of the latter. Another example is when a natural parent "runs interference" or otherwise prevents a stepparent spouse from exercising authority over a child. Assessment should determine the existence of dysfunctional power blocs and coalitions.

Power relations are also involved in decision making and problem solving. Those with power determine courses of action both within the family and in dealing with the outside world. In families with more than one adult, it may be useful to determine who takes the lead with specific issues such as finances, recreation, social relations, sex, home making, child care and discipline, and occupational issues. Is decision making shared, are there spheres of influence, and are the partners satisfied with the process? Dissatisfaction may occur, for example, when a member's relative power is disproportionate to his or her contribution to family resources.

The *style* of the exercise of power in decision making is as important as who has the power. Power can be exercised in an authoritarian manner or more democratically. Who is allowed to provide input to problem solving and what influence do they have? Is power exercised directly or indirectly? For example, a family might assert that the father is the decision maker. But his decisions may be carefully guided or manipulated by another member such as his wife or his parents or his children.

The exercise of power helps to maintain the family pattern. Thus the assessment of power in a client family is essential to understanding the functioning of the family.

FAMILY AFFECT.　Families are characterized by a range of feelings among and between members. Assessment should determine how family members feel about each other individually and about the family group as such. One obvious dimension is like-dislike. This can be tricky: A child might reply, "Well they're my parents aren't they? I'm supposed to love them." Or a parent might assert, "I love all the children equally. I don't play favorites." Statements such as these may be firmly embedded in the family's mythic structure, but assessment needs to go further to determine what is actually the case.

Another dimension is trust-mistrust. To what extent can family members trust each other on a day-to-day basis? Is there a climate of honesty among members? Do members keep their word to each other? Can they be counted on to follow through on promises made? How secure do family members feel that others in their family will provide support and be there for them? How safe is it for a child to express deep-seated concerns to parents? Do family members fear rejection?

Family feelings of cohesiveness, closeness, safety, and connectedness are also important to assess. Often the absence of such feelings contribute to problems as, for example, when an adolescent turns to peer groups or gangs to obtain something that is needed but cannot be obtained from the family. Alternatively, feelings of suffocation and enmeshment can cause members to want to escape from the family setting.

One approach is to look for differences. Are there differences in the way a parent or parents feel and express their feeling for each of the children? Are there differences in the way a given child feels about each of the parents and each of the siblings? Look for differences and the way they are expressed. Also, assess the range of feelings expressed. Some families have rules that do not permit the expression of anger, anxiety, doubt or sadness; only calm or happy feelings are permissible. Some families have rules about the expression of affection. For example, some families are quite physically affectionate while others are uncomfortable with such displays.

FAMILY COMMUNICATION.　Relationships and processes of families, like any social system, are carried in the communication among members. The basic question for assessment is, Who says (or does not say) what to whom about what, in what way?

The communication roles and behaviors that family members display can be thought of as following fairly strict, albeit implicit unexpressed rules, usually outside the awareness of members. However, as they communicate, family members express their views of self and others and express their own perceived status and evaluation of others by the way they talk to each other. Family communication is patterned, not random. Homans' (1961) formulations of Exchange Theory are relevant here: the rules and patterns that exist at any given moment have developed over time as the members interact and mutually shape each other through reinforcement.

Watzlawick, Beavin, and Jackson (1967:51) noted that utterances can be characterized by both their "content" and "relationship" aspects. The content aspect can be thought of as the idea or intent of the speaker. The relationship aspect refers to how the speaker conveys a perception of self and personal status in relation to the person spoken to; for example, how family members talk to each other, rather than what is said, express liking or not, and express whether they feel themselves to be equal, subordinate, or superordinate to the other. Alliances and coalitions are also revealed in the way members communicate.

For example, consider family members sitting comfortably watching a TV program. One says to another in a conversational tone, "I'm thirsty, but I'm too tired to move. Would you mind getting me a glass of water, please?" Alternatively, the speaker might turn to the other and snap in a commanding voice, "I'm thirsty. I want some water." The content aspect of both utterances is roughly the same. That is, the response the speaker wants in both cases is the same: to receive a drink of water. But the two utterances also indicate something about the relationship. In both cases, the speaker feels that it is legitimate to ask the other for the service. However, in the first case, the speaker appears to perceive a relationship of equal status by the manner of speech, that the request may cause inconvenience, and is aware that an explanation for the request is necessary. In the second case, the speaker is expressing a view of the other as subordinate and as one whose convenience is of little consequence. The speaker also reveals a definition of self with respect to the other. That is, the speaker assumes that her or his wants place a demand on the other for services (note that no specific request was made, but was left implied).

In general, the content aspect is carried by the words. The relationship aspect is more often carried by word choice, sentence structure, paralinguistic features (rate, pitch, tone, loudness, etc.) and nonverbal features (eye contact, facial gestures, posture, etc.). Clinicians should be alert to, learn to tune in to, and interpret all these cues as sources of information, generally, and to assess congruence between verbal and actual behavior.

Look for additional cues about family structure from observation of who talks first, who talks most, who consistently overtops others (speaks when they are speaking or breaks into another's speech), who ignores whom or who changes the subject? Who legitimizes or gives assent to what is said, either by overt approval or silent assent? Who structures interaction or acts as moderator? When a member of the family is speaking, do the others listen? Alliances can be observed in terms of who supports whom and who is allowed to argue with whom, and how the others react to such argument. Role definitions are revealed as members interact. For example, is there a member or members who act as conflict suppressors or mediators or whose interactions are meant to placate dissatisfaction by others?

It is also important to notice who does not speak. For example, in assessment sessions with a family of four, the mother and the oldest daughter monopolized most of the interaction. The father and youngest daughter (who was the identified patient) almost never spoke, and when they did it was in response to a direct question or request from either the mother or oldest daughter. For their part, the mother and oldest daughter, age 15, carried on as though they were siblings rather than parent–child. They argued about almost everything and sought to one-up each other. One common topic was the youngest daughter, and the mother's treatment of the youngest daughter. They turned to the father and youngest daughter for support in their conflict. This placed the latter two in an impossible situation of having to support one or the other. Is it any wonder that they tuned out? This interaction pattern is also an example of what Minuchin (1974:102) called "triangulation." The mother and older daughter talk about a third party rather than directly address their relationship. Minuchin called this a "... highly dysfunctional structure" because siding with one party invites attack by the other.

Finally, it is important, as noted above, to note nonverbal behavior. While families may attempt to put on a show for the clinician, their internal states may be more accurately revealed in nonverbal actions. Looks, exchanged looks, eye-contact, posture, and facial expressions may carry important information. One less obvious nonverbal action is the arrangement of seating. Sometimes alliances and subsystems within a family can be revealed by the way the group arranges itself in physical space.

Program Planning

The program planning stage consists of two parts, the presentation of a formulation and negotiation of an intervention plan. The formulation should present a restatement and analysis of the problem and what can be done about it. The problem may need to be restated in terms of observable, measurable behaviors against which progress toward desired outcomes can be evaluated. To evaluate the effect of intervention requires clear, well-formed objectives. It may also be necessary to restate the problem in terms of several discrete objectives. That is, to solve the overall problem may require a variety of changes. For example, in Tony's case, the program may involve a trial of medication such as Ritalin supervised by a child psychiatrist, placement in special education classes at school, parental involvement in a group such as CHADD (Children and Adults with Attention Deficit Disorder), and changes in family interaction patterns and relationships as well as cognitive and behavioral changes by Tony himself.

The formulation includes the integration of assessment data relating facts to present functioning. It should explain what factors control the occurrence of problem behaviors in context: What are the causes and what function do they serve, and for whom; who are the key actors and what part do they play? Strengths, positive factors, and resources should also be included. Finally, the formulation should include options for intervention activities and steps for evaluating progress toward objectives.

It is best to approach your formulation as tentative, a hypothesis, and to present it to clients as equal partners facing a shared concern. The discussion permits clients to offer feedback, to comment and make revisions, additions, and amendments to your formulation. By being open with clients and presenting the results of the assessment, you are demystifying the process, not hiding behind a cloak of professional superiority. Instead of maintaining control, you show respect for clients' autonomy, ability to understand, and to make creative choices.

Following discussion of the formulation, the next step is to plan the program. This involves negotiating agreement on objectives and steps to achieve them. Negotiation of objectives sometimes involves a choice-point for both you and clients. For example, one objective may be that the client will have to abstain from alcohol use. He may decide he does not want to stop drinking even though other objectives are contingent upon abstinence from alcohol. He may withdraw or he may state his willingness to work on some of the other objectives but not quit drinking. This attitude may need to be addressed as an intervention issue or you may eventually have to decide whether you are willing to continue with this client under these conditions.

The program plan itself is a statement of who will do what, when, where, and how, with target outcomes specified. From negotiation and consensus over objectives, the discussion with clients should turn toward negotiation and contracting for the specific action steps. Here the clinician's role is to explain the options for interventions, their reasons, and possible outcomes, both positive and negative. Explanations should be geared to clients' understanding. They should be able to understand the relevance of the options and have an opportunity to provide input and to make choices about what is relevant for them in their context. It is often useful for clinician and clients to collaborate to develop a written plan that includes the objectives, activities, target dates, and specified roles. It is important to negotiate role performance. As Lane (1990) pointed out, it is not the clinician's task to assign what role others will play, but to find out their preference and negotiate acceptable roles for work.

The intervention program should be individualized, not a matter of fitting clients into problem categories and following a prescribed routine of treatment. Each client's context is unique. The task of program planning is to enable clients to develop strategies for change, to add constructive choices to their behavioral repertoire. That is, the goal of intervention is to help clients add constructive choices to their present behavior. Presumably, identification of a need to change indicates that some behaviors are maladaptive. Problem behaviors persist because clients are unaware of alternatives, or if aware, lack the skill to use them, or if aware and skilled, lack incentives to use them. Program planning will need to consider the inclusion of resocialization experiences and include work to overcome barriers that prevent clients from adopting alternative strategies. Intervention should increase the likelihood of more adaptive strategies for behavior.

In program planning at the microlevel, pay attention to the three major action systems: biological, psychological, and social. Assessment should have revealed the contribution of each to the problem. Biologically, the use of medication or other medical procedures, changes in diet, or fitness and health promotion activities may be relevant. Some or all of this may be outside the scope of a clinical sociologist, and collaborative relations with appropriate professionals such as physicians is essential. Psychologically, assessment should have revealed cognitions, feelings, and ideas associated with the problem as well as features of clients' personalities and cognitive styles. Some members of a client system may have identity issues associated with the problem behaviors. Assessment should also have revealed the presence of psychopathology. Socially, attention is directed to relationships and interactions. Since primary relations with significant others have the greatest influence in socialization, they can be of key importance in resocialization, as Bryan (1992) pointed out. More generally, problem behaviors are often associated with role performances. Program planning may need to address specific role performances and relationships.

The mix, and whether one or another of these should be prioritized, is a matter of clinical judgment and negotiation with clients. For example, with a client who has chronic pain or an untreated medical condition as well as personal and relationship difficulties, it may be best to help her find an appropriate resource and deal with her physical condition as a first priority. The same may be true in medically stabilizing a person with a chronic mental disorder or addressing dangerous eating disorders such as anorexia or bulimia or helping substance abusers detoxify.

Program planning must pay attention both to the *intra*personal and the *inter*personal aspects of action. Action is mediated by the internal dialogue, cognitive events that include the actor's internal representation of the situation, of self and others, of own and others roles, and expectation of outcomes that can be obtained in the situation calling for action. The actor's motives include protecting self and one's evaluation of self and either maximizing reward or minimizing punishment to self.

Approaches to Program Implementation

All action, including problematic behavior, is patterned and is caused. For change to occur the pattern must be disrupted and new behaviors in context must be established. Behavior is in response to some set of antecedent conditions and is maintained by its consequences. For change to occur, intervention must address the chain of antecedent conditions that bring on the problem behaviors, the behaviors themselves, and/or the consequences of the behaviors that keep them in place. The creative task is to determine where in the sequence to intervene, the locus of intervention, and how to intervene.

Assessment should also direct attention to the locus/loci of intervention, the place or places at which to direct change efforts. The concept, locus of intervention, refers both to where in the sequence of events and where in the client's world to work for change. The sequence of events refers to the antecedent → response → consequences linkage. Figure 3.3 shows one possible approach, the disruption of the sequence of antecedent conditions.

The sequence of antecedent conditions may include contexts, interactions, cognitions, feelings, and behaviors. The earlier in the sequence that redirection can take place, the better. The key to making this work includes making sure that the person can, indeed, execute the new response and that the new response is more rewarding than the previous response.

Where this approach is not possible, attention turns to the problem behavior itself and its consequences. As Figure 3.4 illustrates, the intervention works to shape a new response to the old sequence and works to establish more desirable outcomes than were previously received. In either case, for new behaviors to be *tried*, actors must anticipate more positive outcomes. For new behaviors to *replace* previous behaviors, they must, in fact, provide more positive outcomes.

The development of strategies for helping people change requires an understanding of the personal and social context for change. We agree with Straus (1982:60) who noted that behavior and our sense of self reflect social arrangements. Individuals are not passive responders but are creative constructors, "doing the best they can to meet their conditions of existence and trying to create a relatively stable, meaningful, and satisfying life for themselves and those with whom they are closely bonded." People as individuals must conduct their daily lives as actors and as objects for their own evaluation, what Mead termed the "I" and the "me." We all take part in many networks and must interact with a variety of others. We try to emerge from these transactions with situations, self, and others

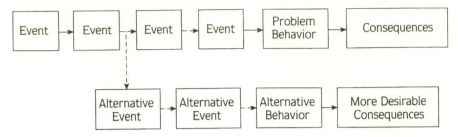

Figure 3.3. Disrupt Sequence of Antecedent Conditions

with an intact sense of positive self-worth and perhaps, having achieved some worthwhile objectives. Behavioral choices, which depend on interpretation of the situation, are made to meet these goals.

The individual is not an empty vessel, but approaches the interpretation of situations and selection of behaviors by applying prior learnings. This learning serves as a predictive base; action is chosen within a defined situation based on anticipated outcomes which are derived from this predictive base. Learning, experiences, growth, offer us the opportunity to enrich our predictive base and add alternative behavioral choices. We change or refine behavior on our own to improve our outcomes. We often seek to change when older, established patterns no longer get us the outcomes we want. In such a situation we may experiment with new strategies until we find out what works for us. This is not always possible for everyone, however. Experimentation is only possible when the person perceives that the cost of failure is relatively low. The situation and surroundings may make predictability more desirable, while experimenting with new behaviors, whose outcomes are unknown, produces anxiety, something to be avoided.

To change, we must be open to change, growth, and experimentation. Sometimes, the situation is such that change is difficult for people. If nothing else, our

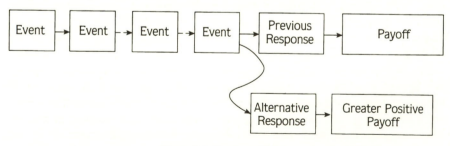

Figure 3.4. Response Change

present actions, strategies, and presentations of self may have relatively predictable outcomes in terms of our coping with our everyday tasks and relationships. Our present strategies may not be the best possible, but they have the feature that outcomes are relatively well known while the consequences of new behaviors may be unpredictable. Thus, change could involve a great deal of ambiguity and risk depending on the circumstances. To change, we have to be open to growth and experimentation, but the demands of the situation may make having predictable outcomes more attractive. Having a poor strategy may be better than having no strategy or an untried strategy. This is likely to be even more the case the more stressful the situation. People wind up consulting clinicians, either voluntarily or involuntarily, when their situation does not support their continued search or when they have exhausted their own resources. For change to occur, they must become aware of constructive alternatives, be able to use them, and they must become aware that they will reliably and predictably lead to better outcomes.

Choices for action also involve taking the role of the other. Behaviors are chosen based on the real or anticipated actions of others. Members of ongoing groups, such as families, generally have developed a predictive base about the likely responses of coactors. Present behavior represents the actor's perception of the best adaptation to the situations calling for action. Change by an individual group member has consequences for others and the individual's relationships with others. The individual's present behavior may be maintained by the outcomes obtained within a relationship or set of relationships such as occurs within a group or family. One of the risks of new behaviors may be the loss of a relationship or important payoffs within the relationship. Change by an individual may also require adjustments by others and the way they relate to and interact with this person.

Clinicians must be alert and aware of an individual's social networks: Change by an individual member may threaten to upset the stable structure of a family or other social network. Long-standing role relationships with the individual, that others found comfortable and predictable, may be upset, or the individual's attempts to change may be threatening to others. Change by the individual may result in punishments or the loss of valued rewards previously obtained from these social relations. Thus, members of a client's social system may be sources of barriers to change. Change by an individual may be resisted by others who exert pressures that work against the individual's attempts to change.

Clinicians must be aware of this process and attempt to counteract it. One simple step is to educate the individual client about the process, explaining how it works and why. As systems theory suggests, change by one member of a social system ultimately means change by the other members and the system as a whole. Working with key members of the client's social system, preparing them for the consequences to them of the client's change, and enlisting their support for the client's change efforts, can also be important steps in facilitating an individual's change.

This will need to be handled with careful planning and sensitivity. For example, family members may feel that the individual "owns" the problem and therefore is the one who must change to improve the situation. They may find it difficult to understand and even more difficult to accept that their own actions toward the individual may contribute to the maintenance of the problem behaviors and that they may also have to change to facilitate improvement in the identified client. Such change also will have to have some positive payoff for them.

Programs for change, then, must proceed on a broad front that includes the internal dialogues of individuals and their interactive behaviors within situations. With regard to the former, the clinician's task could be to help clients understand the role their internal representations play, the content and sources of their present thinking, and help clients find and use more positive thoughts that are appropriate to their background and situation and may result in improved outcomes. Glass (1992) described just such an approach in work with adults raised in alcoholic homes. Of this approach Glass wrote:

> Initially, an individual can benefit from education and elucidation about how painful thoughts, emotions, and behaviors can arise through interaction with family members, i.e., how self is formed. This helps the individual to understand the origin of these painful phenomena, and also makes clear that the thoughts, emotions, and behaviors are all subject to change—the internalized "truth" about self can be challenged. The individual can engage in the redefinition of self. With this information, the individual is able to begin the process of self-resocialization—intentionally replacing negative self-images, attitudes, and behaviors with more positive, life-affirming ones.

Programs must also address the social aspect, the interactive behaviors of members of a client system. Billson (1994:128) stated that

> Practice for sociologists lies in intervention in problems relating to *interpersonal processes* as they appear in *patterned interaction* among individuals *in groups* of all sizes and types. The primary goal of such intervention is to modify *interpersonal behavior* and to ameliorate the negative aspects of *external conditions* that affect interpersonal processes. (Emphases in original.)

As individuals develop more effective ways of communicating and interacting, they may be able to negotiate more positive relationships and they may also develop a more positive sense of self as a result of having more positive consequences from social interactions. For example, changes in dysfunctional interaction patterns among family members can have far-reaching consequences for all members. Minuchin expressed this view in his formulations of structural family therapy. He stated that, "Change is seen as occurring through the process of the therapist's affiliation with the family and restructuring of the family in a carefully planned way, so as to transform dysfunctional transactional patterns" (1974:91). Role-playing sessions with clients are a useful tool here. It gives the clinician an opportunity to teach and help members learn new behaviors. It allows them to experiment with these new behaviors in a relatively risk-free setting and allows for rehearsal to develop some skill and comfort with them.

As much as possible, intervention programs should concentrate on changes occurring in the contexts where changes are identified as necessary. Conversations and sessions in the clinician's office may fit everyone's model of "therapy," but they serve little purpose unless they apply to real behavior changes and problem solutions in clients' own life spaces. We assert that, as best practiced, clinical sociology is not completely a chair-bound, office-centered activity. Subject, of course, to negotiation and contracting with clients, the sociological clinician may play several roles in working toward behavior change and problem solution. And, clinical sociologists must be prepared to "go where the action is."

Thus, in addition to office sessions, a clinical sociologist working with a child such as Tony may make school visits to work with school staff on interaction with the child. This may involve anything from providing in-service training for school staff on topics like conflict mediation, or coaching specific individuals on how to conduct a behavior modification program for a specific child. It may involve work as the child's advocate to obtain special education or other resources from the school or other organizations and agencies.

Intervention programs may also involve coaching family members on alternative interaction patterns and ways to communicate. This might include the clinician modeling alternative behaviors then asking family members to rehearse them to help them learn how to do them.

The clinician's task, then, is to assist clients in altering their internal dialogue. In addition, the clinician's task is to help clients learn problem-solving strategies when again faced with a need to change. From the perspective of individual members of a client system, this means developing alternative responses to familiar situations that will provide better payoffs. To do this, clients must be able to explore new role definitions and role performances and be able to rehearse them in a situation of little or no risk. From the perspective of a total client system, such as a family, members must acknowledge the reciprocal aspects of role relationships and be able to facilitate each other's attempts to change and renegotiate their relationships.

Program Implementation and Evaluation

Program planning should result in contracting for the intervention activities including specification of who will do what when and where. It should also specify target dates and evaluation procedures. Program implementation involves carrying out the agreed upon steps. Program evaluation involves monitoring progress toward the objectives.

The evaluation phase points up the application of the scientific methods of sociology, what van de Vall (1987) called "data based sociological practice." The intervention plan is analogous to a hypothesis to be tested. Continuation with or modification of the plan depends on data collected concurrent with implementation.

Our discussion of the intervention steps—assessment, program planning, program implementation, and program evaluation—has, of necessity, been presented in linear fashion. In reality it is not a linear but a circular process.

Figure 3.5 attempts to show how evaluation fits into the process: Data from the evaluation may show that the program is working as planned and moving toward the desired outcome (positive result). In this case, the decision is to continue with implementation as originally planned. However, data from the evaluation may show that the program is not proceeding as planned or is not showing movement toward the objective (negative result). This may require additional assessment data and/or an adjustment to the program, implementation of the adjusted program, or continued evaluation.

In previous discussions of objectives, we have tried to emphasize that objectives must be stated in operational terms; that they must be observable and

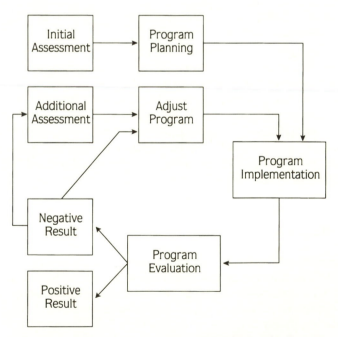

Figure 3.5. Fitting Program Evaluation into the Intervention Process

measurable. Quantification and measurement of specific critical variables are the keys to program evaluation.

Earlier, we suggested that objectives can be subdivided as process objectives and outcome objectives. Process objectives are statements about activities to be undertaken. Process evaluation consists of making sure that planned activities take place when and as planned. Often, clinicians, especially beginners, focus on results and neglect process evaluation. This is not the best strategy. A program is designed that is hypothesized to achieve movement toward a certain outcome. Failure to achieve that outcome may be attributed to the program itself. But that may not be the case. If the program was not implemented as planned, it has not been adequately tested.

Thus process evaluation should be included in the evaluation plan. Data should include whether the steps were taken as planned and in the sequence and time frame planned. Process evaluation may also reveal bottlenecks or barriers to implementation of the planned steps. This may require a return to the assessment stage or the planning stage and further negotiation with clients.

Process objectives are to be stated as measurable variables. For example, process objectives may be stated as:

1. John will enroll in the county GED program by (give date) and attend three classes per week.
2. John will take the high school equivalency test by (give date).

Monitoring these objectives can be as simple as having the instructor sign an attendance sheet each session that John attends.

Outcome objectives are also to be stated as measurable variables. Leitenberg (1973) offered a plan for "controlled investigation of single cases" describing experimental designs for use when n = 1. They depend on operationalizing, observing, and quantifying both problem behaviors and target behaviors. Without considering each design in detail, generally, baseline rates of behaviors are established prior to intervention then measured following the introduction of the intervention that is hypothesized to bring about the desired change. If the rates of problem behaviors do not change following the introduction of the intervention, it would seem clear that program changes are in order.

A simple example of an outcome objective might be:

1. Tony will attend school 90% of the time by (give date).

Given that Tony's present rate of attendance, the baseline rate, is less than 50% of the time, such an objective represents a positive change. It is clearly measurable with a bit of cooperation from either parents or school personnel. (Obviously, attendance alone would not constitute all the objectives for Tony but would be one among several appropriate to the problem. The others must be equally measurable.)

We agree with Leitenberg that this approach is different from the usual uncontrolled case studies where a clinician applies "clinical judgment" on whether an intervention is working or not. The components of this approach involve establishing clear and specific criteria for success and systematic collection of quantifiable data which can be compared to established criteria. It permits more accurate and objective judgment of the intervention steps.

Summary

Clinical sociology is applicable to the problems of individuals and families seen as microlevel social units. Attention is directed not only to intraindividual processes but to social relations and interactive behaviors as well. In addition, sociological practice on the microlevel must maintain an awareness of the interplay of levels—the influences of mesolevel and macrosociological processes on individuals and families. Problems are defined in terms of problem behaviors and problem solving emphasizes behavior change. Intervention is guided by empirical processes including thorough data gathering for assessment and evaluation of operationally defined and measurable outcomes. Clinicians are also guided by humanistic values that show respect for clients' uniqueness and autonomy.

References

Achenbach, T.M., & Edelbrock, C.S. (1983). *Manual for the revised child behavior checklist and profile*. Burlington, VT: University Associates in Psychiatry.

Achenbach, T.M., & Edelbrock, C.S. (1986). *Manual for the teacher's report form and teacher's version of child behavior profile*. Burlington, VT: University of Vermont, Department of Psychiatry.

Ackerman, N.W. (1958). *The psychodynamics of family life*. New York: Basic Books.

Barkley, R.A., & Edelbrock, C. (1987). Assessing situational variation in children's problem behaviors: The home and social situations questionnaires. In Prinz, R. (Ed.), *Advances in behavioral assessment of children and families*. Greenwich, CT: JAI.

Billson, J.M. (1994). Society and self: A symbolic interactionist framework for sociological practice. *Clinical Sociology Review, 12*, 115–133.

Bryan, M.E. (1992). Intervention among children of substance abusers and school success. *Clinical Sociology Review, 10*, 118–125.

Conners, C.K. (1973). Rating scales for use in drug studies with children. *Psychological Bulletin special issue, 80*, 24–34.

Derogatis, L. (1983). *SCL-90R Manual* (revised version). Baltimore: Johns Hopkins School of Medicine.

Dunham, H.W. (1982). Clinical Sociology: Its nature and function. *Clinical Sociology Review, 1*, 23–33.

Glass, J.E. (1992). An alternative understanding of the cognitive, emotional, and behavioral characteristics of individuals raised in alcoholic homes: A clinical theory of the individual. *Clinical Sociology Review, 10*, 107–117.

Haley, J. (1963). *Strategies of psychotherapy*. New York: Grune & Stratton.

Hepworth, D.H., & Larsen, J.A. (1986). *Direct social work practice: Theory and skills*. Chicago: Dorsey.

Hollon, S.D., & Kendall, P.C. (1980). Cognitive self statements in depression: Development of an automatic thoughts questionnaire. *Cognitive Therapy and Research, 4*, 383–395.

Holmes, T.H., & Rahe, R.H. (1967). The social readjustment rating scale. *Journal of Psychosomatic Research, 11*, 213–218.

Homans, G.C. (1961). *Social behavior: Its elementary forms*. New York: Harcourt.

Jackson, D.D. (1965). Family rules: Marital quid pro quo. *Archives of General Psychiatry, 12*, 589–594.

Lane, D. (1990). *The impossible child*. Stoke-on-Trent, U.K.: Trentham Books.

Leitenberg, H. (1973). The use of single case methodology in psychotherapy research. *Journal of Abnormal Psychology, 82*, 87–101.

Lowe, M.R., & Cautela, J.R. (1978). A self-report measure of social skill. *Behavior Therapy, 9*, 535–544.

Martin, P.Y. & O'Conner, G.G. (1989). *The social environment: Open systems applications*. New York: Longman.

Minuchin, S. (1974). *Families and family therapy*. Cambridge, MA: Harvard University Press.

Newman, B.M., & Newman, P.R. (1984). *Development through life: A psychosocial approach*. Homewood, IL: Dorsey.

Rebach, H.M. (1991). Communication and relationships with clients. In H.M. Rebach & J.G. Bruhn (Eds.), *Handbook of clinical sociology* (pp. 81–97). New York: Plenum.

Rogers, C. (1951). *Client centered therapy*. New York: Houghton Mifflin.

Stover, R.G., & Hope, C.A. (1993). *Marriage, family, and intimate relations*. Fort Worth, TX: Harcourt Brace Jovanovich.

Straus, R. (1982). Clinical sociology on the one-to-one level: A social behavioral approach to counseling. *Clinical Sociology Review, 1*, 59–74.

van de Vall, M. (August, 1987) *The methodology of data-based sociological practice*. Paper presented at the 82nd Annual meeting of the American Sociological Association.

Watzlawick, P., Beavin, J.H., & Jackson, D.D. (1967). *Pragmatics of human communication*. New York: Norton.

Recommended Readings

Billson, J.M. (1994). Society and self: A symbolic interactionist framework for sociological practice. *Clinical Sociology Review, 12*, 115–133.

In this article, Billson shows the inseparability of society and the self. The author argues that the maintenance of disciplinary boundaries by psychology, psychiatry, and social work have often relegated the social influence and the interaction process to "background" status. Meanwhile sociology and anthropology have focused on patterns of social organization with individual processes left distinctly subordinate. Billson takes issue with these approaches, asserts the importance of interaction in understanding human behavior, and offers an approach to clinical practice based on symbolic interactionist theory.

Glass, J.E. (1992). An alternative understanding of the cognitive, emotional, and behavioral characteristics of individuals raised in alcoholic homes: A clinical theory of the individual. *Clinical Sociology Review, 10*, 107–117.

In this article, Glass argues for the application of symbolic interactionist theory to clinical work with individuals. The theory describes "how the process of primary socialization can result in the internalization of troublesome cognitions, emotions and behaviors ..." which are "maintained and repeated within the course of individuals' lives." The article goes on to describe the application of the theory to clinical work with individuals raised in alcoholic homes.

Hallowell, E.M., & Ratey, J.J. (1994). *Driven to distraction*. New York: Touchstone Book/Simon & Shuster.

This is an informative and highly readable book about Attention Deficit Disorder (ADD) written by two psychiatrists who also have ADD. The book is not limited to childhood ADD but covers the life-span from childhood to adulthood and offers information on recognizing and coping with the disorder throughout the life span. The authors make extensive use of case materials to illustrate their points. They cover the biological, social, and psychological problems and offer suggestions for treatment and management as well as lists of resources.

Lane, D. (1990). *The impossible child*. Stoke-on-Trent, U.K.: Trentham Books.

David Lane opens his book with the statement: "It was not my intention to study the impossible child. He intruded himself into my work, and would not be ignored." This book represents 15 years of Lane's research and work with problem behavior in schools. The impossible child is one who disturbs the teachers so that they refer the child for "help," but that punishment, sympathy, psychology, child guidance, or residential placement have failed to change the child. The first part of the book is an extensive presentation of research and theory. The second part gives a detailed discussion of intervention that begins with the assumption that behavior "does not exist in isolation from the context in which it occurs," but "is part of a complex web ... that include biological and social/political influences." The approach to programming for children and schools is one that is consistent with the approach offered in this book and one which is consistent with a sociological approach.

4

Problem Solving at the Mesolevel

Introduction

This chapter turns to clinical sociological practice on the mesosociological level. The first section addresses the question, Where is the mesolevel? Since organizational development and community organization constitute two important fields of sociological practice, the second and third sections of this chapter will offer some observations on organizations and community organization. The remaining sections will focus on practice issues.

The Mesolevel of Sociological Practice

At the mesolevel, individuals come together to form larger social structures. The nature of these social systems is influenced by the individuals as they interact and negotiate their social reality. However, the negotiation is influenced by the situation. The social setting presents a structured situation in which individuals' behavior becomes patterned by expectations, role definitions, and other situational demands. Collins (1988:412) stated:

> Human beings have the capacity to create or negotiate whatever they can at any moment in time. But they always act in a structured situation, so that the consequences and conditions of their creativity and negotiation are nevertheless patterned by larger relationships beyond their control.

We think of the microlevel, dealt with in the previous chapter, as fairly tightly bounded, referring to individuals and individuals within primary groups, as well the primary groups themselves. At the other extreme, macrolevel structures often exist at a high level of abstraction. We refer to them with terms like *the normative order*, *society*, or *the sociocultural system* or we refer to social institutions such as the economic order or the political order. The term *macrolevel* refers to the organization of organizations. But people experience society, the macrostructures, in interaction with specific others. It is here that we find the mesolevel.

We have trichotomized the micro–macro continuum as micro-, meso-, and macrolevels. However, the continuous nature of this classification system makes it difficult to describe mesosociological structures with a deft phrase or two. These structures vary with regard to size, scope, and time-frame, but generally encompass bounded organizations rather than organizations of organizations. We could refer to them as involving secondary rather than primary relationships. Mesolevel structures could be characterized by the fact that, at least in principle, members can identify and interact with each other. They may also be characterized by their "reality." In principle at least, mesosociological structures are more concrete than the abstract macrolevel structures mentioned above; they usually refer to specific organizations.

On close analysis, however, some of these distinctions begin to blur. The primary/secondary distinction may be questionable. Certainly, primary-like relationships often come to exist among the members of a work unit who have been together over time. The size distinction also gets murky. For example, a school system within an identified district, a school within that system, and Mr. Brown's second grade class could all be characterized as mesolevel structures. We might also ask, How large does a structure have to be before it is no longer considered meso? Where on our continuum should we place multinational corporations or large metropolitan areas that cut across several political jurisdictions?

Mesolevel structures have in common the fact that they provide people with their everyday experiences. They provide everyday roles that often become intricately linked with our identities and meet a variety of needs beyond those met by family. We usually receive our education and medical care, engage in political or religious activity, and often make our livelihoods as members of organizations. Berger and Neuhaus (1977) characterized mesolevel structures when they discussed "mediating structures." "These structures, small and proximate to individuals, mediate between them and large social, political, and economic forces, including bureaucracies" (Couto, 1989). Mesolevel structures include various kinds of organizations and networks. Examples include work units, boards or managerial teams, corporate business structures, religious organizations, communities, public agencies, neighborhoods, gangs and clubs, and voluntary associations.

As we have consistently maintained, clinical sociologists combine the roles of theorist and researcher with the roles of active interventionist and change agent. Mesolevel practice involves consultation and/or direct intervention to bring about targeted change in networks and organizations. Interventions go beyond individuals and focus on problem solving in specific social systems. For something to be a social problem, two conditions must be met. First, a condition or series of events or pattern of behavior must be identified as a problem or deviation from some norm by observers with the influence to make their interpretations stick. Second, the problem must be additionally defined as based in and/or having an effect on social arrangements. An individual problem exists if you must do without needed medical services you cannot afford. This does not constitute a social problem. But if medical services are rationed and differentially distributed according to social categories based on cultural beliefs that access to medical care is a privilege to be earned, a commodity to purchase by those who have the means, lack of access has its basis in social arrangements. It will become a social problem when significant influential groups define it as a problem to be addressed through social action.

Examples of Mesolevel Sociological Practice

Robinette and Harris (1989) and Miller (1991) described a mesolevel role for sociologists in mediation and conflict resolution. These sociologists noted the centrality of Conflict Theory to sociology and, as Robinette and Harris observed, "conflict resolution is an essential process in creating, sustaining, and modifying social structures." Britt (1988, 1991) called attention to roles for sociologists in organizational development. Stephenson (1994) and Friedman and Friedman (1993) described roles for clinical sociologists in "diversity management." The issue takes note of demographic changes in ethnic distribution in the United States and the integration of minority members into organizations to the mutual benefit of the organization and the individual worker. Couto (1989) reported on what he called "redemptive organizations," a variant of voluntary associations that have an explicitly political purpose of social change and are rooted in local leadership of low income, repressed communities. Bruhn (1987) was concerned with the broker role, and his particular interest was the role of clinical sociologists as health brokers. Hoffman (1985) described a role for clinical sociologists as "acculturation specialists," who have "the clinical role of mediating difficult intercultural transitions, helping to bridge the gap between two potentially incompatible culture patterns."

Hoffman (1987) reported on a clinical sociologist's role as a "culture broker" to develop alcoholism services for Cuban refugees. Through ongoing participant observer research the clinical sociologist was able to restructure a failed program that was based on traditional, Anglo approaches to alcohol recovery in inpatient units. Weber (1991) described a role for sociological practitioners in health promotion based on her work developing a health promotion program for municipal employees in a small city. As Weber noted, the promotion of healthy behaviors in the workplace involves "a combination of educational, organizational, and environmental activities designed to support health conducive behavior within the work setting" (p. 107). Health-conducive behavior differs from disease prevention and involves such things as weight reduction, aerobic exercise, blood pressure monitoring, general health education, nutrition, and stress management. With symbolic interaction as the theoretical base and needs assessments and evaluations as the research tools, the intervention involved work with groups of workers and managers to design and implement a program tailored to the needs of the specific organization. The intervention included organizational changes to produce positive outcomes for both individual employees as well as for the organization.

Stoecker and Beckwith (1992:199) described their roles as activists and community organizers with "projects to increase the organizational effectiveness and urban redevelopment capacity of community-based development organizations in Toledo, Ohio." Their intervention on the mesolevel resulted in the development of citywide organization, the formation of the Working Group on Neighborhoods, and ongoing commitment of the community based development organizations to "make this process work."

Abbott and Blake (1988) took a direct service approach to mesolevel intervention. They described the development of the Street Youth Employment Program for homeless youth ages 16 to 20. Their objectives were to provide part-time employment, stabilized living arrangements, and offer education and on-the-job training. They had the youth participate in program planning and operation. Though they worked with a relatively small group, 70% of the participants got off the streets and into more stable involvement in work or school. Abbott and Blake attributed the successful outcomes to linking stable living to meaningful employment and attention to the youths' physical and mental health needs.

We have attempted, with this brief review, to give a feeling for an answer to the question, Where is the mesolevel? The general approach to clinical work at the mesosociological level is to work with identified members of the client system to define and assess the problem situation and design, implement, and monitor problem-solving activities. The goal is to assist with positive social change in a way that is acceptable to the members of the client system and meets their needs as they define them. We have also tried to give some feeling for the diversity of settings for practice on the mesolevel and the diversity of roles for the clinical sociologist. This very diversity makes it difficult to describe specific tactics for clinical work. Most sociological intervention takes place at the mesolevel, which offers a rich field for the application of sociology and the development of sociological practice.

Organizations and communities are two types of mesolevel social structures that come to sociological attention. In the next sections we will briefly consider a general view of each of these, then turn our consideration to intervention.

Organizations

Sociological practice at the mesolevel is, most frequently, practice within an organizational context. Collins (1988:450) remarked:

> Most social issues in sociology are organizational problems. Deviance, police, corrections, medical sociology, educational problems, ethnic and gender discrimination, as well as the largest-scale issues of citizen control of the military, environmental degradation, industrial accidents, nuclear war, and the operation of democracy, are all largely organizational problems.

Organizations are relatively ongoing social units coordinating positions and the activities of occupants of the positions. They are created to achieve some specific objectives. Business organizations, for example, exist to produce goods or services to make a profit. Government agencies exist to carry out some function established by statute. Voluntary associations and community organizations form for specific purposes as well. These objectives define the "work" of an organization. To do its work, an organization develops a structure, a recurrent and more or less predictable pattern of relationships among members that results in coordination of members' activities and maintains the organization as an intact unit.

Organizational Survival

Organizations are open systems which means they exist in and interact with their environments. The environment of a system establishes the parameters of the system, the conditions that act on and interact with the focal system (Anderson, 1990). Parameters exist for all organizations. They are the constraints that the organization must contend with. Laws, statutes, and regulations that govern the provision of goods and services are an example. The realities of a global economy and global competition are additional examples. As environmental demands change, organizations must be able continually to adapt in order to survive.

As organizations define objectives, they define the type of relationship they would like to have with their environment. Organizations also define boundaries that distinguish between the organization and the environment. They receive a variety of inputs from their environments. Inputs are those things that cross organizational boundaries and affect the system in some way. We can roughly categorize inputs as information, material, and energy-activity. Inputs enter the structure of the organization, are responded to and acted upon in some way designed (it is hoped) to carry out the objectives and promote the continuation (steady state) of the organization. Responses are output as information, material, and energy/activity to the environment. Output affects and becomes part of the environment, which feeds back to further affect the organization.

For example, consider a moderate sized manufacturer. Inputs include raw materials, the capital necessary to obtain machinery, hire workers, and purchase raw materials. They also include the time, knowledge, skill, and energy of the workforce. Orders for products are another set of inputs. Environmental parameters can also be considered inputs. One example is market forces that affect the supply of and demand for products and their price structure. Other examples of inputs include the actions of other organizations, the nature of the competition, technology and technological change, statutes and regulations, conditions in the labor force, and outside control (e.g., banks, owners, investors, government, etc.). The company's continued existence is dependent on its ability to output goods and services to its environment such that it receives as feedback a continued flow of those inputs that support its existence. In a capitalist-type economy, the company's well-being may depend largely on its profitability. It must continue to sell products and services to a clientele at a price attractive to the clientele that also provides a sufficient profit for the company.

The input–process–output model applies to public agencies or service organizations as well. Usually, the objectives and methods of operation of public agencies are established by statute. Some or all of their operating funds come from legislative appropriation. Like the manufacturer, public and service organizations develop their structures influenced by the environmental parameters and their work. Inputs include the resources necessary to carry out their mandate as well as demands for services from a clientele and other environmental conditions. Their survival also depends on receiving continued support from their environment.

In the division of labor, various positions are organized as subsystems. Perhaps the manufacturing company's main subsystems are production and marketing. Each of these may be composed of subsubsystems. For example, a marketing division might be composed of departments such as sales, customer relations, market analysis, etc. These subsubsystems may be further divided into specific work or project units responsible for various functions, with workers in each unit—managers, salespersons, engineers, secretaries, etc.—responsible for definable tasks that carry out the task of the unit and contribute to the overall objective. System analysis for problem solving requires specification of the focal system which defines system elements and environment. Thus, for a department within a division, the elements of the system may be the workers in the various positions. The environment includes other departments. If the division is the focal system, the departments constitute subsystems.

As each unit at each level operates, they process the inputs from the environment with the goal of meeting the objective: to maintain its continued existence. The concept of "steady state" as it applies to organizations needs elaboration. First, the concept denotes a dynamic, not a static state. That is, steady state refers to ongoing negotiation with an environment to survive and maintain stability; maintenance of a steady state means coping effectively with ongoing threats to survival and stability. Ashby (1956:197) used the metaphor of a cat pursuing a mouse to illustrate the concept. The mouse, as a dynamic system can be in a variety of states in its attempts to escape the cat. Some of these states are consistent with the outcome: "mouse survives." However, other possible states of the mouse do not correspond to "survival."

Some states are desired states as consistent with survival and stability and others are not. Referring to inputs as "disturbances," that which moves systems from one state to another, Ashby noted that disturbances threaten the stability of the system. Also, the set of disturbances contains some measure of "variety." The task for survival and stability is to map the variety of disturbances into those states or outcomes that are consistent with the desired states and to do so on an ongoing basis. Ashby called the process "regulation."

Thus, regulation is those actions that process the variety, usually large, of inputs or disturbances from the environment into the set of states, usually small, consistent with survival and stability. Perfect regulation exists if, no matter what the disturbance, it is met with a response whose outcome is favorable to maintenance of the system. Organizational environments establish the conditions to which organizations must adapt, if they are to maintain themselves. These situational demands vary in complexity and degree of uncertainty. Organizational structure is initially designed and evolves according to attempts to meet situational demands. The more complex the environment, the greater the diversity of potential inputs, the more complex the organization must be to cope with environmental variety.

For any given organization, the concept of steady state may have several meanings, but in general, it refers to survival and stability. The concepts of "survival" and "stability" are not necessarily synonymous. Problems may arise within a unit when those things that maintain stability detract from meeting task objectives. An example is a maladaptive conformity commonly called "groupthink." This occurs when members of a group place maintenance of group solidarity above task effectiveness. They may overtly give agreement or consent on an issue or policy though they hold private but unvoiced reservations. A group norm of avoiding conflict to maintain stability can create problems for the group. The way an informal group within an organization protects itself by failing or resisting compliance with formal rules is another example. More generally, stable patterns may emerge within or between social units as members attempt to cope with their social realities. Though this stability may be maladaptive in terms of the goal or the overall organization, members will continue in these patterns and may resist change, needing the stability they derive from the patterns that emerged. Problem solving will need to address both internal structure and situational demands that the structure emerged in response to.

Goal setting and the establishment of structures and practices are the result of decision making designed to ensure the continuation of the organization. (Can anyone point to an organization that willingly ceased to exist?) Profitability or task effectiveness may be a key variable in an organization's survival, but as Collins (1988:461–462) observed, the organization will continue as long as its hierarchy remains intact and continues to pay employees, not whether it carries out its task.

> Ultimately it is the control structure that determines whether and in what form the organization will exist. Functional task pressures may feed into this, but as a secondary influence.

Moreover, how task-effective an organization has to be depends on its environment. An inefficient organization may continue if the environment supports its continued existence. On the other hand, a public agency that has a majority of the members of its governing legislative body howling for its demise, may have a short life, no matter how task-effective it is.

For organizations to maintain a steady state, control and regulation are necessary functions. Environmental conditions as inputs must be processed in such a way that the organization's response as output promotes the well-being of the organization. Control and regulation processes attempt to organize the internal activity to meet input demands and maintain existence. Organizations establish formal systems of control and regulation through a hierarchy of positions. Certain positions have authority over and responsibility for the activities of others and for coordinating those activities. The hierarchy is also the formal communication structure as certain positions report to and receive orders from certain higher positions. Problem solving may need to assess the legitimacy and appropriateness of the hierarchy given the task an organization has to perform.

Control and regulation involve decision making on methods for coordinating the components and meeting environmental conditions. This involves correcting internal conditions that may have become dysfunctional or responding to changing external conditions and demands. Market changes, technological change, changes in statutes and governmental regulation, etc., all require that the company adapt so that conditions are met with responses that maintain the company's well-being, its profitability.

Problems arise for an organization if it does not or cannot adapt to limit the threats to its integrity. Control and regulation can be either reactive or proactive. Reactive regulation is "error" driven and involves responses to problems that have occurred. Proactive regulation involves anticipating challenges to the organization and planning appropriately. Britt (1991) has argued that a proactive stance heightens organizations' ability to cope with challenges to their well-being.

Organizational Structure

Organizational structure is defined by the distribution of power and the mechanisms used for control and coordination and obtaining compliance with organizational goals. The structure is shaped by the work which, in turn, is shaped by the goals which are defined in terms of some interaction with social systems outside the organization—the environment. A chicken processing plant will have a structure that is very different from that of a public outpatient mental health clinic. The two types of tasks represent points on a continuum from highly routine, predictable, and repetitive tasks with standardized outcomes to tasks that feature a high degree of uncertainty requiring professional training, initiative, creativity, and adaptability and whose outcomes are difficult to specify.

Organizations can gain compliance through coercive control, through manipulation of material rewards, or through voluntary, internalized acceptance by members of the organization's goals (Collins, 1988; Etzioni, 1975). Administrative procedures, the methods used to gain compliance are adapted to the work. Administrative devices can be categorized as (1) surveillance, (2) inspecting outcomes, (3) written policies and procedures, (4) information control, and (5) environmental control. Surveillance involves posting "watchers" to see that workers comply. It is likely to produce minimal compliance and then primarily when the observers are present. Inspecting outcomes involves situations with easily measured outcomes but focuses on the product, not the process. Compliance is limited to the measurable outcomes. The use of written policies and procedures is an attempt to rationalize performance but focuses on procedures rather than outcomes. The presence of rules may lead informal groups to evade the rules. Informational control is based on the ability to define the situation such as having "expert" knowledge or skill. The greater the uncertainty in the environment, the greater the control those in possession of specialized information can exert. Environmental control can be exercised by controlling the physical setting to limit noncompliance.

The use of control-type and administrative devices establishes the organizational structure and responds to the goals and work of the organization. For example, if the task is the assembly and sales of fast food, tasks of low initiative with observable outcomes, coercive control, surveillance, rigid rules, and environmental control will work very effectively. This is especially true if there is no need to counter alienation or to have workers internalize the goals of the organization. The availability of an endless supply of teenage workers helps to make up for the high turnover rate of employees in the fast-food industry (see Ritzer, 1993). On the other hand, with tasks that call for initiative and creative adaptation to relatively unpredictable situations, such as the work of most professionals, administrators, or emergency workers, coercive controls are not likely to be effective. Surveillance, rules, piecework, and other coercive measures eliminate worker autonomy which can be alienating, fail to motivate, and not meet the needs of the situation. Internalized control and informational administrative procedures are more likely to be found with these tasks.

Any given organization may have a mix of control and administrative procedures. Workers at the lowest level in the status structure may receive more coercive control while the organization may count on internalized control for members higher in the status structure. Although there are qualifications, the general principle is that "organizations which choose the proper control form for its tasks will survive and prosper" (Collins, 1988:464). One qualification is the nature of environmental demands; how efficient an organization has to be may depend on its environment. However, whether an organization chooses the "proper" control form is itself a result of control and the exercise of power within the organization.

The task and the structure, however, cannot be divorced from consideration of the environment. The goal is framed in terms of the production of goods and/or services to output to the environment. The structure must be responsive to the nature of the demands or disturbances in the environment. As noted above, the structure must be of sufficient complexity to meet the complexity in the environment. Thus, the key to understanding an organization is to understand its work and how it organizes to do its work given the environmental constraints present.

Community Organization

Compared to formal organizations, communities have more diffuse boundaries, show a great deal of variability in the extent of participation and interaction within the system by role-occupants and show a great deal of variability in the degree of organization and structure. Indeed, the term *community* can be ambiguous, sometimes referring to a geographic area including the people who live in that area and institutions that affect their area. Alinsky's (1941/1984) Back of the Yards was such a community, as was Bailey's (1974) South Austin. Or, community may refer to a people sharing a common characteristic and therefore a similar fate. Thus we hear of ethnic communities such as the black, Latino, or Southeast Asian communities. We also hear of gays or seniors or handicapped persons referred to as a community, though the members of these communities do not necessarily live in a specific geographic area.

Community organization often involves the development of a fairly formal organization, usually in response to shared problems facing the members of a community. Rivera and Erlich (1992:3) had ethnic minorities in mind when they defined community organization as,

> efforts to mobilize people who are directly affected by a community condition (that is, the "victims," the unaffiliated, the unorganized, and the nonparticipating) into groups and organizations to enable them to take action on the social problems and issues that concern them. A typical feature of these efforts is the concern with building new organizations among people who have not been previously organized to take social action on a problem.

Thus, by community organizing we refer to methods of intervention in which the professional change agent helps community members, groups, or organizations organize for planned collective action for social change. It may be to address a particular single issue or it may be to develop unity to go on to address a wide range of problems and community needs: maintenance or improvement of physical facilities such as parks, street or sidewalk pavement, housing, street lighting; initiation or improvement of services such as police, sanitation, or fire protection, health and welfare or education; political and economic issues involving policies, legislation, and distribution of resources; social problems such as drug use, crime and violence, teen pregnancy, discrimination, and ethnic conflict.

Community organizing activities vary depending on the nature and needs of the specific community. There may be strong, close ties among members at one extreme to none at the other extreme. Community members may be an advantaged group or may be oppressed, powerless, and disadvantaged or some mix. They may be keenly aware of their problems or have no awareness. In general, community organizing involves helping community members create a relatively formal structure, an organization, with the ability to work toward achieving some defined set of goals. Often this involves confronting a power structure of some sort. The view is that by acting through a formal structure of their own, community members can, to some extent, redress the power imbalance between them and formal power structures.

Roles for community organizers can be labeled "enabler," "broker," or "activist." In the enabler role, the community organizer works directly with a client population, not as a leader but to help facilitate the efforts of local people. In the enabler role, the community organizer tries not to provide answers but may raise questions that help local people gain insights into the problem. The role-occupant does not accept responsibility for organizing but encourages the local people who actually decide what to do.

A second role is that of broker. In this role, the community organizer negotiates with networks with which local people have little information or experience. The broker also puts people in touch with resources. In the third role, the activist, the community organizer takes direct action to organize people and to confront and challenge opposition. Which role to adopt depends on the situation and the orientation of the organizer. In many instances, community organizers may enact each of these roles in the course of work.

Just as community needs vary, approaches to community organization and change vary as well. Rothman (1979) developed three models as pure types while noting that they often overlap. The three models or approaches were labeled "locality development," "social planning," and "social action." In Rothman's analysis, the goals for intervention and the nature of the community suggest different approaches to change as well as different roles for the change agent.

In the first model, locality development, the goal is to organize the community into an integrated, functioning unit with change based on involving "... broad participation of a wide spectrum of people at the local level in goal determination and action" (p. 26). The idea is that for change to take place, individuals first must come to see themselves as a community and learn that, through consensus building and collective action, they can address and often solve problems within their locale. The change agent's role is that of enabling, encouraging, and facilitating community members to come together to get organized. The role may also involve teaching and facilitating group process and teaching problem-solving skills. Immediately confronting power structures may not always be the goal in this model. Often organizing and creating a sense of community can be goals in themselves,

---

Clinical Focus 4.1

Community Organizer Readiness Skills Assessment

Archer, Kelly, and Bisch (1984) reviewed several sources and developed a list of the skills needed by a community organizer. The following list is taken from that source (p. 57). It may be useful to contemplate this list of skills to examine ourselves to see if we are ready for the task.

1. A working knowledge of community organization theory and process
2. Good planning and assessment skills
3. Knowledge of the community in which organization is taking place
4. Awareness of the power structure and the transfer of power in the community
5. Credibility within the community
6. Dedication to an idea or goal
7. Trust in others and in their abilities
8. The ability to share responsibility
9. Good communication skills
10. Leadership qualities
11. Belief in the democratic process
12. Flexibility to be able to react to the situation and respond appropriately
13. Time-management skills to realistically obtain objectives in reasonable time, acknowledging the constraints and resources available
14. Acceptance that the community, not the individual is the client
15. Research skills
16. A sense of humor
17. Patience

---

which may later be applied, effectively, as needs arise, to work internally or to negotiate with outside agents.

The second approach, social planning, features a technical approach to solving specific social problems through "rational, deliberately planned and controlled change...." The change agent's role is that of expert planner who applies expertise to design and implement plans and policies in a cost-effective manner. Participation by community members may vary from a little to a lot; the emphasis is on the technical skill of the expert, including the ability to get desired responses from bureaucracies.

In the third approach, social action, the change agent takes an activist role to organize a disadvantaged community as a conflict structure to confront a power structure, such as government, for social justice and/or redistribution of power and resources. This is the Alinsky model of community organization and change. As Glass (1984) pointed out, Alinsky believed that change comes through power, the ability to act. For the powerless, this means organization.

Rothman and Reed (1984) described mobilizing a community to assess its needs and create an effective plan to address drug and alcohol problems. They noted that communities vary in the extent to which they regulate and support types of drug use. Even experts on drug use and abuse differ on the definition of the problem. Community variability and scientific uncertainty make it presumptuous to prescribe uniform interventions. Just as there are many approaches to intervention in drug and alcohol problems, there are various ways for sociological practitioners to help communities organize to do something about them. One approach was reported by Watts (1989:154), and by Watts and Wright (1991) who endorsed the view that the community level presents opportunities for change, "... greater than at the societal or individual levels." Watts used both qualitative and quantitative research to bring drug problems to the community's attention, leading to mobilization. Watts' activities exemplify the locality development approach.

Watts also called attention to another point relevant for a discussion of community organization. As the intervention agent, Watts' work led to the definition of youth drug use as a social problem where previously it had not been recognized as such. If an individual's abuse of drugs and alcohol disrupts his or her life, that is a personal problem. However, it is a social problem if the pattern exists within the community. Thus, as Watts noted, "The sociologist can help alter community beliefs that contribute to an environment that tolerates drug use" (p. 156). Watts' work introduced the issue of teen drug use into what Hilgartner and Bosk (1988) called "The Public Arena."

Hilgartner and Bosk (1988) rejected the view that social problems are readily identifiable and have an objective reality. They argued Blumer's view instead, that "... social problems are projections of collective sentiments rather than simple mirrors of objective conditions...." (p. 53). Social problem definitions evolve in "arenas" where a situation or condition gets labeled as a problem "in the arenas of public discourse." Arenas include the mass media, both news and entertainment, political organizations, social action groups, religious organizations, professional societies, etc., anywhere people come together on an institutional basis. These arenas are competitive marketplaces where public attention is a scarce resource.

In addition to the competition among problems for attention, competing interpretations of a problem may exist. A problem such as drug use or teen pregnancy could be interpreted as problems of individual responsibility or as social and community problems. Community organization to address a problem thus calls for dramatic activity on many levels to bring the problem to community attention and to develop a shared collective definition that a problem exists and needs to be addressed by collective action. The various arenas in which problems may be addressed, however, have a "carrying capacity," a limit on the number of problems that can be attended to at a time. Timing entry into the field should be included in any strategy.

Hilgartner and Bosk also noted the principles by which social problems are selected for appearance. The first is "drama"; the more dramatically the problem can be presented, the more likely it will compete successfully. Problems must remain dramatic, which requires the introduction of new symbols or events from time to time. Second, problems couched in broad cultural themes compete better. Third, problems framed in terms acceptable to dominant political and economic groups will compete better. Finally, each organization has its own rhythms that influence the timing of its attention to social problems which also affects selection. These include, for example, reporters' and editors' understanding of what is news.

For community organization efforts to be effective, community members must come to define a problem, believe collective action will be effective, and be prepared to give their time and energy to the collective effort. Watts' work in his community accomplished these objectives by dramatically illustrating that a problem existed, that it was a social problem that touched each family, thus encouraging mobilization.

Intervention at the Mesolevel

Orientation

The diversity and uniqueness of settings do not permit detailed description of specific intervention strategies in a chapter such as this. The uniqueness of each group and situation makes it difficult to offer even general change strategies. Each target of change has a unique history, development, and needs. A particular intervention may not "fit" or may conflict with the group's unique situation. Therefore, clinical sociologists must not impose change strategies they may feel comfortable with or assume that these strategies will be appropriate to most groups and situations.

The purpose of intervention is to bring about problem-solving change in social systems based on data collected with the intent of using the data to produce change in a system. One purpose of data is to stimulate discussions and meetings in which members of a social system can express attitudes and feelings about intervention and change. Data help identify problems and provide a basis for discussion. Data also help provide a rational basis for decision making, present possible alternatives, and clarify possible effects of interventions. A third purpose of data is to initiate persuasion and political action by mobilizing a constituency based on understanding of the facts. Data can be obtained from a variety of sources using a variety of methods and can help sharpen the intervention objective and identify conditions favorable to the success of intervention.

The task of a clinical sociologist in organizational development or community organization, is to work with members of a social system, "... to help them to change social structure or modes of functioning or both" (Jacques, 1982:50). It is important to emphasize that social problems must be addressed socially. Because problems appear to be manifested in the behavior of individuals, problems are often addressed by attempts to modify the behavior of individuals judged to be deviant, to "have a problem." Managers and administrators tend to have an individual orientation consistent with our cultural beliefs in individualism. It is also easier to contemplate changing individuals than broad structural and institutional patterns and processes. Thus, Finkelstein (1992) concluded that, in most efforts at addressing social system problems, "the primary unit of analysis remains the individual."

Finkelstein referred to individual and social psychological analyses as restrictive and too narrow. He was critical of "narrowly focussing on the attitudes, beliefs, and subjective states of individuals in order to predict behavior." Individuals are active creators of reality but they construct their reality collectively and adapt to their social systems as best they can. Attitudes and behaviors, motives and motivations, beliefs, values, and commitments are constructed and maintained by social processes within social systems. Feelings of alienation, frustration, and powerlessness derive from social structures and social, political, and economic processes and individuals' roles and status within social structures. Lasting, effective change must address these.

For example, a high school finds a segment of the youth unreachable and unteachable, into drugs and delinquency, and generally incorrigible. Well-meaning individual interventions may include disciplinary action, behavioral management, individual treatment plans, counseling, and tutoring. These often end in frustration since they fail to examine and address the structure and culture of the school, the community, the neighborhoods, peers, and families, and fail to involve the total social system in addressing what are social rather than individual problems. The situation calls for multilevel analysis. The intervention process is an attempt to close the gap between what is and what ought to be. Preparing for change involves what we have called the strategic steps of intervention: assessment, program planning, program implementation, and program evaluation.

People with problems want solutions. When faced with a problem, the temptation is to start generating solutions and adopting one. The danger in this approach may be failure to address the right problem and/or adopting strategies that will not work. Clinical sociologists bring a more deliberate and rational process to problem solving. As we have stated, problem solving requires change. Change requires preparation.

Preparation for Change

Preparation for change begins with the step we call assessment, which involves analysis of a social problem, its nature, and importance. Analysis of a social problem includes the application of sociological methods to the analysis of a social system. It means gathering detailed information on the problem, the social system, and the social system's relationships with other relevant social systems. Assertions are supported by data which define the problem and point toward design and implementation of a program for problem solving. Analysis of social systems involves analysis of structures and processes. It means working with members of a client system to construct a knowledge base regarding the social system and its problems.

Content of Assessment

Many of the principles expressed in the previous chapter generalize to mesolevel cases and bear repeating. The first item for your assessment is whether to take on the task. As before, relevant issues include the demands on your time, your expertise, and your interests. Value issues are also relevant. If the goals are incompatible with your values, it may be best not to become involved. There are some issues you may want to evaluate before getting involved. These issues may affect whether you want to get involved or at least guide the way you proceed. Often you must decide on the basis of a brief contact with a representative of the client system. Is commitment to change genuine? Some organizations may find it useful merely to appear to be addressing problems. Are you being asked to help cool out pockets of discontent rather than genuinely address problems and circumstances that generate legitimate criticism? Are there hidden agendas? Is a business organization's goal to gain tighter control and manipulation of employees? You may also want to evaluate how much control those in authority will have and how much freedom you will have to pursue your investigation. Is the intervention being imposed by those in authority or is there general concern and willingness to address problems? In this section we propose a participatory model of intervention that involves all levels of a system. If you follow this approach it may also be necessary to discover if this is acceptable in this client system.

An important early step is to identify the focal system, the social unit with the problem. This permits further identification of various system levels—sub- and subsubsystems, suprasystems, etc. It also directs attention to boundaries, mapping linkages with other systems, and identification of the relevant environment and the constraints it presents. Finally, it permits identification of the level of analysis. It is important not to confuse system levels. The general principle is that a system must be analyzed at its own level; that is, a system must be analyzed in terms of the interaction and relationships among its elements. No amount of analysis of system components will reveal the nature of a system. This is not to say that analysis of subsystems is not useful. It does mean that, at any level, analysis of components will not explain the unit. Analysis of the interaction and relationships among elements is essential to understanding a system.

If a division composed of several departments is the focal system, analysis of the division means analysis of the structure and interaction of the various departments. Analysis of each department as subsystems may also be necessary for a complete understanding of the problem, but the division itself can only be understood in terms of the relationships among its components. The size and complexity of the focal system is a key variable governing the assessment and all stages of the intervention. Multilevel analysis is essential.

Begin assessment by eliciting a statement of the presenting problem. As Ramondt (1994) observed:

> The clinical approach attaches particular importance to the preliminary investigation, which sets the framework for determining which problems are to be examined. The predominant culture in organizations is not a problem-setting but a solution-oriented one. In many cases this is the major source of problems within an organization; the problem has not been properly identified and poorly defined solutions are tackled.

As is often the case, the problem statement may eventually have to be refined or even reformulated, but clients' accounts represent their understanding and represent what they want you to understand about their situation. Clients' statements of the presenting problem may be a socially constructed reality derived from the interaction network and influential members within it. It may be widely shared by members of the client system. As an element of organizational culture, the shared definition of the problem may affect broad areas of action within the organization and frame attempts to cope with or solve the problem.

Alternatively, an issue for ongoing assessment may be to determine how widely shared this statement of the problem is. It may be useful to keep Murphy's dictum in mind: Where you stand on an issue depends on where you sit. What some may define as a problem may be a coping mechanism for others. It would not be unusual in a formal organization for upper management, middle management, and workers to have very different views on what the problem is, who is responsible, what needs "fixing," and how to "fix" it.

It is not useful to try to find out who is "right." Do not try to reconcile, merge, or average the different points of view. Within any given social system there are cliques and interest groups. Interests may vary across organizational levels and across subsystems. It is useful to observe where consensus and differences exist in problem definition.

A historical approach to problem analysis is sometimes useful. Often social systems' problems have their roots in processes and structures that were once quite rational and effective or were designed for conditions which have changed or no longer exist. More generally, problems often evolve over time; small quantitative changes in response to environmental demands may emerge as the major qualitative changes that have become problematic. Historical analysis may provide understanding of how long the problem situation has existed and how it came to be recognized as a problem. It may also reveal causal factors, though it is important not to oversimplify. Problems seldom have a single cause. Finally, historical analysis may show what has been tried previously to alleviate the problem and what effects these attempts have had, including the responses of members of the social system to attempts at problem solving. Ramondt also suggested exploring critical incidents in an organization's history, the way in which they were handled, and the consequences.

Social problems exist because some group defines a condition or situation as deviating from some norm or desired state. For organizations, created for explicit purposes, deviation may include those things that contribute to reduction in goalward movement such as reduced productivity or the things that threaten stability. For communities, deviation may include those things usually defined as socially deviant—crime, drugs, violence, etc.—or quality of life or standards of living issues.

Problem analysis should discover what official norms govern behavior. Official norms derive from sets of values and perhaps even determinations of morality. Assessment should uncover these. Analyses should also determine the extent of deviation from the norm. This calls for data on the extent of the problem as well as data on the social and economic costs. Organizations may show reduced productivity, employee dissatisfaction, poor morale, and problem behaviors. A school system may show a high dropout or failure rate or instances of weapons being brought to school or instances of violence. Communities may show rates of violence, crime, and drugs as well as physical deterioration or unattended health or mental health problems of residents. Data on the extent of the problem and its social costs can be an aid to mobilization of problem solving activities. For example, we previously showed how Watts' (1989) data on drug use identified a social rather than an individual problem.

Problem analysis should further locate the social causes of social problems. Durkheim's (1895/1966) "Rule" is still valid: social facts should be explained in terms of other social facts. Social problems are the consequences of social arrangements. Study the social system. With organizations, the key is the work. The input–process–output–feedback model suggests an approach. It is necessary to identify the important variables that describe the input. However, the issue for analysis is the process; how does the organization organize to do its work? Thus, Ramondt argued for analyzing organizations in terms of their organizing behavior and what they *do* rather than what they are. This reveals the relationship between structure and process. It was also Ramondt's view that structure must follow the process.

Analysis of the task structure includes analysis of the task itself. What is to be done and how is it to be done? How are tasks organized and coordinated and controlled? Who has the responsibility and who has authority over what specific operations? As they emerge from the work, attention to other structures is necessary. Specific structures include the communication structures, both formal and informal: who talks to whom about what, when, and how? The power structure is another: What are the formal and informal influence, authority, and reward structures? What positions have the responsibility for what decisions? Questions for assessment also include the following: Who are the key actors, both individuals and groups? What are the control, coordination, and regulation mechanisms in organizations? Who are the decision makers and legitimizers? What is the nature of power relations? What are the processes of power and control? How do they work? How is power and influence distributed within the system? What are the formal and informal structures and how do they operate? How do their goals, norms, and values differ? Are there needs for training and personnel development? Do members have the resources including the ability necessary to carry out their roles? What are the communication styles and patterns? How does the system manage conflict and tension, planning and goal setting? How are decisions arrived at? What is the pattern of social relations? Are persons mistreated?

Additionally, French and Bell (1984) presented a laundry list of assessment questions for formal organizations. The following list is derived from that source:

- What are organization norms and values?
- What are the attitudes, opinions, and feelings of members toward system goals, management, and procedures?
- What is the internal climate? Authoritarian or democratic? Oppressive or open? Controlling or trusting?
- How effective are the organization's procedures for monitoring and preparing for oncoming or potential problems?
- For subsystems, how do they relate to the whole? What are the unique demands placed on each subsystem? How do they interface and are there differences in their performance levels?
- Are subsystem goals compatible with system goals?
- Do members know how to do what is expected of them?
- Is good use made of resources?
- What are intergroup relations like and what effects do these have on the overall system?
- How does the system interface with its environment and with other systems?

Much of the above applies when the object of intervention is community organization. The analysis must include the problem, the environment, the structure of the social system, and the possibilities and readiness for change. Like assessment with organizations, assessment of communities should locate power, influence, and authority structures, for example. Additional questions for assessment include, what is the nature of the community, the demographic characteristics? What naturally occurring networks exist? What, if any, interest groups exist and what is the nature of their interaction? Do their interests conflict? What are their concerns? What are the communication networks and where are they? Who are the gatekeepers and legitimizers within the community? Where are the rallying places where people come together? What are the outside agencies that impact on or provide services for the members of the community and what are relations with them? What socioeconomic and political issues exist within the community. What are the cultural norms and values that guide the community; for example, an ethnic community?

Alinsky's report (1941/1984) of community organization in the Back of the Yards area in Chicago around 1940 serves as an example. Community members determined that chronic social problems existed: unemployment, disease, child welfare issues, delinquency, and poor housing. They also determined the solution to their problems depended on themselves. Demographically, the Back of the Yards area had great ethnic variety. Though 90% were Roman Catholic in religion, each ethnic group had its own church. Additionally, most community residents were economically dependent on the Stock Yards as well. Thus, through organizing efforts, the Church and organized labor managed to bring the diverse groups together and became central organizations in providing leadership and legitimacy for community organization. The result was the Back of the Yards Neighborhood Council, "rooted primarily in the fundamental institutions of the community," whose members had "a vast fund of intimate knowledge regarding those subtle, informal, and personal aspects of the communal life of Back of the Yards." Through this Council, the problems of the community were addressed with many positive achievements.

An assessment of a social system is conducted from within it. The rules of good research should govern the assessment task. Various research strategies can be used as the following list suggests:

1. Survey research with structured questionnaires and rating scales has the value of covering a large organization or community and developing useful data quickly and efficiently. Panel studies or repeated waves can be used to monitor trends and other aspects of the time dimension.
2. In-depth interviews with selected role occupants at all levels of the system can also be useful to flesh out details that questionnaires often miss.
3. Focus groups with members sampled across levels of a social system can also be useful to get more in-depth insights into members' views and concerns. The method has the advantage of allowing contact with more respondents than one-on-one interviews and represents efficient use of time.

4. Specific meetings with a whole team or work unit or other intact group within the social system can be useful to observe the functioning and interaction patterns of the unit.
5. Both participant and nonparticipant observation can provide data on actual activity in the naturalistic setting.
6. Review of documents, policy statements, plans, budgets, evaluations, mission statements, and tables of organization, documents usually available with formal organizations, can be an essential step. They represent formal statements of what ought to be that can be compared to how things are actually done. Are policies and procedures rational and consistent? Do they facilitate achievement of desired outcomes?
7. Monitoring the flow of communication, both written and nonwritten, can also be useful. Pay attention to both the formal and informal networks. How is information disseminated and how effective are the existing networks? Where appropriate, include mass media in the analysis.
8. Diaries and record keeping by selected members of an organization can also be a useful source of information. For example, one technique involves having members record their activities at random intervals.

The Process of Assessment: Participatory Research

The process of assessment is a clinical research task designed to reveal the structure and processes of a social system, help define and clarify the problem situation, and point toward pathways for change. It differs from scientific research in its intent and often in its methodology. The clinician cannot take the role of disinterested scientist. The goal is to produce positive social change. The methodology we offer here was labelled "action based" by Finkelstein (1992). Couto (1987) called the approach "participatory research" and Whyte (1989) called it participatory action research (PAR).

The technique recognizes first the dynamic nature of social change. That is, neither the intervention agent nor members of a social system can control all the factors influencing change. In addition, as change begins, secondary changes may occur that may alter the change process itself. Thus, change is not likely to be brought about by simply introducing a sequence of planned activities and letting them take their course. The change process needs continual guidance by people able to adapt creatively to reach the desired outcome. Thus, Whyte (1989:368) stated, "Success in organizational change is not achieved simply by making the right decision at a particular time but rather through developing a social process that facilitates organizational learning."

Couto's model of participatory research seems to have community organization in mind. He stated that, "Its central concerns are research, knowledge production, and empowerment related to the position of oppressed people, poor people, people with political or economic disadvantage." The intent is to mobilize people affected by a problem, with research and action both part of the change process. Thus, Couto indicated the characteristics of participatory research:

- The problem under study and the decision to study it have origins in the community affected by the problem;
- The goal of the research is political or social change derived from the information gathered;
- Local people control the process of problem definition, information gathering, and decisions about action following from the information; and
- Local people and professional researchers are equals in the research process. They are both researchers and learners. (Couto, 1987:84)

In this model, the role of the clinical sociologist is to maintain constant dialogue with and train and assist local people to conduct and use credible research that clarifies and documents the problem and clarifies what needs to be done to solve the problem.

Whyte (1989) applied what he called participatory action research (PAR) to organizational change and problem solving. In this approach, professionals work together with organizational members "in designing projects, gathering and analyzing data, and utilizing the findings in action projects." By their participation in the process, organizational members and decision makers control and own the change process by shaping it to their needs.

As Whyte (1989) described PAR the "research design is a joint product" of the clinical worker(s) and organization members. The latter "carry a major responsibility for gathering and evaluating data, and serve as ... the experts on technical matters ..." related to the work of the organization. "The professional researchers assume responsibility ... for helping [organization members] integrate the socio- with the technical to develop a socio-technical model of the change process" (p. 374). Whyte went on to argue, quite persuasively, based on his extensive experience, that effective organizational work must integrate the social and the technical systems:

> Since the social system shapes ways in which technology is developed and applied, and the technological system shapes and channels social relations, analyses that focus on only one of these two systems are bound to be theoretically misleading and of limited practical value. (p. 376)

Putting PAR into practice would seem to involve putting together the research team drawn from the various components of the focal system. Organizational members of the team should represent the technical expertise relevant to the work of the organization. Sociological members of the team can assist through group facilitation, and providing information on the operation of social systems as well as providing training and advice on research methodology. The process is one of ongoing dialogue among all members of the team, both organizational members and clinical sociologists.

Planning for Change

Change is a process. Some change will occur with or without intervention. But if change is to be directed and controlled, it must be developed. Therefore, an intervention should involve a carefully crafted plan about the direction and speed of change, and how change will affect the members of the social system following the intervention. Responsibility for the effects of an intervention should be acknowledged and accepted by all parties involved in the effort.

The assessment research should provide an analysis of the problem, the social system, and what needs to be done to bring about change that solves problems. The next step is the planning of an intervention program. The intervention program can be viewed as having five major needs: (1) conceptualizing and developing the parts of a change effort; (2) preparing a strategy designed to get change accepted; (3) implementation of the strategy; (4) follow-up to determine whether or not the strategy worked; (5) ability to adapt based on these findings. The most consistent aspect of sociological intervention is that it is data based. An intervention plan is based on a thorough assessment of the problem situation and the social system. Progress is monitored throughout implementation through ongoing evaluation both of process and outcomes. The fourth and fifth parts are often neglected in the overall plan or the agent leaves the field before effects can be assessed. Sometimes change may be slow and cumulative and therefore it may be impossible to observe any obvious effects in a short period following the intervention (Netting, Kettner, and McMurty, 1993). However, every effort must be made to monitor an intervention program so that guidance of the process, step 5, is based on evidence. Thus, planning must include an evaluation plan.

Preparing for change should include assessment of a system's readiness for change. Not all members of a client system will conceive of change the same way or even see the need for change. Change may mean new role relationships, changes in formal or informal status structures, or changes in interaction patterns. Change may mean a new task structure. Members may also come to feel their security is being threatened. Some will see change as a threat to stability and resist. The intervention agent, whether inside or from outside the system, must be careful not to impose change. To do so could result in anger, hostility, and resistance. It is important to learn attitudes toward change, the sources of support and resistance, and the values and priorities of the target of intervention. It is possible that the time is not right for intervention and change, but it is essential that a consensus for change arise and be supported; that intervention not be imposed. Thus, program planning involves negotiation and consensus building with regards to goals as well as means.

Interventions can be one-time only or take place over time; they may occur more than once over time and in more than one way. Some interventions require little or no effort on the part of the recipient(s) while other interventions need substantial time and commitment; e.g. completing food diaries, interviews, and tests. The nature and duration of interventions must be made known to the members of the client system. Furthermore, it is advantageous for the intervenor to get input at periodic intervals. This will help insure an open and trusting relationship and assist in retaining people in the intervention effort.

Preparing for change requires that the intervenor carefully conduct an assessment that includes a group's prior experience with change, attitudes toward change, and the group's perception of what needs to be changed and their degree of investment in bringing about change. Imposed change will bring about opposition and hostility. Preparation for change requires time, patience, and touching base with those who will be affected by change. The best situation is if the targets of change participate in helping bring it about.

Preparing for change may also involve what Ramondt (1994) referred to as an analysis of a social system's capacity for change. This refers to the energy and resources available to apply to a change process and what else is competing for the use of these resources. Ramondt further suggested that analysis of capacity for change should recognize critical domains within the social system and how much energy is invested in each domain:

- The political domain: Who decides and who cooperates with whom in the allocation of scarce resources?
- The cultural domain: To what extent does consensus exist on norms and values relating to key policy areas?
- The technical domain: What is the "design of the central processes for realizing a desired output?"

In some instances analysis of readiness for change and capacity for change may lead to the conclusion to hold off. However, in most cases they should be viewed as affecting the change strategy. Knowledge of readiness and capacity for change in a social system may affect the timing of various steps. It may show the need for efforts at persuasion and influence of or negotiation and compromise with various constituencies to get key actors "on board" so that further movement can take place. All too often resistance and other barriers to change are attributed to individuals. However, analysis of readiness and capacity for change should include the structural factors of a social system that produce individual member's attitudes towards and participation in change efforts.

Change efforts in organizations should focus on the work and the process by which the work is done. The social organization, as Ramondt (1994) stated, should be compatible with the design of the process. Planning, implementation, and evaluation of change efforts should be based on a real partnership between the professional change agents and the organization members. Sometimes a show of participation is used as a manipulative tool to gain compliance. But organization members' experience, knowledge, and skills with the organization and the work are an important resource. If they are given a real role to play in the change process, the design is more likely to address needs and they are more likely to have the motivation to carry out the activities to make it work.

Program planning, therefore, continues the collaborative effort that includes the clinical sociologist(s) and system members to produce what Whyte (1982) called "social inventions" which focus on outcome objectives. For organizations Whyte described the PAR approach in which "the social scientists structured the social and technological learning process." Organization members from a variety of positions—managers, supervisors, workers, union leaders, etc.—worked with the social scientists "in designing new physical, technological, and social organizational arrangements." The social scientists shared control of the process with key organization members.

This approach to organizational problem solving is often called "sociotechnical" to emphasize the close association between the technological aspects of the task and the social organization of the task-process. Policy and program development must consider both aspects. As Whyte (1989) described PAR, organization members had the responsibility for gathering and evaluating data and providing technical expertise on matters pertaining to the task. The social scientists helped organization members "integrate the socio- with the technical to develop a sociotechnical model of the change process."

Program planning must also consider how, when, and where implementation will begin, i.e., the steps for transition. Where appropriate, pilot programs may be useful. Finally, program planning must establish the evaluation procedures. It must establish measurable process indicators which will determine whether the plan proceeds on course as planned. Outcome indicators must also be established to determine if the plan moves the organization toward the objective. Evaluation should also be alert for unintended negative effects. Time frames should be established for deciding whether to continue a course of action or to consider modification based on the results of evaluation.

Planning for change in community organization work is also a collaborative activity to achieve a goal that is also mutually defined. That is, the goals and the steps to achieve the goals are established by active, ongoing involvement of the people affected by the process. The clinical sociologist(s) participate as members along with the community members. The plan to be developed should specify what is to be done, by whom, when, and why.

Planning must begin with consensus on the goals, the desired outcome for the community. This itself may not be a simple task. The more diverse the community and the more diverse the interests of the various constituencies, the more the need for negotiation, compromise, and consensus building. The systemic nature of all social systems reminds us that any change affects all components of a system as well as the total system. Planning for change must make every effort to include all the elements of a community in a truly collaborative effort. This includes recognition of cultural and linguistically diverse groups, class differences, and minority group status. Archer et al. (1984:24) were quite succinct about the professional's role here:

> Collaboration can only take place among people who participate. In deciding on the community's desired future, consultants must be constantly alert for the interests of those who are to be affected by change but who for whatever reason are not participants in the process.

Steps in planning include defining the target population that should be included in the planning. That is, planning should be done by and for the people affected. Planning should consider the roles change agents must play and the model of community organization: How much confrontation will be necessary and how much confrontation are people comfortable with? Planning may also require consideration of stages, steps to be completed before additional steps can be taken.

Finally, planning must include planning the evaluation activities. Evaluation represents the feedback loop that provides information on the progress and direction of change-related activities. This means that planning must provide for valid and reliable indicators that the program is on course and is not creating unintended negative consequences. This stage of planning should also provide for agreements for ongoing involvement of the planning group. As plans move forward, it is necessary to evaluate progress and continue to guide the process based on the feedback.

Sengstock (1987) reported on her work with a community intervention to design and implement a service plan for abused wives that offers one model of how to do it. Sengstock's work exemplifies the combination of all three of Rothman's models. The project started in 1980 at a time when there was little public knowledge or awareness of the problem and very few services for abused wives in the community. Thus, one of Sengstock's tasks was to introduce the problem into appropriate public arenas and get the problem on the public agenda. Sengstock described three broad, sociologically based strategies that resulted in successful outcomes:

1. Provision of information about social structure and its consequences, enabling individuals and groups to use knowledge of social structure to develop more effective plans for group action.
2. Use of sociological principles and data to make people aware of aspects of the social situation of which they had previously been unaware.
3. Involvement of the individuals/group members in the planning process to maximize the likelihood that they will have an investment in the outcome.

Analysis of the social structure of the community directed attention toward those segments that could help achieve the goal. Sociological analysis was also used to determine what task forces were needed. It also helped to identify key individuals that played important roles in the various public arenas to include in planning and implementation committees. These individuals had to have sufficient interest to get involved in the problem and who were in agencies or had contacts that could influence the initiation of services for abused women. In many instances their public image required that they cooperate and through participation they became invested in the project. Sociological knowledge was also applied as guides to problem definition and goal selection. It was found that people lacked information about woman abuse and a variety of methods were used to present information on spouse abuse and about services needs and providers. This often meant the dissemination and interpretation of research results in a way that was meaningful to the people who needed this information.

The goal of the project involved changing the way community agencies acted. This necessarily meant including key members of these agencies. Research shows that individuals will be more committed and change is more likely to occur if these individuals are included in the planning and implementation of change. Much of the actual work took place in committees and task forces. Members' commitment and their personal involvement in problem solving, as well as their willingness to be guided by social science findings, were enhanced by the application of social psychological principles of group process. The clinical sociologist can play a role by facilitating group process and teaching members about groups and group processes. Sengstock's report thus demonstrated the application of sociological theory, research, and methods in community organization.

Cautionary Notes

Sometimes reasonable interventions run into the rigidity of social systems and create new problems. Howard (1995) reported several examples of system rigidity:

- Mother Teresa wanted to build a homeless shelter in an abandoned South Bronx building. New York City insisted the building have an unnecessary $100,000 elevator. The nuns gave up; they said the money was better spent on soup and sandwiches for the poor.
- A rigid federal law required a Virginia company to spend $31 million to prevent a small amount of benzene from escaping from a smokestack. Therefore, the company could not spend the money to clean up tons of harmful benzene emissions that came from a nearby source.

- A plan for sidewalk toilets in New York City had wide support. But it ran afoul of disabilities-rights regulations because wheelchairs could not fit the kiosks. A compromise plan to have attendants at disabled-only kiosks failed. No one used them.

These illustrations point out that sometimes problems remain unsolvable, at least with reasonable solutions, because of the potency of the social systems involved. In these examples, direct problem solving was impeded by laws. Sometimes, even compromises are impossible, especially when laws are involved.

Summary

The mesosociological level refers to those social structures that mediate between people and the larger social, political, and economic forces within society. We make our livings, receive health care, education, and a host of other community services, practice our religions, take political action, and often seek social contact as participants in mesolevel social structures. The practice of clinical sociology at this level involves addressing problems within these structures as social problems rather than as problems with individuals.

Social problems arise as products of social structures, their cultures, and the dynamic interaction processes within them. Individual members may be affected as they attempt to cope with and adapt to the situations. However, problems are seen as located in the social arrangements. Problem solving involves clinical sociologists working as partners with members of client systems to bring about planned social change. The clinical sociologist can make a variety of skills available to the client system. Research skills assist members of the client system in understanding the nature and scope of the problem and in understanding the social system as well as monitoring the effects of change-related strategies. Group facilitation skills are useful in helping a working group with its task. Finally, perhaps the most important contribution clinical sociologists can make is providing information on the operation of social systems. The clinical sociologist provides members of the client system with access to the knowledge base of sociology, as sociologists and members of client systems work together for social change.

References

Abbott, M.L., & Blake, G.F. (1988). An intervention model for homeless youth. *Clinical Sociology Review, 6,* 148–158.

Alinsky, S. (1941/1984). Community analysis and organization. *American Sociological Review, 46,* 797–808. Reprinted in *Clinical Sociology Review. 2,* 25–34.

Anderson, R.C. (1990). A technique for predicting intraorganizational action. *Clinical Sociology Review, 8,* 128–142.

Archer, S.E., Kelly, C.D., & Bisch, S.A. (1984). *Implementing change in communities.* St. Louis: C.V. Mosby.

Ashby, W.R. (1956). *An introduction to cybernetics.* New York: Wiley.

Baily, R. Jr. (1974). *Radicals in urban politics: The Alinsky approach.* Chicago: University of Chicago Press.

Berger, P.L., & Neuhaus, R.J. (1977). *To empower people: The role of mediating structures in public policy.* Washington, DC: American Enterprise Institute.

Britt, D.W. (1988). Analyzing the shape of organizational adaptability in response to environmental jolts. *Clinical Sociology Review, 6,* 59–75.

Britt, D.W. (1991). A clinical perspective on organizational development. In H.M. Rebach & J.G. Bruhn (Eds.), *Handbook of clinical sociology.* New York: Plenum.

Bruhn, J.G. (1987). The clinical sociologist as a health broker. *Clinical Sociology Review, 5,* 168–179.

Collins, R. (1988). *Theoretical sociology.* San Diego, CA: Harcourt Brace Jovanovich.

Couto, R.A. (1987). Participatory research: Methodology and critique. *Clinical Sociology Review, 5,* 83–90.

Couto, R.A. (1989). Redemptive organizations and the politics of hope. *Clinical Sociology Review, 7,* 64–79.

Etzioni, A. (1975). *A comparative analysis of complex organizations.* New York: Free Press.

Finkelstein, M.S. (1992). Taking back a rich tradition: A sociological approach to workplace and industrial change in the global economy. *Clinical Sociology Review, 10,* 182–197.

French, W.L., & Bell, C.H. Jr. (1984). *Organization development,* 3rd ed. Englewood Cliffs, NJ: Prentice-Hall.

Friedman, N.L., & Friedman, S.S. (1993). Diversity management: An emerging employment/consulting opportunity for sociological practitioners. *Clinical Sociology Review, 11,* 192–199.

Glass, J.F. (1984). Saul Alinsky in retrospect. *Clinical Sociology Review, 2,* 35–38.

Hilgartner, S. & Bosk, C.L. (1988). The rise and fall of social problems: A public arenas model. *American Journal of Sociology, 94,* 53–78.

Hoffman, F. (1985). Clinical sociology and the acculturation specialty. *Clinical Sociology Review, 3,* 50–58.

Hoffman, F. (1987). An alcoholism program for Hispanics. *Clinical Sociology Review, 5,* 91–101.

Howard, P.K. (1995). *The death of common sense.* New York: Random House.

Jacques, E. (1982). The method of social analysis in social change and social research. *Clinical Sociology Review, 1,* 50–58.

Miller, J.S. (1991). Clinical sociology and mediation. In Rebach, H.M. & Bruhn, J.G. (Eds.), *Handbook of clinical sociology.* New York: Plenum.

Netting, F.E., Kettner, P.M., & McMurtry, S.L. (1993). *Social work macro practice.* New York: Longman.

Ramondt, J.J. (1994). Methodological observations on clinical organization research. *Clinical Sociology Review, 12,* 83–101.

Ritzer, G. (1993). *The McDonaldization of society.* Thousand Oaks, CA: Pine Forge Press.

Rivera, F.G., & Erlich, J.L. (1992). *Community organizing in a diverse society.* Boston: Allyn & Bacon.

Robinette, P.O., & Harris, R.A. (1989). A conflict resolution model amenable to sociological practice. *Clinical Sociology Review, 7,* 127–140.

Rothman, J. (1979). Three models of community organization practice, their meaning and phasing. In Cox, F. M., et al., (Eds) *Strategies of community organization,* (3rd ed.). Itasca, IL: F.E. Peacock. (Original work published 1968).

Rothman, J., & Reed, B.G. (1984). Organizing community action to address alcohol and drug problems.

In Cox, F.M., Erlich, J.L., Rothman, J., & Tropman, J.E. (Eds.). *Tactics and techniques of community practice*. (2nd ed.). Itasca, IL: Peacock.

Sengstock, M.C. (1987). Sociological strategies of developing community resources: Services for abused wives as an example. *Clinical Sociology Review, 5*, 132–144.

Stephenson, K. (1994). Diversity: A managerial paradox. *Clinical Sociology Review, 12*, 189–205

Stoecker, R., & Beckwith, D. (1992). Advancing Toledo's neighborhood movement through participatory research: Integrating activist and academic approaches. *Clinical Sociology Review, 10*, 198–213.

Watts, W.D. (1989). Reducing adolescent drug abuse: Sociological strategies for community practice. *Clinical Sociology Review, 7*, 152–171.

Watts, W.D., & Wright, N.B. (1991). Drug abuse prevention: Clinical sociology in the community. In Rebach, H.M. & Bruhn, J.G. (Eds.), *Handbook of clinical sociology* (pp. 363–381). New York: Plenum.

Weber, L.R. (1991). The sociological practitioner in organizational health promotion programming. *Clinical Sociology Review, 9*, 106–124.

Whyte, W.F. (1982). Social inventions for solving human problems. *American Sociological Review, 47*, 1–13.

Whyte, W.F. (1989). Advancing scientific knowledge through participatory action research. *Sociological Forum, 4*, 367–386.

Recommended Readings

Archer, S.E., Kelly, C.D., & Bisch, S.A. (1984). *Implementing change in communities: A collaborative process*. St. Louis: C.V. Mosby.

This book presents a most thorough and detailed treatment of community organization. The authors as health educators with community nursing backgrounds, have targeted students and practitioners in health and human services disciplines. However, the material generalizes to all forms and purposes of community organization. The perspective is the same as advocated here for clinical sociologists. From systems theory as a theoretical base, the authors describe a participatory model, one of collaboration between professional change agents and local people. The book is excellent as a textbook or as a how-to-do-it manual of community organization.

Conyne, R.K., & O'Neil, J.M. (Eds.). (1992). *Organizational consultation: A casebook*. Newbury Park, CA: Sage.

This volume is centered around five case studies: (1) reducing racism and sexism in a university setting; (2) health promotion policy development in a hospital setting; (3) facilitating change in a financial service company in transition; (4) implementing school-based consultation services; and (5) consultation with a human service agency to improve management practices. At the end of each case the personal reflections of the authors on the consultation experience and training implications are given.

Gallessich, J. (1983). *The professional practice of consultation*. San Francisco: Jossey-Bass.

This is a handbook for consultants, trainers of consultants, and consumers of consultation services. Part I lays the foundation for the book by defining consultation and examining its roots and the milieu in which it evolved and is currently practiced. Part II outlines diverse approaches to consultation such as clinical, mental health, behavioral, organization, and program. Part III discusses the common processes, principles, and practices of consultants. Part IV offers the problems and prospects of consultation, a professional code of ethics, and future patterns for training.

Rivera, F.G., & Erlich, J.L. (1992). *Community organizing in a diverse society*. Boston: Allyn & Bacon.

This is a book of 12 chapter-length readings on community organization with minority communities. Included are a reasonable cross section of ethnic minorities. The editors state that the book is about "what communities of color are doing to protect their integrity and build their power." Social problems—drugs, unemployment and underemployment, inadequate housing, teen pregnancy—fall heavily on these communities composed of poor minority members who have the fewest resources to combat these problems. In addition, public attention has been shifting away from concern for these groups and problems. The book stresses that, among ethnic groups, the issues of race and culture transcend those of social class.

5

Problem Solving at the Macrolevel

Introduction

The distinctions between macro- and microsociology have been debated for sometime (Eisenstadt and Halle, 1985; Knorr-Cetina and Cicourel, 1981). As Huber (1991) pointed out there is controversy among sociologists about the meaning of the words *micro* and *macro*. There is a tendency to equate micro with individual and macro with collective level events. Whether one focuses one's efforts at the individual or personal level or at a broader social systems level, both are linked. The nature of macro–micro linkages is increasingly important as the etiologies, prevention, and solutions to contemporary societal problems, in the United States and elsewhere, lie in understanding the interfaces and linkages between individual behavior and factors at the societal level. While the emphasis in this chapter will be on problem solving at the macrolevel, it is our premise that problem solving cannot be effective if it is based on what it includes or excludes. Rather problem solving should be interactive between levels of human behavior, and this requires an interdisciplinary perspective (Sanderson, 1988).

Macrosociology: A Working Definition

We define macrosociology as the study of large-scale social patterns. In the United States macrosociological problems include violence and human abuse; quality of life issues such as environmental pollution; effects of the changing workplace such as downsizing, technology, and diversity; and issues related to the accessibility, availability, and affordability of health and human services. Macrosociology is concerned with the causes and trends of large scale problems, and the impact of larger social issues on groups such as families, and, of course, individuals. Macro- and microsociology are interrelated phenomena. It is of particular interest to the clinical sociologist to intervene or prevent deleterious effects from the larger system impacting on smaller components.

What Is Macropractice?

Macropractice involves consultation or direct intervention to bring about targeted change in agencies, organizations, communities, or society as a whole. Macrointerventions go beyond individual and group interventions but are often based on needs, problems, and issues identified at the microlevel. Macropractice can encompass many types of roles including those of planner, community organizer, manager, administrator, policy-maker, or direct service provider. Macropractitioners do not work at the broader levels without an understanding or involvement with microconcerns. Micro- and macroroles are interconnected. Clinical sociologists are change agents, and therefore, they are sensitive to the reciprocal effects of change in any situation in which intervention occurs (Netting, Kettner, & McMurtry, 1993).

Indeed, clinical sociologists frequently find themselves brokering different levels of interaction (Bruhn, 1987). This could involve mediating between an individual or group and administrators in their workplace, or between two institutions, or between communities. Or the clinical sociologist could become involved in helping to formulate social or health policies which cut across the matrix of a community. Or the clinical sociologist could become involved in efforts to control gang violence in cities on the U.S.–Mexico border.

Sherman and Wenocur (1983) discussed various dilemmas of the practitioner who becomes involved in macroissues. Taking on larger issues can add many hours of work and can lead to frustration about some things that cannot be changed. Yet, to ignore macroissues means that practitioners have to work within established norms. To become an activist attempting to create change could put the practitioner in a position of being labeled as noncooperative. The practitioner who deals with macroissues must become masterful in orchestrating differences in values, goals, and objectives of many usually traditional and carefully protected social systems. Therefore, macropractitioners must have great patience in seeing the results of their work, which is often not under their control.

Macroproblem Solving: General Issues

Sociology as Intervention

Laue (1989) argued that doing sociology is social intervention, and that all intervention is a type of advocacy. In terms of such actions' effect on power configurations within the social systems involved, there are no neutrals: all social action is value-laden and political. Intervention is usually interpreted narrowly as meaning the use of coercion, force, or pressure. Lyons and Mastanduno (1993) pointed out that intervention extends along a continuum ranging from the exercise of influence through negotiations to the physical crossing of boundaries or borders. What is important, however, are the intentions of the intervenor and the perceptions of the party receiving the intervention. Also how intervention is perceived can change with time and events. For example, in-depth investigations into human rights violations, considered "intervention" by governments in the 1960s and 1970s, are now accepted as standard practice (Leinberger & Tucker, 1991). Alternatively, what looks to the intervenor as unobtrusive or benign attempts to influence another may appear to be blatant intervention or an infringement on rights or sovereignty. International intervention in its various forms has always been a part of international relations. Macroproblems and interventions tend to be better known because they affect more people and receive publicity. Macroproblems are also likely to involve more than a single intervenor because of their scope and complexity. Macroproblems are also networked; that is, they are intertwined with other problems. Therefore, it is important to identify and establish ties with the social networks or support systems that are related to the problem being studied.

Power, Politics, and "The System"

Clinical sociologists are members of the macrosystem. As such they are not free of bias and bring to any situation their own set of values and ideas about the nature of intervention or change needed. In addition, the clinical sociologist is usually a member of a power structure, such as a university, a clinic, or an agency and brings the biases of that affiliation to situations of intervention and change. Politics is a pervasive influence, direct and indirect, in any situation involving macrosociology. No matter how hard the clinical sociologist might try to avoid politics it is inescapable. Funding and politics are usually linked to both the causes and solutions of macrolevel problems. It is common for laypeople and professionals to criticize "the system" as the culprit for many of our societal problems, yet "the system" is made up of many players with interest in protecting their positions, funds, or their degree of control, and we are all players in some way making "the system" what it is. In addition, "systems" are difficult to reengineer; they have a life cycle of their own. As such, clinical sociologists should not be misled into believing that they have answers or solutions that only need implementing to change "the system" for better. It is likely, depending upon the problem, that the clinical sociologist must be satisfied with creating an awareness of a problem at the very least and perhaps assist in resolving a part of a problem at the very most. An example will help to illustrate the limits of macroproblem solving.

A large private foundation established a grant program to stimulate creative approaches to establishing community partnerships with health science centers in an attempt to redesign the delivery of health services, especially to underserved populations. Two large universities in a southwestern border city were jointly funded by one of these multimillion dollar grants to redesign the curriculum in medicine and nursing, enabling students to spend some part of their clinical training in community and school clinics working in teams to learn about primary health care problems among barrio residents. There were also several community partners who agreed when the grant was written to work in collaboration with the universities in achieving the grant objectives. The major objective of the grant to the university project directors was redesigning the health curriculum to teach students in a community setting. The major expectation of the grant to several but not all, of the community collaborators was the more expedient and free delivery of primary health services to barrio residents. These two sets of objectives were not mutually exclusive and became a major source of dissention between the universities and one of the more aggressive community groups as the project evolved.

The first year of the project was concerned with hiring personnel, establishing the Advisory Board, and working with various committees within the universities to gain approval and set in motion the interdisciplinary, community-based clinical experiences. The struggle to obtain curricular change was greater in the medical school than in the nursing school, but was accomplished by the second year of the grant. The project directors worked with several local community school boards to establish school-based clinics which the grant funded in part. The clinics were to remain and be funded by the schools after the grant expired.

The power and politics of one of the strong community organizations, which had the backing of the Catholic church, began to emerge when the Advisory Board was being selected. The two project directors were members of the Board in addition to one faculty representative and one administrator from each university. One of the representatives was a clinical sociologist. The community groups each had one representative but several of the collaborating clinics were not represented on the Board. A project administrator was appointed who was a compromise candidate to all Board members after the university and community groups each advocated for and encouraged applications from persons they knew would represent their respective interests.

As the project entered the second year, the two Board members representing the church-backed community group pressed for Board membership to be broadened to include other barrios which were not represented but were in the project area. In addition, the Board began to act like a policy-making group instead of an Advisory Board. The two project directors became more assertive stating that they were ultimately responsible for the grant funds and therefore they were the primary decision makers. The community representatives were angry and, since they were members of the budget committee of the Board, were responsible for marathon long budget meetings, questioning the allocation of funds to the universities rather than to community personnel. These aggressive community representatives were also responsible for long Board meetings and, as a result, attendance at the Board meetings diminished. Calls had to be made by a secretary each meeting to determine whether there would be a quorum. The church-backed community group held a meeting with one of the university presidents to protest the diminished role of "community" in the project. The project administrator was often conflicted between the universities and the community in her decision making. As a result, the project administrator gradually lost the confidence of the project director and her contract was not renewed. Monies allocated for project activities each year were often not fully expended because of the lack of consensus among the Board, and funds were carried over to the subsequent year. Debates on the Board arose as to who (what group) would take over the project when the grant period ended. The church-based community group made strong attempts to assure their future control. Indeed, the community group called the private foundation and asked for a representative to meet with all parties, in hopes the foundation would take sides. The foundation refused to take sides.

The project directors gained approval from the Advisory Board to add representatives from the local school districts cooperating with the project. This further diluted the control of the church-based community group. As a result, their members stopped coming to Board meetings and were dropped from the Board for nonattendance. The project continued throughout years 3 and 4 and was quite successful in educating teams of health professional students in primary health care in the barrios. In the fourth year one of the project directors retired and the other project director made plans to submit a grant for the continuation of the project. A new project administrator was hired who proved effective in bridging the universities and community groups, but the issue of the future of the projects' activities after grant funds ended is yet to be resolved.

The clinical sociologist in this example was an administrator representing the university on the Board of Advisors to the project. The clinical sociologist gave his opinion and offered advice about group dynamics, representation, decision making, etc. as problems arose, yet as a representative of the university he was also seen by community representatives as "the enemy" when issues were discussed. All issues involved power, politics, and "the system." This vignette represents, on a small scale, the issues involved in reshaping our health delivery system on a societal level, and why attempts continually fail. Power and politics counterbalance positive attempts at change no matter how good the motive or goal. Indeed, power and politics often become more important goals to the players than the common problem they are seeking to correct.

Had the clinical sociologist not been a member of the Advisory Board, and had instead been hired as a consultant to the project, it is possible that his advice might have prevented some of the problems that arose. For example, the clinical sociologist could have given guidance regarding the following:

- A clear set of goals and objectives for the project
- A Board of Advisors with representation from all participating parties from the project onset and a clear set of expectations of Board members
- Mediation when conflict arose between Board members, and between one of the Project Directors and the Project Administrator
- A method of evaluating project outcomes

- An overall plan for the project with timetables linked to activities and funding
- Plans for continuation of the project beyond the grant
- Brokering the expectations of the universities and community groups

The clinical sociologist should not always operate from a crisis mode. Unfortunately, many projects do not build consultants into the budget and consequently advice from outside experts is often an afterthought. A clinical sociologist can function best when not a member of the project team as advice is more easily disregarded from an insider and members of the project team should be loyal to the project, although not necessarily noncritical.

Macroproblems can be limited to the boundaries of one society or country, such as the problem of providing equal health care to minorities and the disadvantaged in the United States, or macroproblems can broaden from national problems to international ones, such as the case of skyjacking, other forms of terrorism and crime, and environmental pollution (Redclift & Benton, 1994).

Some macroproblems originate at microlevels, as in the case of AIDS and other infectious diseases, where individual behavior is the cause of the problem, and become national and international problems. On the other hand, problems which originate at the macrolevel, such as war or a country's support of terrorism, have repercussions at the microlevel, as witnessed by the needed airport security around the world since terrorism became more common. Macro- and microproblems are linked in cause and effect. It is the scope and complexity of macroproblems that make them difficult to study and to solve. There are several factors that make macrolevel problems more complex than those at the micro- and mesolevels:

- Boundaries of all types increase in number and complexity.
- Social and cultural differences increase.
- Laws governing human conduct may clash.
- Values, customs, and priorities for living differ.
- National characters may clash.
- Resources for solving problems differ.

Several examples of macro level problems will be presented to illustrate these factors.

Examples of Macroproblems

Equal Health Opportunities for Minority and Disadvantaged Americans

A national representative survey (Davis, 1995) conducted for the Commonwealth Fund by Louis Harris and Associates between May 13, 1994 and July 28,

1994 among 3,789 adults, 18 years of age and older, included 1,114 white, 1,048 African American, 1,001 Hispanic, and 632 Asian American adults (including 205 Chinese, 201 Korean, and 201 Vietnamese Americans). Some of the key findings were:

- Thirty-one percent of minority adults, ages 18 to 64, do not have health insurance, compared with 14% of white adults in the same age group.
- Among individuals, ages 18 to 64, lapses in health insurance coverage were more common for minority adults (20%) than for white adults (15%) during the past 2 years.
- Just 56% of working minority adults, ages 18 to 64, receive insurance through an employer, compared with 66% of white adults in the same age group.
- Twenty-nine percent of minority adults report having "very little" or "no" choice in where to get health care compared with 16% of white adults.
- Forty percent of minority adults have major problems paying for medical care, compared with 26% of white adults.
- Twenty-one percent of all minority adults have problems with language differences in receiving care, with about one-quarter of those who do not speak English as a first language needing an interpreter when seeking care.
- Getting specialty care is a major problem for 18% of minority adults, compared with 8% of white adults.

A conference on the disadvantaged in American health care (Brown, 1991), held in 1989, defined the disadvantaged in terms of demographic age groups (the elderly and children), in terms of illness (AIDS, mental illness, chemical dependencies), and in terms of market and governmental failure (the homeless, the hungry, and the medically uninsured). Other groups who lack access to specialized markets include the disabled, the retarded, the chronically ill, the poor, and immigrants. We find ourselves with all of these special groups because as a society we do not share a universal claim about the essential nature of health, equal distribution of services to maintain or restore it, and a plan to universally provide such services. We have a health policy for each of these special client groups, with each group at various times proclaiming a crisis.

The lack of an equitable distribution of health services to all segments of the American population is a sociological problem, yet debates about ways to reform our current "system" of delivering health and social services focus first on economics and how power will be distributed among providers of care. More rhetoric is heard about the kind of health care system we do not want than on the kind of system we want or, at least its essential structure and components. Cost is only one of the several agendas in the health care reform debate. Race is an issue; class politics is involved; and the tension between individual and collective values and between self-interest and shared interests are present (Brown, 1991). There is a societal reluctance to address the issue of shared risk and a refusal to share resources equally.

Health care inequities is a tough problem for the clinical sociologist. A sociologist is sensitized perhaps more than most citizens by macrodebates and is affected as a patient when health care is sought. What can a clinical sociologist do about our health care delivery problems? First, a clinical sociologist cannot envelop a whole society. A broad perspective is helpful in understanding problems, but corrections or solutions cannot be grandiose. Therefore, a clinical sociologist must approach societal problems from a more realistic view, especially if solutions are to be tried and evaluated. The larger the population the more difficult it is to implement change and assess the effects of an innovation because there are too many variables at work, some of which may be unknown. Building models of change with large populations may not have applicability in all situations, but building models of change with very small populations and attempting to generalize to larger populations also has its drawbacks. That is why most sociology is practiced at the mesolevel of analysis. The midrange level is practical because it is possible to "get a handle" on the majority of variables affecting a problem and its solution, and therefore, "envelop" the unit under scrutiny. An example of an international problem that does not have a single solution is provided by AIDS; it is even doubtful that a vaccine would prevent AIDS in all its forms. The epidemiology of AIDS takes on different forms in different societies and cultures, and AIDS prevention and education programs cannot be universally applied. Therefore, an approach to preventing AIDS would seem to be most manageable, and perhaps effective, at the community or county level. Programs which envelop larger populations than this often cannot tell why they succeeded or failed and are usually not generalizable (Kelly & Lawrence, 1988).

A clinical sociologist developed a preventive model for AIDS at the community level and implemented it (Bruhn, 1990). Even at the community level it was noted that AIDS and its casualties presented so many needs it was difficult not to try to deal with all of them. Recommendations were made for establishing a successful community-based AIDS program. While the program described here is unique to a given geographical area, it is not unique as a community-based program. Thus, macrolevel problems are being dealt with at the mesolevel. Since AIDS is a changing disease it is important that any approach be flexible and adaptable to meet the changing needs of a population. Ultimately all attempts at AIDS education must effect attitudes and behavior at the macrolevel.

Violence and Anger

Violent crime is one of the most serious problems facing American society. In 1991 there were over 1.9 million violent crimes reported to the police. This includes 106,000 reports of forcible rape, 108 million assaults, and over 24,000 murders. The number of murders has continued to increase with an increasing number committed by teenagers against teenagers. The profile of the typical offender is that he is a young black or Hispanic male, has grown up in poverty, and has not received the nurturance of a close family. His values and morals are typically learned from television and peers. He tends to be a drug user and a heavy drinker who takes no responsibility for his unlawful, socially unacceptable ways. The problem now is that there are not only angry individuals but angry groups, organizations, institutions, and countries. Anger has become a macroproblem. For example, terrorists have made anger a transnational problem. Ways of expressing anger have become more innovative (planting packages of nuclear waste in a Moscow park), more destructive (the bombing of the Federal Building in Oklahoma City), and challenge the systems of justice of countries to cooperate to control the actions of angry groups. Angry people purposefully cross boundaries to gain attention whether it be an angry artist or angry terrorist; the former may violate professional rules or offend a few art lovers, the latter violates national laws and threatens the safety of many.

A clinical sociologist is not expected to solve problems with anger at international, national level or regional levels. However, the clinical sociologist can be effective in helping to discover the reasons or motives for anger in institutions and organizations and to assist these clients (when they seek help) in directing their anger in constructive ways; e.g., organizing coalitions such as Mothers Against Drunk Drivers, to change laws on a national scale. Clinical sociologists can be helpful in diagnosing the anger titer in large entities and work in a preventive way to circumvent destructive behavior (Roberts, 1994). Reported violence is only the tip of the iceberg. The number of rapes, acts of human abuse, and assaults that are unreported, if known, would probably be staggering. New prisons and jails have not solved the crime problem. Roberts (1994) pointed out that prisons and jails are human warehouses for the new underclass: the thousands of drug-abusing, unemployed, and repeat offenders. Prisons are overpopulated and recidivism rates are high. Many prisons have become schools for crime, places where offenders become more incorrigible and violent as a result of unsanitary, degrading, and inhumane conditions.

One of the key factors underlying committing violent acts is anger—directed toward another person or persons for failing to respond in an expected way (assault), or toward an institution or agency which espouses or represents an opposing view (abortion clinic bombings). The ways in which we can express anger in America and get by with it have become more direct and violent. There appears to be a high titer of anger in our society (Skolnick & Currie, 1985).

A clinical sociologist, whose environment is also enveloped in anger, may also have been a personal target of some type of violence. A clinical sociologist is also likely to have worked with angry clients and helped them express their anger in socially acceptable ways. Just as a "blow-up" at work can negatively affect a person's credibility and chances for promotion, adversarial groups earn a label of "troublemaker" (environmental and animal rights groups), and thus block positive avenues for mediating their anger. And, some hate groups, such as the Ku Klux Klan and skinheads, exist because they achieve a level of satisfaction from their anger which, if resolved, would negate the raison d'être for their existence.

Approaches to Anger Control

There are several approaches a clinical sociologist can take in helping shape the course of anger. Figure 5.1 presents a paradigm of anger control. There is a "zone of the prevention of violence" when anger can be mediated, contained, and perhaps resolved or directed into nonviolent behavior. It is important to point out that anger should not be prevented. Anger is a legitimate emotion. It is violence that needs to be prevented, hence anger must be contained and directed. One of the key elements in preventing violence is that the angry unit must ask for help with anger. Obviously terrorist groups are not going to ask for help with their anger, but there are many groups whose anger is less extreme and perhaps less focused, which are debating about how to use their anger. These units are ripe for intervention because their use of anger is still ambiguous and can be redirected or mediated. To intervene, uninvited, into the lives of angry people will make you another target of their anger. Therefore, a good approach toward an angry group might be a "neutral" group which is nonthreatening and invites dialogue with the angry group, which could lead to mediation.

Environmental Pollution

The physical environment is the most important determinant of human health. Protection of the environment is the most fundamental step in preventing human illness (Cortese, 1993). Many of today's environmental problems, such as acid rain, high urban ozone pollution, and pollution of seas, are both regional and

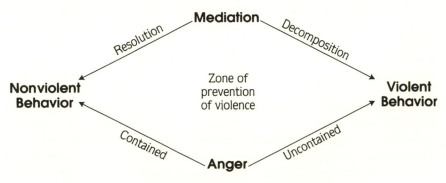

Figure 5.1. Paradigm: Anger Control

international in scope. The cumulative effects of rapid increases in population and rapid industrial growth with the attendant pollution and resource depletion are causing changes on a global scale. We are altering the physiology of the planet. Tropical forest destruction, soil erosion, toxic pollution through man-made emissions of sulfur, nitrogen, lead, cadmium, and zinc are examples.

Fundamental human beliefs have produced this environmental transformation. We treat our natural resources as free and inexhaustible and have concentrated on simplistic, quick, technological fixes for environmental problems. These solutions often do not deal with the root causes of the problems. In addition, approaches for controlling pollution have varied nation to nation, and within nations the kinds of pollution have been addressed inconsistently.

Leichter (1991) pointed out that we can no longer afford the costs of foolishness and must assume responsibility for our environment and our individual and collective health. The world now faces a threat to human health and survival from changes in the global environment—stratospheric ozone depletion, habitat destruction, species extinction, global warming, and the poisoning of air, water, and soil by toxic and radioactive substances. The less developed nations experience the most severe water-related health problems. An estimated 2 billion people in these countries presently lack an adequate water supply (Page, 1987). This is predominantly a rural problem with 86% of these estimated 2 billion people living in rural areas of the less developed nations. Both the less developed and the developed nations will continue to experience some water-related health problems in response to the ongoing processes of urbanization and industrialization. The increasing use of products composed of or containing toxic substances also contributes to the threat of water-related disease. We do not fully know what substances are in our water supplies and their toxicity.

The primary emissions of sulfur oxides, nitrogen oxides, carbon monoxide, particulates, and metals (e.g., lead and cadmium) are severely polluting cities and towns throughout the world. Smog has been shown to induce asthmatic responses in adults and children. In addition to particulates, urban air also contains aromatic hydrocarbons, arsenic, and asbestos. Exposure to these compounds is associated with increased rates of lung cancer. Indoor air pollution is also a significant cause of death. Atmospheric pollution has now reached a level that threatens not only the health of entire populations, but their survival as well. Various national regulatory approaches have not, so far, succeeded in controlling air pollution on a global scale (Christiani, 1993).

Perhaps one of the more frightening environmental threats to health and survival is radiation. At least three major nuclear reactor accidents have occurred since the advent of nuclear power. In November of 1995 dissidents unhappy with the resolution of the war in Chechnya planted several packages of nuclear waste (cesium) in Moscow. Radioactive waste has polluted large areas in and near nuclear weapons production plants across the United States and Russia. Although

---

Clinical Focus 5.1

Crying Wolf

An issue affecting both popular and official reactions to environmental health
policies is the portrayal of each problem
as the most serious health threat. Air
pollution, nuclear waste, global warming, and acid rain have all been labeled as
the major public health issue. This hyper-
bole has hurt the cause of health promotion because it has not been taken seriously and because it has been taken too
seriously. Not every health problem can
be the most serious of our time. However, legislators fear that public hysteria
may demand extraordinary actions. There
is also the risk that the public will become anesthetized to the claims of risk.
There is the potential that government
will either do too much and thereby reduce
individual freedom, or too little, and contribute to personal tragedies and social
costs associated with avoidable deaths
and illnesses. What is a reasonable relationship between health promotion, policies
and personal freedom at the macrolevel?

---

the relation between low doses of radiation and cancer is still unresolved, there is
little argument about the effects of high and moderately high doses of radiation
(Lichtenstein and Helfand, 1993). There is also medical concern about nuclear
power plants, including waste disposal, reactor accidents, and low-level radiation
exposures.

Macrolevel Approaches

Introduction

Shostak (1985) suggested five mental tools the clinical sociologist can use in
his or her work. One is to stay alert to *reversal ideas*, those that prescribe novel and
desirable roles for groups and individuals that are rarely considered. Looking at
common problems in new ways can often open opportunities for new approaches
to problem solving. A second tool is *irreverent* ideas. These are ideas that
challenge the status quo or the boxes or stereotypes that lead us to look at people
and situations in paradoxical ways. A third tool is *wild ideas*. For example, a wild
idea might be to use city, county, and federal prisoners in maintaining the grounds
of universities, colleges, and public schools thereby reducing the costs of maintenance. If prisoners can be used to shovel snow in a university stadium so that a
football game can be played, certainly there are other wild ideas involving a long-
term, constructive way to utilize our growing prison labor to benefit society. A
fourth tool involves *encapsulating ideas*. Conferences, reports, white papers, etc.,

can be used to consolidate and analyze particular problems in-depth with appropriate brainstorming of new approaches to resolve issues. This is easier to do when the issue or situation is encapsulated and at least mentally isolated from distracting competitive problems for a short while. A final tool is to utilize *anticipatory notions*, that is, predictions or forecasts to help guide or direct change. This encourages futuristic and proactive thinking about issues and problems. These "tools" emphasize innovation and creativity in problem solving. This is essential as few problems today are simple, contained, and discipline-directed. They are complex, diverse, and interdisciplinary. A successful clinical sociologist in the future will be somewhat of an entrepreneur in "packaging" approaches to solving problems. Additional approaches or tools which are available are discussed below.

The Superordinate Goal

In the classic Robbers Cave Experiment, Sherif and his colleagues (Sherif, Harney, White, Hood, & Sherif, 1961) showed that conflict between groups can be reduced and cooperation increased by the introduction of goals which cannot be ignored but are beyond the resources of each group acting alone. The superordinate goal of survival is an example. This experiment offers suggestions for reducing conflict and hostility between social groups: (1) the introduction of a "common enemy"; (2) the dissemination of information to correct prevailing group stereotypes; (3) the channeling of competition for highly valued rewards so the focus of competition is directed away from the group level to the individual level. At the macrolevel the alternative to war, peace, is a powerful superordinate goal. However, the time must be right for warring groups to seriously entertain a superordinate goal. Examples are plentiful in today's world, e.g., Bosnia, Ireland, Chechnya, Africa. The superordinate goal can be an important tool for the clinical sociologist at the meso and macro levels.

Empowerment

Individuals, groups, organizations, communities, and nations can feel impotent, ignored, not heard, not players in decisions that affect them. At the macrolevel there are numerous destructive ways that nations can call attention to themselves in order to feel powerful, e.g., Libya, Iran. Empowerment is not something that is bestowed, it is not a right, but rather it is an acknowledgment of the voice of a group. Empowerment is in some sense "earned" by the past actions of a group, a historical readiness for the group "to be heard from," the size of the group, and its persistence and activities. In earlier years such groups were known as interest groups or lobbies. Since World War II such groups have grown in number and sophistication in organization. The *Encyclopedia of Associations* lists 20,000 such groups. Environmental groups alone number an estimated 7,000 (Fisher &

Schwartz, 1996). The number of public interest and grass roots groups have grown to more than 40 million individuals and collect more than $4 billion per year for their organizations (Rauch, 1994). Porritt (1995) reported that the National Trust, a British environmental organization with 2.2 million members, held a conference in Manchester, England on the future of the countryside. The overwhelming message from the conference was that members are ready and waiting to be called into lobbying action.

Empowerment can be used as a tool by the clinical sociologist to "call" macrogroups to act on their own behalf. Sometimes groups feel they have to be told that they are empowered or are eligible candidates for empowerment. Empowerment, however, is not only being vocal about a group or nation's interests, it also carries a great deal of responsibility and accountability—responsibility to act in legal ways or be subject to consequences (e.g., Greenpeace's efforts to block France's nuclear testing in the Pacific) and accountability to those who support and contribute to a group or nation's interests (e.g., mismanagement does not gain a group or nation creditability in the world community).

Benefits from empowerment can include:

- Educational programs, conventions, meetings
- Information dissemination through publications and the World Wide Web
- Networking among members
- Campaigns to influence opinion
- Funding for projects
- Promotes legislative action and reform of public policy
- Cooperation across geographic boundaries
- Litigation for violating laws

Prevention

The Preventive Paradigm

Prevention, as an approach or tool, is a challenge because nations or institutions usually do not plan ahead, and therefore, most operate from a crisis mode. This reactive style of behavior makes it necessary to solve problems as they arise, often the same type of problem, rather than establishing a structure or process to prevent problems. So much time is spent in "putting out fires" that there is little or no time for thinking about the future. This style of behavior can lead to pessimism and burnout because there is little positive energy being expended. The future is today's problems.

To get macrolevel groups to plan, do forecasts, and to visualize the future they would like to work towards is difficult because planning is often thought of as "merely a paper exercise." But without a plan, the future is merely how the forces of change shape the future.

National culture has an effect on the propensity to engage in planning, since there is evidence that some nations are more inclined to favor it than others (Mintzberg, 1994). Enterprises which have a strong internal culture (like Japan) seem to discourage action planning. They emphasize vision and mission more than a central plan. In an international study (Steiner and Schollhammer, 1975) planning was found to be most common and most formalized in the United States, followed by Britain, Canada and Australia with Japan and Italy at the other end of the scale. Thus, the propensity to plan seems to be Anglo-Saxon.

Problem solving with a preventive philosophy and planning are compatible activities. These approaches are closely tied, however, to values. It is difficult to get some countries, e.g., Mexico, to plan for the future with a preventive approach to solving some of its public health problems when the most pressing problems are unemployment, poverty, and infectious diseases. Therefore, while the preventive paradigm is a useful tool for the clinical sociologist, it must be introduced in the context of the culture and values of the macrolevel group.

Environmentalists often use the slogan "think globally, act locally." There is a need to make significant shifts in our mindsets in adopting a preventive approach; it requires a shift in the time frame. In our society we are used to making decisions and seeing short-term payoffs. Many international problems will not have short-term solutions. Hall (1990) suggested that we use about one half of a human life—about 35 years—and use that as a scale on which to measure macrolevel interventions. The preventive framework itself does not give final answers, but to paraphrase David Tracy, a theologian, "It makes us ask better questions" (Hall, 1990).

Arbitration, Mediation, and Collaboration

In earlier chapters we have suggested arbitration and mediation as tools of the clinical sociologist in dealing with micro- and mesolevel problems. These tools are also appropriate at the macrolevel.

Black (1987) has suggested that there are hard paths to solving problems (using technology) and soft paths (considering values, special interests, and agendas). Macrolevel groups do not approach problems without consideration of power, values, economic interests, control; "soft" issues and concerns are usually the key factors underlying a conflict. There are some hard path threats, such as nuclear and fusion power and chemicals, confronting our international society. Some of the solutions involve greater regulation of indoor and outdoor air pollution by changing the use of biofuels etc. But we need to transcend labels when examining macrolevel problems. We need to directly address realities which involve arbitrating and mediating values so that all parties collaborate to win (Straus, 1987).

Conflicts come in many forms at the macrolevel. Consider the list of words that are often used to mean conflict: disagreement, argument, controversy, dispute, debate, quarrel, strife, strike, row, brawl, police action, war. An underlying basis for conflicts can result in differences about:

- How things work
- How we can make them work better for us
- How I can make them work better for me

Straus (1987) believed that focusing on disputes isolated from the context in which they arose obscured and deflected attention away from the objective of resolving the conflict. Conflict arises when something has gone wrong with a balance. For example, single-issue activism can become pathological; i.e., if an environmental group focuses on only a solution for water pollution in a given area. In our increasingly complex world we need to find holistic and comprehensive solutions where possible. Furthermore, the quality of our decisions, not just winning a conflict, should be our goal.

Mediation is an old method for resolving conflicts. The difference between mediation and arbitration is that an arbitrator has the power to make a decision, while a mediator must use his or her skills to get the parties to reach their own agreement. All forms of dispute settlements assume that the participants are adversaries. In addition, disputes are confronted at the end of a process. There is a need for a paradigm shift when collaboration and nonadversarial methods are the norm in macro level processes. As Straus (1987) suggested, we need to manage complexity, not arbitrate and mediate it. Collaborators assume that a joint analysis of a problem will lead to a better decision about it. Rivlin (1971) pointed out that collaboration should not be oversimplified. Single approaches should be avoided. For example, health service systems cannot be judged simply by the number of patients who use or don't use a particular service. Multiple measures and sources of information are needed so as not to distort the system being looked at. She suggests that technology (the computer) might be helpful in modeling or simulating solutions for complex problems. Modeling can be a first step in gaining a perspective in a conflict, amendments can be inserted, and new versions of the model examined by the collaborating parties.

Simon (1983) noted that macrolevel institutions must often attend to major problems one at a time. Therefore, important and controversial issues require that legislators direct their attention to one issue at a time. But in complex issues, like environmental protection, this can be a serious block because environmental protection cannot be reasonably considered without considering many aspects of a country and its relationship to its neighbors (United States and Mexico). There is a growing recognition that we need collaboration as the tool to help us manage interconnected macro issues. No matter how hard we try to achieve rationality in decision making, there will always remain a hard core of irreconcilable values. What is important is to be up-front with our differences so that these can be

---

Clinical Focus 5.2

Takeover

Two large educational institutions resided in a metropolitan area; one was a community college, the other an upper division and graduate-level university. The community college provided about 35 to 40% of the students who entered the university each year. Relationships between the administration of the two institutions were excellent, resulting in the signing of an historic dual admission agreement. Students could enter the community college and obtain associate's, bachelor's, masters, and doctoral degrees without ever leaving the area.

However, the mayor of the city wanted a 4-year residential college in the downtown area, stating that this was the trademark of a progressive capital city.

The area is surrounded by numerous private colleges in addition to the community college and university. Rumors grew that the university and community college should be merged into one institution. The university's Board of Advisors wanted the university and community college to merge. The community college president opposed a merger, while the president of the university suggested closer working relationships rather than a merger. Rumors of a merger have dampened the historic dual-admission agreement and have created the seeds of suspicion among faculty and administrators at the community college. A collaborative opportunity has turned into a situation requiring mediation.

---

discussed and resolved as much as possible. While conflict resolution will always be an important tool for the clinical sociologist, collaboration should increase as a dominant method in our complex world.

Summary

Macrolevel problem solving involves using some of the same tools as used at the micro- and mesolevels. However, the larger the social grouping, e.g., nations, the more complex the problems and the solutions. What is proposed in this chapter are some uncommon and innovative approaches to solving macroproblems such as the superordinate goal, the preventive paradigm, empowerment, and collaboration.

References

Black, J.S. (1987). The technological solution: Hard and soft paths, scientific uncertainty, and the control of technology. In M. R. Greenberg (Ed.), *Public health and the environment: The United States experience* (pp. 207–229). New York: Guilford Press.

Brown, L.D. (Ed.). (1991). *Health policy and the disadvantaged.* Durham, NC: Duke University Press.

Bruhn, J.G. (1987). The clinical sociologist as a health broker. *Clinical Sociology Review*, *5*, 168–179.

Bruhn, J.G. (1990). A community model for AIDS prevention. *Family and Community Health*, *13*, 65–77.

Christiani, D.C. (1993). Urban and transboundary air pollution: Human health consequences. In E. Chivian, M. McCally, H. Hu, & A. Haines (Eds.), *Critical condition: Human health and the environment* (pp. 13–30). Cambridge, MA: MIT Press.

Cortese, A.D. (1993). Introduction: Human health, risk, and the environment. In E. Chivian, M. McCally, H. Hu, & A. Harris (Eds.), *Critical condition: Human health and the environment* (pp. 1–11). Cambridge, MA: MIT Press.

Davis, K. (March, 1995). *Minority Americans do not have equal health opportunities: A briefing note from the Commonwealth Fund*. New York: Commonwealth Fund.

Eisenstadt, S.N., & Halle, H.J. (Eds.). (1985). *Macro-sociological theory: Perspectives on sociology theory* (Vol. 1). Newbury Park, CA: Sage.

Fisher, C.A., & Schwartz, C. (Eds.) (1996). *Encyclopedia of Associations*, Vol. 1: *National Organizations of the U.S.* (30th ed.). New York: Gale.

Hall, R.H. (1990). *Health and the global environment*. Cambridge, UK: Polity Press.

Huber, J. (Ed.) (1991). *Macro-micro linkages in sociology*. Newbury Park, CA: Sage.

Kelly, J.A., & Lawrence, J.S. (1988). *The AIDS health crisis: Psychological and social interventions*. New York: Plenum.

Knorr-Cetina K., & Cicourel, A.V. (Eds). (1981). *Advances in social theory and methodology: Toward an integration of micro- and macro-sociologies*. Boston: Routledge & Kegan Paul.

Laue, J. (1989). Sociology as advocacy: There are no neutrals. *Sociological Practice*, *7*, 110–122.

Leinberger, P., & Tucker, B. (1991). *The new individualists*. New York: Harper-Collins.

Leichter, H.M. (1991). *Free to be foolish*. Princeton, NJ: Princeton University Press.

Lichtenstein, K., & Helfand, J. (1993). Radiation and health: Nuclear weapons and nuclear power. In E. Chivian, M. McCally, H. Hu, & A. Haines (Eds.), *Critical condition: Human health and the environment* (pp. 93–121). Cambridge, MA: MIT Press.

Lyons, G.M., & Mastanduno, M. (1993). International intervention, state sovereignty and the future of international society. *International Social Sciences Journal*, *45*, 517–532.

McMurtry, S.L., Kettner, P.M., & Netting, F.E. (1993). Strategic choices made by nonprofit agencies serving low-paying clients. *Community organization and social administration: Advances, trends and emerging principles*. New York: Haworth Press.

Mintzberg, H. (1994). *The rise and fall of strategic planning*. New York: Free Press.

Netting, F.E., Kettner, P.M., & McMurtry, S.L. (1993). *Social work macro practice*. New York: Longman.

Page, G.W. (1987). Water and health. In M. R. Greenberg (Ed.). *Public health and the environment: The United States experience* (pp. 105–138). New York: Guilford.

Porritt, J. (1995, October 7). Outdoors: The National Trust: A pussy-cat that could turn tiger. *Daily Telegraph*, p. 3.

Rauch, J. (1994, June 6). The hyperpluralism trap: What "We the people" has wrought. *New Republic*, *210*(23), p. 22.

Redclift, M., & Benton, T. (Eds.). (1994). *Social theory and the global environment*. New York: Routledge.

Rivlin, A. (1971). *Systematic thinking for social action*. Washington, DC: Brookings Institution.

Roberts, A.R. (1994). Crime in America. In A. R. Roberts (Ed.), *Critical issues in crime and justice* (pp. 3–18) Thousand Oaks, CA: Sage.

Sanderson, S.K. (1988). *Macrosociology: An introduction to human societies*. New York: Harper & Row.

Sherif, M., Harvey, O.J., White, B.J., Hood, W.R., & Sherif, C.W. (1961). *Intergroup conflict and cooperation: The Robbers Cave experiment*. Norman, OK: Institute of Group Relations, University of Oklahoma.

Sherman, W.R., & Wenocur, S. (1983). Empowering public welfare workers through mutual support. *Social Work*, *28*, 375–379.

Shostak, A.B. (1985). How can we all survive? Managing social change. In R. A. Straus (Ed.), *Using sociology* (pp. 172–182). Bayside, NY: General Hall.

Simon, H.A. (1983). *Reason in human affairs*. Palo Alto, CA: Stanford University Press.

Skolnick, J.H., & Currie, E. (Eds.). (1985). *Crisis in American institutions* (6th ed.). Boston: Little, Brown.

Steiner, G.A., & Schollhammer, H. (April, 1975). Pitfalls in multi-national long-range planning. *Long Range Planning*, pp. 2–12.

Straus, D.B. (1987). Collaborating to win. In M. R. Greenberg (Ed.), *Public health and the environment* (pp. 271–292). New York: Guilford.

Recommended Readings

Aday, L.A. (1993). *At risk in America: The health and health care needs of vulnerable populations in the United States*. San Francisco, CA: Jossey-Bass.

This book provides a framework for identifying and studying vulnerable populations, data on their needs, and the trends and correlates of their growth over time. The author discusses issues regarding the access, cost, and quality of their care and policies and programs that have been developed to address the needs of vulnerable populations.

Amick, B.C., Levine, S., Tarlov, A.R., & Walsh, D.C. (Eds.). (1995). *Society and health*. New York: Oxford University Press.

The authors raise social factors and social processes into sharper focus as determinants of health. Individual chapters range from the effects of health on such factors as the family, the work situation, the community, to the influences of gender, racism, social class, political economy and culture. The book concludes with some policy considerations.

Fuchs, V.R. (1993). *The future of health policy*. Cambridge, MA: Harvard University Press.

This book is a sequel to *The Health Economy* (1986). The author discusses what health means and the reason pricing health is problematic. He details the many factors that contribute to the growth of health spending and explains why no simple solution is available. The evidence concerning the effects of national health insurance on the cost of care and the health of the population are reviewed. Economics can help to understand the trade-offs, but only a commitment to resolving our political and social dilemmas can break our present impasse.

McKinley, J.B. (Ed.). (1981). *Issues in health care policy*. Milbank Reader 3. Cambridge, MA: MIT Press.

This edited volume is arranged in four sections: background issues, specific areas of health care policy, some dubious policies, and rationing health care resources. The 16 authors provide a wide range of views and therefore the book is a rich resource for general and specific issues affecting health care policy.

Patrick, D.L., & Erickson, P. (1993). *Health status and health policy: Quality of life in health care evaluation and resource allocation*. New York: Oxford University Press.

This book advocates the use of health and quality of life outcomes to measure the benefits of health expenditures. The authors focus on health-related quality of life as the most relevant and comprehensive outcome measure for comparing costs. Because health-related quality of life incorporates social values, life expectancy, and a comprehensive description of health, it addresses the trade-off between how long people live and how well they live. The authors bring the fields of health status and health policy together to assist health decision makers and researchers in the formation of policy and its implementation and evaluation.

Sills, Y.G. (1994). *The AIDS pandemic: Social perspectives*. Westport, CT: Greenwood Press.

This book gives the reader an overview of the social, economic, and political aspects of AIDS throughout the world, especially the developing world. Of particular interest is the international response of global mobilization against AIDS, including the World Health Organization's global programs and international forums. The chapter on the task of changing social behavior which addresses ethnic and cultural biases, life-style dynamics and sexual behavior is especially helpful in understanding this macroproblem.

6

Program Evaluation

Introduction

Throughout our discussions of intervention, we have consistently maintained the importance of program evaluation as an integral part of the intervention process. The purpose of this chapter is to focus specific attention on the evaluation stage. It should be noted that program evaluation is almost a discipline in itself and many sociologists and other social scientists are often employed as program evaluators. Their task is to evaluate ongoing programs for clients who call upon them for this specific activity. This chapter is not intended to be a treatise on program evaluation from that perspective. Here, our concern will focus on a subset of the broader world of program evaluation: program evaluation as a part, a stage in an overall intervention. That is, we direct your attention to the situation where the clinical sociologist works with a specific client/client system to design and implement a specific problem-solving intervention.

Our purpose in including a chapter on evaluation is based on our working experience that the evaluation step often gets neglected or ignored completely. There are a variety of reasons for this. Evaluation is often a difficult task and the more complex the social system that is the target for change, the more difficult the evaluation becomes. In some cases, the nature of the change process is such that effects take time to accumulate. Clients may be eager to get a program underway but may not be willing to commit the resources necessary for a long- or even midrange evaluation. It may also be difficult to sustain the interest and energy of those involved to conduct a proper evaluation. It may also be difficult to maintain a commitment to evaluation because those who planned and implemented the intervention program are content with what they see happening; they claim to "know" the intervention is "working" (though they are seldom able to articulate *how* they know). Finally, evaluation may get short shrift because intervention program activities, which may compete for time, energy, and other resources, are given first priority.

We insist that to ignore evaluation or to relegate it to an afterthought status is to do an incomplete job. Our view of evaluation, as we discuss it here, is guided by the following:

1. Program evaluation should be an integral part of program planning.
2. Program planning, as derived from the assessment step, should include clear, operationally defined, and measurable objectives.
3. Program planning should include the evaluation steps as part of the implementation process.
4. The timetable for program evaluation should begin when program implementation begins.
5. Program evaluation should provide a steady flow of feedback on the course of the implementation of an intervention program.

This chapter will address the questions, Why evaluate? What to evaluate? and How to evaluate. Evaluation is a fascinating and complex application of sociology and other social sciences. Here we try to present an overview.

Why Evaluate?

In the broader world of evaluation, there have been times when evaluators have been viewed with suspicion. As Weiss (1972) suggested, in one of the early, classic works on evaluation, evaluation has been used for political purposes as part of power struggles in agencies or organizations. The goal of such evaluations was seen as supporting or attacking various cliques and interest groups that were for or opposed to certain policies or courses of action. In other contexts, evaluators were seen as tools for justifying decisions already taken. Where these have been staffing decisions, staff members have felt their positions threatened by evaluators' findings. Sometimes, conducting an evaluation has been seen as a way of delaying or postponing decisions. And sometimes, evaluations have been used as public relations moves. We follow Weiss's view that these are inappropriate uses of evaluation.

The definition of a problem and the development of an intervention indicates a resolve to take some action to ameliorate the problem. The purpose of intervention is to achieve some predetermined outcome. The policies and programs are hypothesized to achieve the desired outcome. Intervention can be viewed systemically. Assessment, problem definition, and objectives can be viewed as input. The planning and implementation of policies and programs can be viewed as "process." The activities and consequences are the output. Evaluation is critical to this cybernetic model as the feedback loop. Evaluation is a feedback mechanism for "course correction." As we have consistently stressed (See Figure 3.5, page 106) evaluation may prompt a need for further planning, and/or additional assessment with concomitant adjustment of program activities. Figure 6.1 suggests the role of evaluation.

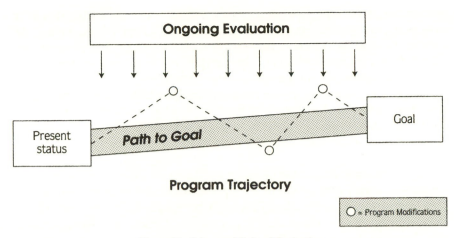

Figure 6.1. Scheme of Role of Evaluation

Shadish, Cook, and Leviton (1991:21) described the role of evaluation in similar terms:

> Evaluation is just one part of a complex, interdependent, nonlinear set of problem-solving activities. Such evaluations have always been with us and always will be, for problems will always occur, solutions will always need to be generated, tests of their efficacy will need to be done, and the test results will have to be stored if they are to help.

In this passage, Shadish et al. point to another important role of evaluation: storing the results and thus contributing to institutional memory. Both the client system under study and the clinical sociologists stand to gain from the information generated in the course of evaluation. All can learn what works and what does not work. What is learned from evaluation can be used for improvement of developing programs. The client system benefits as it learns more about its problem-solving options. Evaluation also provides accountability for use of resources. Clinical workers gain in experience that may transfer to other situations and may also contribute to theory development generally. Evaluation also provides information for program diffusion. As Rossi and Freeman (1982:126) wrote:

> In order to be able to reproduce the essential features of an intervention in places other than where it originated, it is necessary to be able to describe the program in operational detail. Critical points in implementation need to be identified, solutions to managerial problems outlined, qualifications of successful program personnel documented, and so on.

Finally, evaluation is important to intervention to uncover unintended consequences. Efforts for change in a social system or any of its parts may produce other undesirable effects. One such effect may be resistance to change. For example, a system of merit pay increases was introduced into a school system intended to recognize "superior" teachers and efforts in the classroom. The program was intended to improve the quality of teaching. However, the result was divisiveness and reduced morale within the system. Staff members who did not receive the recognition and merit increment responded with anger and hostility. They asserted that they worked as hard as those teachers who did receive the increment. Eventually, the "merit" increments were given to all staff thus defeating the original idea. Planners had apparently not anticipated the broader results of their plan.

Some attention to possible "side effects" during the assessment and planning stages will certainly be helpful. In the above example, the merit pay idea was an idea of the school administration. They might have achieved a better outcome for the merit pay plan had they involved teachers and perhaps the county teachers association (union). More generally, they might have achieved a better outcome for the improvement of classroom instruction with better planning and broader participation to include teachers, parents, community members, specialists, and perhaps even students. Generally then, clinical sociologists and others involved in change need to try to be alert for *other* consequences as they plan and implement intervention programs and investigate them as part of evaluation.

It is not possible, however, to anticipate all and perhaps not even most other consequences of intervention. Thus Weiss (1972:33) pointed out that efforts might address one aspect of a complex problem. "Even if they achieve good results in their area, the more important effect may be to throw the original system out of kilter." The systemic nature of all social systems compels us to look for unintended consequences.

In sum then, the answer to the question, "Why evaluate?" has several parts:

1. To keep a planned intervention on course toward the goal by revealing a need for additional assessment data, or additional planning, and/or changes in the program;
2. To learn about the intervention as it develops to be able to improve it;
3. To reveal dysfunctional unintended consequences brought on by the various parts of the intervention;
4. To contribute to the problem-solving efforts of the client system and to the development of the field generally.

What to Evaluate?

Evaluation is a research task that can tap the full range of experts' knowledge of research methods in social science and their ingenuity and creativity as well.

Here, by way of introduction, we provide an overview and recommend that as needed, readers consult one or more detailed sources such as those suggested at the end of this chapter.

Two considerations govern our approach as developed here. First, it is our view that evaluation is an integral part of the intervention process that includes the assessment, planning, and implementation stages as well as the evaluation stage. This means that evaluation is built into the design of the intervention program. The assessment should point the way to a definition of the problem, establish a baseline, and clarify what needs to be changed and how to change it. In addition to planning intervention components, program planning should frame concrete statements of objectives, timetables, and identify stakeholders, decision makers, and other consumers of evaluation results. The evaluation should be designed as the program itself is being designed. Those responsible for the evaluation should be a part of the project team at the outset and evaluation should begin early in the overall process. This is the moral of the story in Clinical Focus 6.1.

The second consideration is in line with our general view that the clinical sociologists' role is one of partnership and collaboration with clients. The clinical sociologists' role with regard to evaluation is to negotiate the evaluation procedures at the time that other intervention components are negotiated. It should be part of the contracting with clients. It is also the clinical sociologists' role to contribute expertise and advice on the technical aspects of the design of evaluation materials and procedures and to offer instruction in their use.

In our discussion of mesolevel practice in Chapter 4 we called attention to the views of Whyte (1989) and others on participatory action research. We hold that the process continues into the evaluation stage. Thus, Guba and Lincoln (1989:11) called for *"full participative involvement"* of stakeholders and others "as equal partners in every aspect of design, implementation, interpretation, and resulting action of an evaluation...." For Guba and Lincoln this means *"political parity* and *control"* as well as *"conceptual parity"* among professionals and members of the client system. The professionals are advisors and team members. They take part in ongoing dialog with members of the client system who are the ones who own the intervention including the evaluation.

Weiss (1972:20) addressed the issue of whether evaluation should be conducted by outside evaluators or in-house members of the client system. Outside evaluators may sometimes have more credibility with certain decision makers and may be thought to be somewhat more objective. However, evaluators who are part of the client system and part of the working team may have greater understanding, easier access to information, and be more readily able to apply the information. Weiss was referring to the larger practice of program evaluation. In our model here, which is concerned with evaluation of problem solving intervention and participatory research, we suggest that the evaluation component is part of the project from the start. It is the contribution of the clinical sociologists to see that good evaluation

Clinical Focus 6.1

Drug Program

Katherine Williams, Ph.D., is a clinical sociologist who works with youth gang and drug prevention programming. She was an outside evaluator of the project described below and began her evaluation on the last day of the project year.

This federally funded youth gang drug program for adolescent females is operated by the public housing authority in a large Eastern city. Six housing sites were selected for this program due to the presence of female gangs. The application for funding describes the program as a multistage intervention program that addressed risk factors and provides interventions on multiple levels. Staff positions include a Program Coordinator, six youth workers, and three "specialists" who provide services to all six sites. Meeting space is provided for the girls and the youth worker at each site.

The program is to include daily alternative activities such as recreation, sports, and field trips for girls organized by the youth worker at each site. In addition, there are two "specialists" who rotate through the sites each week providing the girls in the program with personal growth and development workshops. The "Personal Growth Specialist" provides sessions on self-esteem, physical fitness, personal hygiene and grooming, birth control, and self-confidence. The "Leadership Specialist" focuses on informational sessions and activities that develop leadership skills. The third specialist position is to provide family support services although this position has remained vacant during most of the program.

Interviews with staff and site-visit observations indicate that the program outlined in the formal description was not being implemented in a consistent fashion. Several factors hampered the successful implementation of the planned program including conflicts between program staff and tenant councils, a lack of consistent supervision, and a significant lack of communication and cooperation among the staff.

In order for the program to maintain a consistent presence at a site, the program needs a stable meeting space that

(*continued*)

is planned and conducted as well as used. If a real participatory model is developed, the members of a client system will support and want the results of evaluation.

The evaluation phase must find out: (1) if the planned intervention steps are occurring as planned and if not, why not; (2) what are the consequences of the intervention, both intended and unintended. The design of the evaluation stage, then, requires the development of data on these issues. The key to good evaluation, as in any research, is conceptualization of the research task. By now it should be

---

Clinical Focus 6.1 (*continued*)

the girls can begin to associate with program activities. Often the relationships between the Housing Authority and the Tenant Associations were problematic. The relationship between the youth worker and the Tenant Association in her site was critical to the continued existence of the program at the site. One youth worker was banned from the site by the Tenant Association and others had difficulty finding sufficient meeting space to hold program activities. When program activities stop due to lack of meeting space, the girls lose interest and find other activities.

Lack of communication among staff also hampered program implementation. As one worker stated "at meetings people never share ideas and talk about problems so other staff members can offer advice." The lack of communication and cooperation was particularly acute between the specialists and the youth workers at each of the sites. The Personal Growth Specialist indicated that "probably the most frustrating and aggravating thing that I've encountered since my stay, is showing up at a site to conduct a

workshop and no one is to be found. Youth workers ignoring my schedule and take their kids on a field trip happens frequently. I only visit each site once a week for about 2 hours. You would think the youth workers could set aside that time for me so I could perform my workshop." The Leadership Specialist echoed this same frustration. "I didn't perform any workshops this week at the sites because when I showed up to teach, no one was to be found. Youth workers constantly ignore the schedule I submit to them at the beginning of every month."

Identifying problems in program implementation is one very important function of evaluation. Williams' study of the program revealed personnel problems and problems of liaison with important stakeholders. Workers were frustrated, resources wasted, and conflicts existed. These problems affected the ability of the program to reach the target group and to carry out the intervention program. If evaluation had been an early and regular component of the plan, these problems could have been identified and possible solutions found.

SOURCE: Williams, K.L. (1995). Personal communication (HMR).

---

clear that the evaluation is driven by the statements of the objectives. As we address the question, "What to evaluate?" three subordinate questions arise:

1. Are the planned intervention steps occurring as planned?
2. Are the planned intervention steps producing movement toward the objectives?
3. What were the consequences?

These are the questions that underlie the three types of evaluation to be described here: Process Evaluation, Program Monitoring, and Impact Evaluation.

Process Evaluation

Process objectives state what must be accomplished to achieve the changes desired. They should be stated in terms of units of activity by designated role-occupants. Evaluation design should provide for early and frequent assessment of process issues. Obviously, the specifics of data collection will be dependent on the level—micro, meso, or macro—and the nature of the client system, whether individual, family, organization, or community, as well as the specific purpose of the intervention. Thus, here we will suggest some general points for process evaluation.

When a program plan is developed, it should specify who does what when. It should also produce quantifiable goals and objectives. The purpose of process evaluation is to determine whether or to what extent the planned events occurred as planned. Process evaluation should include assessment of any materials that might be used in the intervention program. Are the materials appropriate to the task? Are they suited to those who will use them? For example, if training is to take place, as a step toward the desired change, evaluation of the curriculum and curriculum materials will help estimate whether training will be effective. Is the curriculum appropriate to the training objectives? Are the content and materials at a level that can be comprehended by the target audience; are they too simple for the level of the target audience? Are those persons who will do the training qualified, familiar with the curriculum, and competent with the materials? This type of evaluation can be used to "fine tune" the materials themselves and their adaptability to those who will use them.

Program planning should clearly state the various process objectives in unambiguous, measurable terms. Thus an example of a process objective might be:

> To conduct 10 2-hour training sessions for 15 workers in the _____
> department each Wednesday afternoon from 3:00 to 5:00 P.M. in _____.

Process evaluation will need to determine if, indeed, the training occurred as planned. Was each session held? Did the identified workers attend regularly?

If an objective such as the example was included in the plan, the retraining program for these workers must have been deemed necessary to achieve a successful outcome. Thus in guiding the program, it is important to assess whether this step occurred. More generally, the evaluation should note what events or activities are supposed to occur and in what sequence, and should determine if they occurred as scheduled. If they are directed at an identified target audience, evaluation should also assess whether that target audience was reached. Additionally, if there are budgetary matters, process evaluation should assess whether or not funds are being used appropriately and if budgetary constraints as well as accounting and documentation requirements are being adhered to.

If the events did not occur as planned, evaluation must also attempt to discover why. Questions for study might include: Did those responsible have the resources and training, knowledge, and skills for carrying out their responsibility? Did they lack motivation? If so, why? If the target audience was not reached, what were the reasons? Was the time schedule appropriate (e.g., working moms may not be able to come to parenting classes as scheduled in the morning). Are there cultural, physical, or other barriers such as a need to have transportation or child care?

Attention to possible cultural barriers is important. Often well-meaning programs directed toward ethnic minorities or the poor or homeless fail to connect with the target audience because sponsorship, materials, and activities are not culturally syntonic. Inclusion of members of the target population in the planning process can sometimes help.

The task of process evaluation is made more difficult if the program is to be conducted at more than one site. Not only must evaluation determine issues of delivery but issues of standardization may need to be assessed. These will have to be weighed against needs to adapt to variations in local conditions.

Process evaluation, then, is an important part of conducting any intervention. Steps are planned that are hypothesized to lead to problem solving. If the objective is to be achieved, the steps must be carried out as planned if they are to have a chance to work. Often programs fail, not because of poor design, but because they were not executed according to the design. Process evaluation is the source of feedback to project managers and the client system on whether or not the problem-solving steps are occurring as planned.

Process evaluation should cover every phase of program delivery. That includes analysis of management strategies, interaction among participants, materials, activities, personnel appraisal, and client acceptance. This assessment is an important aid to program development. Planners need to know, not only whether plans were carried out, they also need to know what is happening so that obstacles and barriers can be quickly identified, addressed, and perhaps eliminated.

Clinical Focus 6.2 describes a project whose outcomes could have benefited from attention to process evaluation. The moral of the fable is the need for process evaluation and the need for early involvement of evaluation.

General issues for process evaluation include:

1. Are intervention activities occurring as planned?
2. Are target groups or individuals being reached?
3. How do stakeholders, project personnel, and target persons respond to intervention activities?

With individuals and families, the use of diaries and record keeping can help provide data on compliance with agreed-upon activities. These, of course, are subject to all the flaws of self-report data. Reports may be incomplete or inaccurate for a variety of reasons. It is helpful if clients clearly understand the importance of

---

Clinical Focus 6.2

Drug Program (continued)

The program described here was an after-school program for middle-school youth who lived in a public housing project near the school. It was intended to target youth who were at high risk for school failure and dropping out. Teachers and administrators at the school were given certain guidelines and asked to identify children for referral to the program. Most of the children lived in single-parent homes.

One feature of the program was the requirement that children's parents had to participate for the child to continue in the program. Children taken into the program were given the responsibility for informing their parents and getting them to attend evening sessions, first scheduled every other week and later scheduled once a month. Program staff eventually tried sending notes home with the children, but apparently no staff tried direct contact or outreach to the parents. Children whose parents failed to attend were eventually dropped from the program. The program finished out the year serving primarily children who were not the original target group. All of this was learned as program evaluation began after the program had ended for the first year.

Reference to project documents revealed that one of the process objectives of the project was parental involvement including parents' regular attendance at the scheduled evening sessions. As noted above, these were originally planned as bi-weekly but attendance was so light that this was changed to once a month in an effort to improve attendance.

Earlier involvement of the evaluator and earlier attention to process evaluation may have helped to identify problems related to the lack of parental involvement and have permitted adjustments that would have kept more of the target children in the program. It might also have permitted staff to work with the parents and spared them the disappointment and the feeling that "these parents just don't care enough about these kids."

Moreover, the parents are key stakeholders in this project. It seems that all planning took place without participation with parents which, itself, was a process problem that detracted from the chances of success for the program.

Recommendations were made for changes in methods for getting parents involved and for having evaluations begin immediately for the following year.

---

this task and if they own the intervention. They will certainly be more resistant to data collection if they feel that it is something imposed upon them by an outside authority. Where possible, self-report data should be augmented with observation. Where institutions are involved in efforts to change an individual's behaviors, outside sources of data can sometimes be obtained with written permission from clients and negotiation with these sources. For example, liaison with school personnel may provide both process data as well as data on behavioral changes of children and adolescents.

The diversity of meso- and macrolevel interventions makes generalizations about process evaluation procedures difficult. However, these interventions have in common the fact that they often designate a target group or population. Intervention activities must reach this target group and members must participate in sufficient numbers for change to occur. Thus, concern for process evaluation may include whether or not the target group has access or is being reached, and continue participation or drop out. Some types of programs may involve outreach activities or recruitment of participants. Process evaluation will need to determine the effectiveness of these efforts.

Rossi and Freeman (1982:128) discussed evaluation of the coverage of community based interventions involving health or social services delivery. By "coverage" they meant the extent to which a program reached the intended target population, those persons in need of program services. Assessment of coverage includes determination of bias, the extent that certain subgroups of a target population show differential participation. Assessment of coverage also includes determination of the extent to which persons not designated or not in need also obtain services. For example, consider a school-based catch-up program designed for students who are identified as behind in reading skills of three or more grade levels. The objective is generally to improve reading skills. However, if only or primarily good readers are enrolled in the program, outcome measures will make the program look good but it will not have reached those in need. On the other hand, if teachers use the program as a dumping ground for behavior problems, regardless of their reading ability, the program is not serving its intended audience and outcome evaluations will be irrelevant to the original objective.

Coverage issues also involve access. The question for access is, Can members of the target population or group readily participate or are there barriers? Rossi and Freeman (1982:137) identified *eligibles*, *utilizers*, and *dropouts*, those who are members of the target population but do not participate, those who do, and those who start but do not continue. Data on the differences among these groups is useful for process evaluation.

Data collection methods include direct observation, records, surveys, interviews, and group meetings. Direct observation, either participant or nonparticipant observation, can be useful in determining how intervention activities are conducted. The observer needs to be trained in what to look for and the use of standard forms for recording may also be helpful. The scope of the intervention, however, could make this approach expensive and time consuming. In addition, the presence of the observer may alter the behavior of those being observed. Frequent contact can reduce this to some degree. More important, if appropriate relationships are established at the outset, and the participation model is followed with cooperation and participation agreements secured, the potential threat of the observer's presence can be reduced when those being observed understand that it is not they but the intervention that is being studied. Direct observation of the intervention program can be a rich source of information on how it works and where the glitches are.

Various forms of records will also help, either those normally kept by an organization or those designed specifically for the purpose of process evaluation. Examples include records of events, number and nature of participants, activities conducted, units of services provided, problems encountered, etc. Care needs to be taken that record keepers are trained as necessary to provide accurate and complete records. Care also needs to be taken that the record keeping system is not so cumbersome or time consuming that it competes with or interferes with other activities including the performance of intervention activities.

Surveys of various kinds are another data source for process evaluation. Items and the samples to be surveyed will, of course, depend on the purpose and location of the intervention. Such things as awareness or perceptions of intervention activities and level of participation can be obtained through this method. In small projects, it may be possible to survey all persons affected. In larger projects, samples from a target population can be used. For example, a survey may help a program discover differences among eligibles, utilizers, and dropouts, and provide input as a guide to activities to improve coverage of the target population.

Less structured interviews and group sessions can help flesh out the results of other data collection techniques. Participants may include project managers, staff, target groups, members of the working group, etc. These sessions can add details and impressions on the course of program activities.

In sum, then, process evaluation covers a variety of activities designed to determine if the planned activities are occurring as planned and provide feedback to planners and decision makers on the course of intervention. The best planned interventions will not achieve their desired outcomes if the plan is not carried out.

Program Monitoring and Impact Evaluation

The objective of all problem-solving interventions is to bring about specific changes. At the microlevel, with "Tony," introduced in Chapter 3, objectives included improvements in an individual's school behavior and academic performance. At the mesolevel, organizational objectives might include such things as increased productivity, reduced conflict, improved communication, or improved health and safety of workers. Community objectives might include improvements in schools, improvements in infrastructure such as streets, lighting, housing, or sanitation, or improvement in health and social services. At the macrolevel, objectives may include health-care reform, racial justice, reduction of homelessness, or redress of economic inequities. Whatever the level, whatever the problem, the purpose of program monitoring is to see if the hypothesized policies and programs are producing change in the desired direction.

The general purpose of program monitoring is to determine whether an intervention program is achieving the intended effects. A program plan has the functional status of a hypothesis; it is hypothesized that implementation of the policies and/or programs will achieve a specified objective which is the solution to an identified problem. The objective can be considered the dependent variable while the new policy or program can be considered the independent variable. As implementation gets underway, decision makers have to decide whether to continue to pursue the present course of action or to modify their strategy. Generally, outcomes may include (1) change is occurring in the desired direction; (2) no change is occurring; (3) undesirable change is occurring. The task, is to establish a credible link between intervention activities and observed outcomes. This is akin to the problem of establishing a causal inference in scientific research.

Just to remind readers, there are three criteria which must be met to support a causal inference. The first is *concomitant variation*; it must be shown that variation in the antecedent conditions, the independent variable, is associated with variation in the consequent, the dependent variable. The second is *time order*; it must be shown that the variation in the presumed antecedent occurs prior to that of the presumed consequent. The third criterion is *alternative explanations must be ruled out*; it must be shown that variation in the consequent is attributable only to variation in the antecedent and not to other influences. Of the three requirements, the third is usually the most difficult to meet.

The more complex the social system in which intervention is being conducted, the more difficult it will be to establish a valid causal inference, particularly in establishing the third criterion. Thus, as Rossi and Freeman noted (1982:167), in the complex social world there are multiple causal factors operating in addition to an intervention that may affect social systems. In addition, with larger social systems, effects of the introduction of new policies and programs may be small and occur slowly.

To confound the evaluation task a bit more, interventions are often a "work in progress." In scientific experiments no one decides to change the experimental stimulus in the middle of the experiment. Intervention programs are often developmental and decision makers may not be willing or able to await outcomes before changing the intervention.

Impact evaluation is concerned with results, of finding out how well the intervention worked. One basic question for impact evaluation is, Were the objectives met? In addition, it is also useful to sort out the contribution to results of various components of the intervention. For both theoretical and practical reasons, it may be useful to learn which components of a program are essential, which are merely nice to have, and which are unnecessary or perhaps even counterproductive. As with program monitoring, the task for impact evaluation is to demonstrate a cause-to-effect relationship between program steps and components and observed outcomes. We recommend wariness regarding premature closure. Just because the evaluation shows desired effects, it does not mean that the occurrence of an intended outcome had anything to do with the intervention.

In addition to the course of planned changes, evaluation must assess other effects of the intervention on the client system, on other social systems, and on individual members. Impact assessment also refers to efforts to determine the nature of unintended outcomes of intervention as well as long-term effects. Here again, the research task searches for a credible link between a possible or observed impact on one hand, and the intervention elements themselves and the planned changes on the other. Weiss (1972:33) recommended brainstorming "… in advance about all the effects, good, bad, and indifferent, that could flow from the program." If the range of likely outcomes is planned for, "What were unanticipated consequences are now … unintended but anticipated."

Program monitoring and impact evaluation start with the statements of objectives. One of the requirements of the planning stage is the articulation of clear statements of outcome objectives in terms that are observable and measurable. The task is to design research with appropriate indicators that assess whether or not objectives are being met. Below, we will address the design issue, but note that the task of ruling out alternative explanations is the most difficult part of the task.

Problem-solving interventions are some set of planned activities designed to bring about behavior change on the part of designated role-occupants, the target group, which in turn, alter a problematic situation. Figure 6.2 presents the situation graphically. As the figure shows, there are nine paths as pure types. The issue is

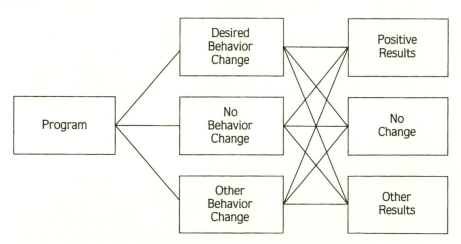

Figure 6.2. Paths of Probable Outcomes

confounded since overlaps can occur. Other behaviors in addition to the target behaviors may change. Other outcomes in addition to the target outcome may also occur.

Program monitoring and impact evaluation are used to determine the extent to which the planned implementation led to outcomes and consequences that they were designed for. We recommend that quantitative methods are central to the research task but that evaluators should include qualitative research methods as well. The latter add richness of detail and experience to the evaluation. Research designs include observational studies, case studies, single-case designs, quasi-experimental designs, experimental designs, and survey designs. The more powerful designs are those that provide for comparison. Here we will review each briefly. Readers requiring greater detail should consult additional sources such as those listed as suggested readings at the end of this chapter.

Naturalistic Observation

Much can be learned about what is happening in a setting by simply observing the setting, becoming familiar with the context, its patterns, and rhythms, and being open to discovery. Conversations with various key respondents add to an observer's understanding of participants' meanings for events and activities and what they feel is important. The more varied the social location of such key respondents, the broader the picture an observer can get.

In this method, the observer is the data-gathering instrument. Guba and Lincoln (1989:176) asserted that:

> Humans collect information best and most easily through the direct employment of their senses: talking to people, observing their activities, reading their documents, assessing the unobtrusive signs they leave behind, responding to their non-verbal cues, and the like.

Guba and Lincoln also referred to the "tacit knowledge" that observers can employ; our own experiences, skills, knowledge, and training provide the ability to understand and judge the materials of observation. Our tacit knowledge provides the basis for making an informed judgment. Observers drawn from the social system, as well as professionally trained sociologists, can contribute useful insights. Preparation of observers through training will always improve their performance.

Naturalistic observation gives richness and context which, when combined with systematic quantitative data enhance an understanding of the effects of interventions. However, the presence of the observer always adds an element that may influence what or who is being observed. This can be softened to a degree by the observer's frequent presence. As the observer becomes familiar, a part of the woodwork as it were, the effect of his or her presence may be reduced. The value of the observation can be increased if observation was part of the assessment stage or can begin sufficiently prior to the implementation stage so that the observers have some idea of "baseline" behavior in setting. It is also helpful if observers have some systematic method of recording observations which usually range from open-ended narrative to structured checklists and rating scales.

The disadvantages, as pointed out by Rossi and Freeman (1982:154) are that naturalistic observation can be time consuming, is not easily taught to untrained observers, and may produce data that are not easily summarized or analyzed. We do not recommend this as the only approach but as a useful approach in concert with other approaches that provide for comparisons. However, naturalistic observation is an especially good step in getting to know the setting and the program.

Case Study

A case study is a detailed description of a single case, individual, group, community, etc. The value of a case study is determined by the extent of the details reported. O'Leary and Wilson (1987:362) stated that the basic criteria for case studies include complete and precise description of intervention methods to permit replication, the complete specification of the problems to which the methods were applied, and specification of characteristics of clients. However, case studies are generally uncontrolled and have limited value in drawing causal inferences from intervention to outcome.

The ability to draw some inferences from a case study can be improved to a degree according to O'Leary and Wilson if (1) the study includes objective evidence of change instead of anecdotal reports; (2) the study relies on continuous or repeated assessment rather than single pre- and postevaluation; (3) reasonable projection of the course of the problem if left unattended is made (some problems might go away whether or not an intervention takes place); (4) change is coincidental with specific interventions, the larger the effect the more persuasive.

The drawbacks are the lack of control. The case study method does not rule out alternative explanations for the observed outcomes. As noted above, some problems simply get corrected with the passage of time, the maturation of persons or systems involved, or changes in social, political, or economic trends. In addition, change might be due to the well-known Hawthorne or placebo effect: Just paying attention and/or appearing to do something may induce changes; however, the specific intervention program may, in fact, have had little to do with the changes that occurred.

Single-Case Experiments

Single-case experimental designs help to overcome some of the disadvantages of case studies by introducing some control. In these designs the case acts as its own control. These designs were developed as a feature of behavior therapy and were intended as a way of monitoring the effects of behavioral psychotherapy with individuals. However, they are offered here with the view that they may be applicable by clinical sociologists not only with individuals but with other cases as well.

To be useful, single-case designs require a clear, well-defined objective criterion measure. Examples of criterion measures include frequency of problem or preferred behaviors by an individual or group, measures of time, dollars, test scores, number of units of output, etc. The logic of these designs is similar to that of time-series analysis.

The simplest design is characterized as the AB design. After a period of baseline measures (the A stage) of the criterion, the intervention or treatment is introduced with continued monitoring of the criterion. The intervention is said to be working if the criterion shows measurable change. Figure 6.3 gives an example. The baseline period acts as the control.

The X line (X—X—X) shows the intervention appears to have been effective since the upswing in the curve appears to have been coincident with the onset of the intervention. The bottom line (designated by o—o—o) shows no effect of the intervention. The middle line (▲—▲—▲) shows a steady increase in the criterion

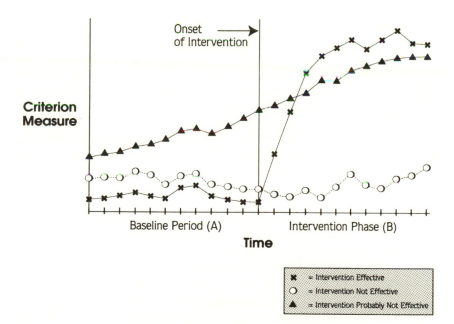

Figure 6.3. Example of Simple AB Design

measure but that it is likely not to have been attributable to the intervention since the baseline trend merely continued upward.

A modification in this design is the withdrawal or "baseline, ABA" design (Leitenberg, 1973) in which, after a baseline period, the intervention is initiated for a period, withdrawn for a period, then reinstated. If the intervention is inducing change, withdrawal should be accompanied by a return to baseline and should show effects again when reinstated. Figure 6.4 illustrates. This design, if it comes out as illustrated here in Figure 6.4 gives stronger evidence for making a causal inference about the intervention than does the simple AB design. However, not all interventions are reversible. Either because of the nature of the intervention or for ethical reasons it may not be possible to use this design.

Where an intervention has several components to address several criterion outcomes and which can be initiated sequentially, multiple baseline designs can be used. Figure 6.5 illustrates multiple baselines across behaviors (Leitenberg, 1973; O'Leary and Wilson, 1987:365). For each target behavior, criterion measures are taken. After a baseline interval taking measures of all three behaviors, the first intervention component is initiated for one of the problems. The others are left unaddressed. They continue as baseline and are addressed sequentially. If no change occurs until each intervention is initiated, we have some basis for a causal inference.

We can also have multiple baselines across individuals or cases where intervention is to be initiated at more than one location. In this case, baseline data are kept on all cases and interventions are initiated sequentially with each individual or unit. If each case or individual shows similar response to the initiation of the intervention, there is some basis for causal inference.

These designs have certain limitations. First, they will not reveal the contribution that the uniqueness of the case has to the effect of the intervention. This will, of course, affect the generalizability from one setting to others. Second, findings are fairly unambiguous when there are stable baselines and dramatic or at least steady changes following the onset of intervention. When these conditions are not clearly met, interpretation may be more difficult. Finally, these designs do not totally rule out Hawthorne or placebo effects.

However, these designs can be particularly useful in program monitoring. They offer some evidence of the effects of the intervention while it is underway. They may be less relevant to impact evaluation, especially of longer term effects. However, as Leitenberg (1973) suggested, "Long-term follow ups are not precluded." The use of controlled monitoring can be an aid in determining if planned intervention steps affect the outcome variables of interest.

Experimental and Quasi-Experimental Designs

Most of us have been taught that experimental designs are the most powerful designs when attempting to establish a causal inference. These designs require

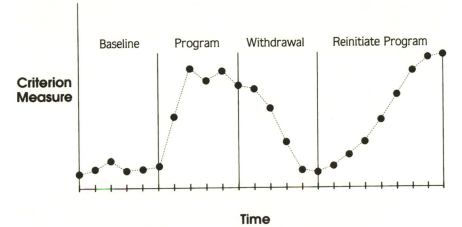

Figure 6.4. Example of "Baseline ABA" Withdrawal Design

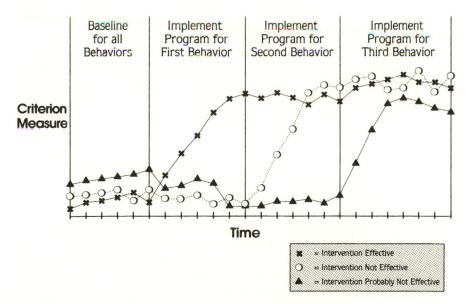

Figure 6.5. Example of Multiple Baseline Design

random selection of subjects or at least random assignment of subjects to treatment groups. They also require careful control of presentation of the various levels of the independent variable or treatment, and the presence of one or more control groups that receive no treatment and/or placebo-type treatment. The control groups provide the basis for comparison. Random assignment of subjects to treatment and control groups supports the assumption that groups are similar at the outset and that the only difference between them is the treatment. These procedures are attempts to control the sources of invalidity identified by Campbell and Stanley (1963)—history, maturation, secular trends, selection bias, etc.—which amounts to ruling out other causes.

True experimental designs have limited applicability to the type of evaluation discussed here. The following hypothetical example comes close:

A local health department includes both a mental health and addictions treatment unit. Aware of the frequency that psychiatric disorders and addictions disorders co-occur, the department prepares a dual-diagnosis program. Each new intake is then randomly assigned to the new program, former treatment, or is placed on a waiting list for treatment at a later date. Patients are assessed at intake on some common criterion measure. The purpose of premeasures provides data to test the assumption of similarity among groups. The various treatments are conducted, patients are reassessed at some later date, and results compared among the various groups, including those placed on the waiting list who acted as a no-treatment control group.

Similarly, it may be possible in some school-based or other institutional setting to randomly assign persons to groups and include or withhold a specific program element to test its impact. It is possible but our experience suggests that it is unlikely. For instance, the dual-diagnosis example raises both ethical and legal issues associated with withholding treatments from certain individuals for the sake of having a control group. The random assignment requirement may be possible in total institutions such as hospitals or jails where health, mental health, or other vital treatments are not an issue.

The term *quasi-experimental designs* describes designs that do not meet all the criteria for true experiments. The so-called intact-groups design is an example. In this design, the program or treatment variations are presented to one or more existing groups with one or more groups left as no-treatment comparison groups. It helps if groups can be randomly assigned to treatment conditions. Criterion measures are collected on all treatment and no-treatment groups both prior to and following treatment and comparisons are made. These designs might be reasonably applied to interventions in school systems, for example, where classroom groups are the intact groups. A sufficient number of groups from within a system and random assignment of groups to treatments may provide a reasonable basis for a credible causal inference about an intervention program.

The further one deviates from the experimental model, the weaker the causal inference. For example, the less like the treatment group that the comparison group is, the less comparable the outcome measures and the less credible the inference from the comparison.

Survey Designs

Surveys involve the use of standardized questionnaires administered either as cross-sectional or longitudinal designs. Cross-sectional designs refer to single administrations. Longitudinal designs refer to repeated administration over time. A panel study is a type of longitudinal design in which the same respondents are contacted on several occasions. An alternative longitudinal design is repeated sampling from the same target population.

Cross-sectional surveys, in which data are gathered one time only, can provide some information for impact assessment but require the use of statistical controls. For example, a target population may include persons who participated in program activities, those who started but dropped out, and those who did not participate at all. The survey instrument includes outcome measures as well as measures of other variables considered relevant, including level of program participation. Outcome measures are tested for a relationship with differences in the extent of participation and with the effects of other, relevant, possibly confounding variables held constant through statistical procedures.

Another application of this design might be the case where at different time periods or at different locations, there were differences in the intervention program. Statistical controls could be used to sort out these effects.

Well conducted cross-sectional studies as impact evaluation permit the collection of a lot of data relatively fast, easily, and inexpensively. They are useful in situations that do not permit before and after designs and do not permit experimental or quasi-experimental designs. They are useful especially where the target population is large. However, to be most effective, they must include adequate measures of the key variables. In the example given above, level of participation was the independent variable. Participants, dropouts, and nonparticipants self-selected themselves. To differentiate them effectively means being able to tap the key variables influencing self-selection in order to control for this effect.

Longitudinal survey designs collect data on more than one occasion. For example, a needs assessment may be used as baseline with a follow-up survey to determine extent of change. One such design involves repeated surveys of the same sample of respondents. This has the virtue of being able to chart the course of changes over time. Problems with this design include the attrition of respondents and sensitization. Attrition refers to loss of respondents from the pool. They may drop out, move, refuse to continue participation, etc. It is usually difficult to estimate in what significant ways they differ from those who remain in the pool.

Sensitization refers to the fact that being in the respondent pool may alter the behaviors of the respondents in some way that cannot be estimated.

Repeated random samples from a designated target population also permit estimates of changes over time. This is particularly useful in controlling for the possibility of sensitization. It is also useful in situations where respondents' anonymity is a strong consideration. For example, adolescents who know that they will have to be identified to be recontacted may be less than frank about their use of alcohol and drugs.

Survey methods can be particularly useful where it is possible to specify a clear independent variable as well as potential confounding and dependent variables. They allow for comparison of outcomes based on status of the independent and control variables. However, where an intervention is aimed at a total social system—what Rossi and Freeman (1982:183) called full coverage programs—it may be difficult to specify values of an independent variable on which to base comparison among members. The method of time-series analysis may be applicable.

Time-Series Analysis

Time-series analysis is essentially a statistical procedure requiring baseline data sufficiently extensive and of sufficient duration to develop a model to project the course of a problem situation if not subject to an intervention. The results of postintervention data are compared using statistical analyses of values projected by the model if no intervention occurred. While the technique is powerful, it requires strong theoretical understanding to model the phenomenon and an extensive preintervention database to construct the projections.

Data Collection

To this point we have not said much about data collection and have simply implied that data will be collected. Here again we must resort to general description and refer readers to detailed sources on instrumentation. The creative aspect of data collection is choosing the sources of data that will answer the necessary evaluation questions. Some of the choices for collecting quantitative data are (1) behavioral observation; (2) tests, questionnaires, checklists, or rating scales; (3) archival data.

To be useful, measures must be reliable and valid. Babbie (1986:109) defined reliability as "a matter of whether a particular technique, applied repeatedly to the same object, would yield the same result each time." Thus reliability refers to the stability or consistency with which a measurement device yields results. "Validity refers to the extent to which an empirical measure adequately reflects the *real meaning* of the concept under consideration" (Babbie, 1986:112). Note that the two dimensions are different. A measure may be reliable—that is, it may consistently produce the same results—but not be valid. It may measure something very well but not what it is intended to measure. To be valid, however, a measure must also be reliable. Both features of a measure are necessary.

Behavioral Observation

Data can be obtained through the direct observation of behaviors. This can range from relatively low-judgment, concrete tasks of simply observing the presence or absence of a particular behavior or to counts of the frequency of occurrence to more abstract and difficult judgments of qualities. Obviously, the former may produce greater reliability and validity than the latter. In the latter case, for example, interactive behaviors may be judged as supportive or antagonistic or somewhere in between. Validity and reliability can be improved with training of observers, furnishing observers with operational cues of what to look for, and providing well-designed data recording sheets. The use of more than one independent observer can also provide a check on intercoder reliability. The more the observation task requires judgments, the more important it is to have multiple observers.

A variation of behavioral observation is analysis of the results of behaviors as in content analysis of documents. Again, the use of multiple coders who have been trained what to look for and who have a clear statement of the coding categories will improve the data.

Tests, Questionnaires, Checklists, and Rating Scales

Tests, questionnaires, checklists, and rating scales may be self-administered or interviewer administered. These instruments present the respondent with some kind of question to which a response is desired. For some purposes, standardized instruments exist. Various kinds of academic achievement tests are an example. Where standardized instruments exist and are appropriate to the evaluation task, they can be useful because their reliability and validity values have been established. Performance norms may also exist which provide a basis for comparison. Uncritical use, however, should be avoided when applying such standardized instruments with groups culturally disparate from those they were designed for and normed on. Class, race, ethnic, and language differences may make such an instrument invalid or at least make application of norms inappropriate.

Instrument construction should be undertaken with great care. It requires careful conceptualization of the dimensions of the variable of interest and how to measure them. Developers should also consider how respondents in the target group will react to being asked certain kinds of questions. This is especially relevant where culturally diverse groups are in the respondent pool. Such groups may have different meanings for terms or norms about revealing personal information or information about family members. More generally, an issue may not be relevant or salient for respondents, but when given an opinion item they may express an opinion on an issue they have not thought about previously. Some issues may be sensitive and items meet with resistance. These and other issues may invoke a socially desirable response; people respond to the items the way they think they ought to respond or the way they think the questioner wants them to respond. Finally, there is always the issue of what people say and what they actually do. Persons' self-reports may be more or less accurate depending on the issue and how, when, and where the question is asked. We call attention to these points to indicate that instrument and questionnaire development is not a simple task of writing up a set of questions and heading out to collect data.

Instruments constructed for the evaluation purpose should be subjected to a rigorous development process. The items should bear a conceptual link to the variable they intend to study; items, language, and reading level should be appropriate to the respondent pool; biased and "double-barreled" wording should be eliminated; ambiguous or vague terms should also be eliminated; response choices should make sense in the context of the item. Overall, the instrument should consider the response cost; if it is too long or fails to hold respondents' interest, they may not respond with due consideration to all the items.

A completed draft of the instrument should be pilot tested on respondents similar to those for whom it is intended. This will provide information on problems of administration and understanding of items. If properly conducted, pilot testing can also provide data for estimates of reliability and validity through analysis of the items. Any text on measurement will describe these procedures.

Archival Data and Social Indicators

Given that most organizations, government agencies, and political subdivisions routinely collect data, these data can be applied to evaluation of mesolevel and macrolevel interventions. Housing data, crime rates, economic indicators such as household incomes, employment data and workforce participation, productivity data, health, mental health, and social services data are only a partial list of what can be obtained.

Users of official data need to be alert to their limitations. For example, with crime rates, these usually refer to crimes known to police. It is generally known that this underreports the actual number of crimes. Not all crimes are reported to police. In addition, organizations and governmental units sometimes change their reporting and/or measurement procedures so that there appear to be dramatic changes in an indicator when, in fact, the change is due to changes in procedures. Still, these data can be useful if handled with care.

Summary

If this chapter is to serve any purpose, it was meant to call attention to the need for including the evaluation step in any intervention. Evaluation is a guide to the development of intervention programs and an assessment of both their intended and unintended consequences. A well-conducted evaluation requires that its planning be an integral part of planning the total intervention. Evaluation activities should begin when implementation of the program plan begins.

With evaluation as with all other phases of intervention, the interests and needs of stakeholders at all levels need to be identified and addressed. Evaluation should include stakeholders and participants from the beginning and as part of an overall client-centered approach to intervention. All concerned parties should participate in establishing the goals and objectives. They should be clear on the necessity for evaluation and participate in planning and implementing the procedures. As with all other phases of intervention, cultural sensitivity should be a part of evaluation. Respect for persons as individuals and as members of cultures and social systems must guide all our activities.

There are some caveats that should be noted as we close this discussion of evaluation. This short list of issues is by no means exhaustive nor does the order of presentation carry any implication.

The Pilot Study Problem

It is sometimes the case that the decision is to mount a pilot program or demonstration project before turning to a full-scale intervention. The reasoning is clear. A small-scale program is tried to see if it works, to become familiar with the program, and to work out the kinks. All of this makes sense, especially where resources are limited. Evaluation is conducted on the pilot program, and the outcome is used to develop the full-scale program. This is where caution needs to be exercised.

Often pilot programs are run under optimum conditions. Program planners are particularly motivated and vigorous in their attempts to make it work. They pull out all the stops. Resources, both material and human, are abundant. The pilot program may be run by highly trained and qualified professionals. The small scale of the program may mean small staff-to-participant ratios. However, the operation of the full-scale program may be turned over to others, perhaps paraprofessionals or indigenous personnel. Ratios of staff to participants may be significantly greater than was true of the pilot program. In short, the experience of the pilot program may not reflect the actual conditions of the full-scale program. Evaluation of the pilot program needs to allow for the transfer of the program from test conditions to the actual conditions to be found in the field.

Implementation/Research/Competition

Weiss (1972:7) called attention to the fact that evaluation must take place in an action setting which may cause conflicts between program and evaluation activities. Personnel responsible for providing data, record keeping, etc., may also be responsible for program activities. Given conflicting demands for the worker's time and energy, the program is most likely to get priority—as it should.

Conflict may exist even where there is some division of labor between program workers and evaluation workers. Time for data collection, access to records, participants, and workers and other evaluation steps may be controlled by the program workers who may see evaluation as unimportant and little of value stemming from evaluation.

It happens that evaluation is not uniformly loved and valued. Persons working hard to bring about change and committed to their efforts may see evaluation as evaluating them and their efforts. In some situations they may see evaluation as a threat to their jobs or threats to programs and activities they believe in. These factors may make them less than industrious and cooperative; they may feel it is in their interest to withhold or fudge data.

Following the participatory model we espouse, some of this can be dealt with in the planning stage. In addition, problems such as these can be addressed in group sessions and ongoing dialogue among those involved.

Role-Conflict

A potential role-conflict is the tension between sociologist-as-social-scientist and sociologist-as-clinical-worker. We are all usually thoroughly versed in the canons of the scientific methods of our field. But evaluation is often messy work done under time pressures. The designs are not always clean, the procedures and the data not always up to the standards of academic research. Moreover, unlike the academic researcher, the clinical sociologist does not have complete control over the research. However, answers are needed and on time. This tension between scientific rigor and the realities of evaluation can be a source of uneasiness. A possible answer is to strive for the best and learn to live with the possible.

References

Babbie, E. (1986). *The practice of social research*. (4th ed.). Belmont, CA: Wadsworth.

Campbell, D.T., & Stanley, J.C. (1963). *Experimental and quasi-experimental designs for research*. Chicago: Rand-McNally.

Guba, E.G., & Lincoln, Y.S. (1989). *Fourth generation evaluation*. Newbury Park, CA: Sage.

Leitenberg, H. (1973). The use of single-case methodology in psychotherapy research. *Journal of Abnormal Psychology, 82*, 87–101.

O'Leary, K.D., & Wilson, G.T. (1987). *Behavior therapy: Application and outcome*. Englewood Cliffs, NJ: Prentice-Hall.

Rossi, P.H., & Freeman, H.E. (1982). *Evaluation: A systematic approach* (2nd ed.). Beverly Hills, CA: Sage.

Shadish, W.R. Jr., Cook, T.D., & Leviton, L.C. (1991). *Foundations of program evaluation: Theories and practice*. Newbury Park, CA: Sage.

Weiss, C.H. (1972). *Evaluation research: Methods for assessing program effectiveness*. Englewood Cliffs, NJ: Prentice-Hall.

Recommended Readings

Guba, E.G., & Lincoln, Y.S. (1989). *Fourth generation evaluation*. Newbury Park, CA: Sage.

This book takes its title from the fact that the authors propose a paradigm shift in evaluation from positivist to constructivist. Their basic premise is that evaluation is basically human, social, political, and value-oriented. They use the term *constructivist* in that evaluation is a social construction involving negotiation. The book argues for the new paradigm and describes the conduct of evaluation from this perspective.

Orlandi, M.A., Weston, R., & Epstein, L.G. (Eds.). (1992). *Cultural competence for evaluators*. Washington, DC: U.S. Department of Health and Human Services, Public Health Service, Office of Substance Abuse Prevention. DHHS Publication No. (ADM)92-1884.

This volume integrates the cultural dimension with program evaluation. The chapters offer conceptual frameworks and practical suggestions for working with programs for various ethnic and racial minorities within the United States. The focus is on prevention programming for alcohol and other drugs, but that is not a limitation in this book. The ideas generalize.

Shadish, W.R. Jr., Cook, T.D., & Leviton, L.C. (1991). *Foundations of program evaluation: Theories and practice*. Newbury Park, CA: Sage.

This book offers a thorough review of theory and practice in the evaluation field. It is a thoughtful, detailed analysis of the contributions of seven theorists to the practice of evaluation research.

Weiss, C.H. (1972). *Evaluation research: Methods for assessing program effectiveness*. Englewood Cliffs, NJ: Prentice-Hall

This is one of the classic books in the field of evaluation and was written by a sociologist and from a sociological perspective. The fact that a book is a classic, however, is not always a good reason to read it. The issues that Weiss addressed and her perspectives and recommendations are timely and informative as a guide to evaluation.

Values and Sociological Intervention

Introduction

Values are the core of professional practice. According to Simon (1972), professional practice is the process of changing existing situations into preferred ones. When professionals attempt to change situations they confront people with their values. The proposed change is "known" by the professional to be best for the client. Clients also "know" what is best for them. The process of "knowing" involves the assessment of values, directly or intuitively. The strength or depth of commitment to the values of a professional and a client, and the congruence between their values, will determine whether intervention is possible and, if so, the ease with which it can be carried out. It is often assumed by professionals that the interventions they propose are "right" and that the rejection of an intervention by a client means the client is not serious about change. Indeed, professionals' assessments of why clients reject interventions or why interventions were not successful, are value judgments. Clients and professionals rarely mention value conflicts as reasons for failure.

Probably the most common, if not the most important, role of values is that of standards for judgment (Kilby, 1993). As Kluckhohn (1961) observed, humans are evaluating animals. Certain moral values are necessary means for leading individuals, voluntarily, to do what they must. Maccoby (1980) has compiled a list of eight problem situations that exist in all societies for which definite rules, usually in the form of moral values, are prescribed:

- Endangering self or others
- Protection of health
- Respect for property
- Control of aggression
- Control of sexual activity
- Self-reliance and work
- Telling the truth and keeping promises
- Respect for authority

Other values could be added; for instance, the care and protection of children and elders. These values help to define the conscience or morality of a person, but each person's array and prioritization is unique. For this reason, the early exploration and discussion of values and expectations is necessary in any relationship that involves intervention. Intervention usually involves one or more problem situations; these situations may take different forms or be expressed differently in different cultures.

We tend to include or exclude people on the basis of the likeness of their values to ours. Sometimes professionals assume that clients who want something or someone to change, and seek help to make that change, will, themselves, be willing to change. All interventions and all perceptions about the consequences of interventions are value-laden. The "rightness" or fit of an intervention is a "fit of values" between professional and client. For example, it has been shown that therapists tend to give more positive ratings to patients whom they feel have assimilated their values, than those who have not. Indeed, the similarity of therapist–patient values has been found to predict positive outcomes in psychotherapy (Kelly & Strupp, 1992).

The purposes of this chapter are to examine (1) how values are involved in sociological interventions; (2) how value conflicts can be resolved; and (3) how primary prevention can help to minimize value conflicts.

Values and Intervention

Value Neutrality and Sociology

The scientific objectivity of sociology depends upon an adherence to value neutrality. Yet all disciplines, including science, are motivated by values. The choice of a profession or a specialization within a profession is the result of a value judgment. The value neutrality dictum insists that this is not the *role* of the sociologist. Value neutrality suggests a distancing from values that are necessary to the practice of a science. If "values" involve beliefs about what is worthwhile, sociology, and other disciplines, must contemplate values (Seubert, 1991). When values are being examined, it is essential that sociologists keep their roles as social scientists distinct from the role of moral philosopher and theologian. Seubert (1991) suggests, therefore, that sociologists limit their expertise to theories that can be evaluated by empirical observation. This does not underestimate the importance of values, discourage their study, or prohibit their employment. Rather, it serves as a reminder that practicing sociologists must be honest with themselves in asserting that sociology is "value neutral," not "value-free."

Sociologists are taught to be aware of their own values and sensitive to those of others. This is especially important for sociologists who "practice" sociology as consultants, therapists, mediators, or administrators because their practice involves social intervention, usually to modify or make more congruent individual, family, organizational, community, or institutional values.

Intervention can change values. A client may reprioritize values as a result of therapy. Intervention also attempts to make values more congruent with behavior. Clients seek professional help when they feel discomfort between what is and what they feel ought to be. The interventionist's task is to help clients reduce the discomfort level by changing their perceptions, changing their mode(s) of adaptation, or changing their expectations. Awareness of values is essential in helping clients minimize discrepancies between expected and real behavior.

Sociological Intervention

Sociological intervention can be defined as any planned act that alters the characteristics of an individual or the pattern of relationships among individuals. The range of acts covered by this definition includes everything from macrophenomena, such as technical assistance to a country on population policy, to microphenomena, such as individual therapy and counseling. Often, the greater the scale and impact of an intervention, the less likely is the intervenor to have knowledge of, much less control of, the intervention, its application, and its effects. In fact, even small scale, carefully planned interventions may have systemic effects. We tend to expect microinterventions to be more controllable and measurable than macrointerventions. However, that does not necessarily mean that microinterventions are more effective. The major focus of the discussion in this chapter will be on interventions undertaken by sociologists at the request of clients.

Values and Intervention Outcomes

All interventions are value laden. It is easy to be misled by expectations that an intervention will be beneficial. The clinician makes the initial assessment of a problem, which involves value judgments. The problem definition influences the clinician's choice of intervention. These processes are not value neutral. We give some kinds of clinicians a greater degree of freedom than others. For example, we give physicians a great deal of latitude in prescribing drugs when we are experiencing pain. A label or diagnosis also is value laden, and the consequences of the label or intervention, such as hospitalization, elicit additional value judgments. The technical and scientific aspects of clinical work and its justification tend to overshadow issues related to values (Zola, 1975).

Four aspects of any social intervention raise value issues: (1) the choice of goals to which a change effort is directed; (2) the definition of the target of change;

(3) the choice of means used to implement an intervention; and (4) the assessment of the consequences of an intervention. The issues that arise at each of these steps may involve conflicting values. An intervention is designed to maximize a particular set of values and minimize the loss of other values (Warwick & Kelman, 1973). Sometimes it is difficult to predict which, if any, values an intervention will change.

Jenkins (1992) pointed out that the ultimate purpose of all health interventions is to enhance the quality of life. Extending the duration of life is not an appropriate goal if the extended survival is painful and qualitatively less human. He argued that judging the quality of any health intervention requires measuring the postintervention health-related quality of life. Jenkins suggested that quality of life has three key attributes: *feelings* (subjective sense of well-being), *functions* (activity, skills, fulfillment, and productivity), and *futures* (prognosis for future feelings and functions). Quality of life also includes at least five levels of human life: biological, psychological, interpersonal, social, and economic. These attributes and levels have different hierarchies of importance depending on one's cultural beliefs and values. Of ultimate importance is whether an intervention is effective in the context of the culture within which an individual or group must live. Interventions are not exclusively successful or unsuccessful. Therefore, the essential questions by which an intervention should be assessed are: How effective was the intervention in making the client more adaptive? How has the quality of life changed?

Becker (1993) suggested that the health promotion/disease prevention movement has created or exacerbated a number of undesirable developments. These include: the devotion of large scale resources to searching for risk factors for disease; exhortation of the public to adopt numerous health-related behaviors with a lack of success, frequent reversals of advice, and unfulfilled promises of effects; a confused and skeptical public; an introspective approach to health that fosters victim-blaming and stigmatization; a tendency to ignore other critical environmental, economic, and social contributors to disease and mortality; and a superreactive media. Kaplan (1985) noted that reductions in mortality from heart disease through dietary changes were balanced by increases in deaths from other causes. This underscores the fact that every planned change is counterbalanced by one or more unplanned changes. For example, Langenhoven and his associates (1991) found that individuals who were at low risk for coronary heart disease benefited as much from a community intervention to increase health knowledge as individuals who were at high risk for coronary heart disease.

Paradoxes of Intervention

Sometimes interventions have unintended, harmful or reverse effects. Sieber (1981) noted that there can be reverse effects only if the consequences of an intervention are assessed. Many of the results of interventions are unknown or indeterminate, the data equivocal, or the effects only temporary. Therefore, our values often are the criteria by which we assess the effectiveness of an intervention. Sieber (1981) described seven ways in which "well- and ill-intentioned meddling can produce results opposite from that intended."

The first type of reverse effect of intervention is *functional disruption*. The functional requirements of nature and society are so interdependent that an intervention in one system might not only rebound negatively on another, but might worsen the condition that one hoped to protect or enhance. Interventions also can create an imbalance if secondary needs are not met or if a conflict in needs makes it possible to serve only one. Furthermore, interventions and change may create new needs that are not addressed by the intervention, thereby creating a new balance in the system. New laws, alternative schools, and deinstitutionizing the mentally ill are examples of functional disruption.

A second type of reverse effect of intervention is *exploitation*. All interventions mobilize resources and opportunities, which may exceed those needed by the interventions. These resources or opportunities can be used by competing target groups. Examples include the diversity of health professional groups engaged in health promotion and health education, efforts to restrict smoking in public places, and gun control legislation.

The third type of reverse effect of intervention is *goal displacement*. This occurs when the benefits of the intervention become diverted from the intended goal, e.g., plea bargaining was to help reduce the clogged justice system by reducing jury trials; however, it tends to subvert the criminal justice process.

A fourth type of reverse intervention is *provocation*. The inability of prison sentences to deter crime, the Brady crime bill requiring a waiting period to purchase a hand gun, and the Supreme Court ruling on abortion (*Roe v. Wade*), have all mobilized special interest groups to reverse intended interventions.

A fifth type of reverse intervention is *classification*. Intervention can lead to new groupings or classifications that require new bureaucracies, agencies, or systems for dealing with them; e.g., mainstreaming handicapped children in public schools, affirmative action hiring, and basic skills tests on admission to college.

A sixth type of reverse intervention is *overcommitment*. Interventions may exhaust resources, and raise expectations beyond the capacity of the interventions to meet them. Perhaps the best examples are the lack of resources to deal with environmental problems and the "right" of everyone in the United States to health care.

A final type of reverse intervention is *placation*. Many interventions are a means of pacifying people. Interventions which are proposed to solve problems can lull dissident groups to achieve their support. A revamped health care system in the United States has involved almost all competing interest groups in continuing discussion. One consequence of placation is that the symptoms of problems, not the solutions are addressed.

Clinical Focus 7.1

The Chicana Counselor

Like the client, the Chicana counselor faces peer pressure to maintain traditional Hispanic values, not only from professional colleagues but from family and friends. Those Chicanos who do not understand the techniques of psychotherapy or counseling have gone so far as to deny that psychotherapy is beneficial to them. In addition, many Chicanos have rejected group therapy. Another aspect of peer pressure is the push from colleagues to meet expectations of their own mind-sets. Given early socialization to be other-directed, the Chicana counselor is confronted with a dilemma when asked to take on additional work. For fear of refusing services, the Chicana counselor may accept additional assignments, becoming overextended. In an urban area with a large population of Spanish-speaking inhabitants, the counselor's professionalism can be at risk in trying to meet the needs of the Spanish-speaking community. For example, in the case of wife beating, the Chicana counselor, realizing the plight of the isolated female with no place to go, may give her home telephone in case of emergency need.

These types of reverse intervention effects are not independent of each other nor definitive, but emphasize the fact that interventions are not unitary in their effects, even when carefully controlled. This schema also emphasizes that interventions, no matter how objectively contrived, do not have value-free effects.

The question of whose values, the client or patient's, or the intervenor's, should prevail, exists in every type of intervention, even when all parties are involved in planning. The issue is not only whose interests are being served, but also that of the conceptual framework that generates the definition of the problem and setting of goals (Warwick & Kelman, 1973).

The goals of social intervention are based on certain value assumptions that presuppose not only the desirability of change, but a preference for certain kinds of change over others. A certain consistency must exist between planned change and human needs. The needs of individuals should take precedence over the good of society. Furthermore, social intervention presumes that changes that involve violence, coercion, or the destruction of traditional values, are unacceptable except in unusual circumstances.

In recognizing the role of their own value preferences, clinicians should not attempt to neutralize or abandon them. Awareness of their own value perspectives allows for more direct discussion with the client. Ethical issues in the choice of goals for an intervention revolve around the values to be served by the intervention and whether they are the "right" values for the client. No change program will meet all of the different needs of an individual or institution. Therefore, it is critical that as many constituencies as possible be represented in the planning.

Intervention as a Specialized Role

A sociologist who chooses to be a clinician has chosen a specialized role as a change agent. A change agent is usually given authority to produce change, and control over people and situations to make change occur. But authority and control do not insure change. Change is the result of an interaction or relationship. The clinician must engage the recipient of a proposed change as a partner. Without the cooperation of the recipient of change, no intervention can be sustained. This is why Schön (1983) proposed that clinicians and their clients develop a reflective contract.

In such a contract, professionals are directly accountable to the client and seek to open their special knowledge to public inquiry. The professional gives up some familiar sources of satisfaction and becomes open to new ones. The rewards of unquestioned authority, the freedom to practice without challenge to competency, the comfort of invulnerability, and the gratifications of deference are relinquished in favor of new discoveries about how professionals practice. The client or patient becomes a participating partner in the professional encounter. Bayles (1983) pointed out that the appropriate ethical conception of the clinician–client relationship allows clients as much freedom to determine how their life is affected as is reasonably warranted on the basis of their ability to make decisions. As clients have less knowledge about subject matter, the special obligations of the professional become more significant.

Bidwell and Vreeland (1977) discussed the issues of authority and control in client-serving organizations. While there are similarities to the dyadic professional–client relationship when a client seeks intervention through an organization, such as a social service agency, hospital, or school, the client usually is looking for a specific service or skill. Organizations may not be sensitive to the values of individual clients, or if they are, they may be bound by organizational culture, tradition, pressures from peers, or time constraints, not to deviate from a structured protocol for dealing with categorized problems. Client-serving organizations are responsible for both their staff and their clients. Many client-serving organizations serve a mandate from a community, county, or state and must legitimize what they do in order to attract funds. Therefore, professionals working in a client-serving organization may not be in a position of power or have much autonomy in their workplace. This will profoundly affect the entire process of interaction with clients and the degree of freedom the professionals have to give choices to their clients. The client-serving organization, in general, is not one that initiates or accepts change easily. Clients of organizations may not have the choice of other sources of help. The relative inflexibility of client-serving organizations and the limited options of their clients often create an intervention that is "forced" to fit the generic value systems of clients.

When clients are viewed within generic value systems their uniqueness as persons and perhaps their unique problems are categorized. The options for intervention are limited by the organization and the client's life circumstances. This presents a challenging dilemma for the clinician between what the client may need according to the clinician's evaluation, what the client expects based on past experience or heresay, and what the organization will permit the clinician to do. There is no set protocol to guide a clinician's professional behavior in such dilemmas. The best approach is to do no harm by not intervening to escalate a client's problem. The clinician may have to wrestle with the urge or felt pressure "to do something." It might be helpful to ask clients what they expect and to address these expectations within the constraints of what the organization will permit the clinician to do (see Clinical Focus 7.1).

Phases of Intervention

Intervention can be separated conceptually into four phases: *selection, process, outcome, and follow-up.* Most kinds of intervention involve these phases in this order.

Selection: Exploring Value Similarities and Differences

Values are important determinants of behavior because they provide criteria for decision making. Each individual brings to each situation a perceptual filter through which events are interpreted to define a problem, generate and evaluate alternatives, and make a choice. While the filter helps individuals to make decisions by limiting alternatives it also complicates decision making in situations where values are not shared, creating misperceptions, making communication difficult, and making consensus impossible (Liedtka, 1991).

Clients may seek the services of sociologists because their values have become misaligned with those of other persons, families, peers, social groups, or social institutions. Clients may request that sociologists restore certain desired social conditions. Thus, the clients come with the expectation that the sociologist will intervene, directly as a mediator, or indirectly as a giver of advice, or otherwise "do something" to help resolve a current situation. The clients also come with the expectation, implicit or explicit, of a time frame for change to occur. The clinical sociologist, on the other hand, has expectations of clients, namely that they will share information, assume some measure of responsibility for the situations that brought about the request for assistance, and cooperate in reaching a decision or resolution.

The assessment phase of a proposed intervention is to gather data that will help the clinician understand the client and the problem. A values assessment occurs when the client and the sociologist first meet. It may require several meetings before values and expectations can be mutually explored. If a clash in values and expectations is too great, the sociologist should refer the client. The client should not be expected to "come around" to accept the clinical sociologist's values. Decision making about the "degree of fit" is not the exclusive domain of the sociologist. It is an assessment accomplished by interaction. Some differences or conflicts in values or expectations can be resolved. However, it is not ethical for either party to mislead the other into believing that values can easily be changed.

Values are mutually assessed by taking into consideration an individual's dress and physical appearance, manner and style of speech, promptness, personality, previous clinical history, and other factors. When the consultation is with an agency, group, or institution, the personal assessment is made between the representative of the firm or group requesting consultation and the sociologist. The group or firm will have checked out the reputation and professional experience of the sociologist. The sociologist will have obtained information on the firm or group's history and reputation, and may have talked with persons who are members of, or know about, the firm or group.

The first encounter between the client or patient and the sociologist is critical; it sets the stage for meeting expectations and begins to "cement" the working relationship. Liedtka (1991) has pointed out that values at many different levels come into play at the time of initial value assessment. *Societal values*, such as individual rights, informed consent, and confidentiality, pervade all relationships involving interventions. *Institutional values*, such as those of hospitals and schools, are the product of corporate cultures where decisions are affected not only by the personal values of the decision makers, but also by the values of others to whom the decision makers feel obliged to respond. For example, Nystrom (1989) found that the variance in ethical values *within* hospitals was larger than the variance *between* hospitals. An institution may be fragmented into numerous coalitions with the relative power groups determining whose value system the organization will reflect (Cyert & March, 1963). *Professional values* are important because they convey the work ethic of the intervenor. Professionals enjoy certain roles, such as that of guardians of confidential information. Some roles are better known than others, for example, that of licensed physicians who are given permission to carry out physical examinations. The roles of consultants or mediators might not be as well known, especially among the lay public. It is critical that the clinician and the client discuss the boundaries of their respective roles from the onset. *Personal values* occur within the context of the value systems mentioned above. The individual is the link between these value systems. The complexity of values is reflected in an individual's behavior. Personal values have been observed to be gender-related and explain the differences between men and women in their response to similar situations (Gilligan, 1982). Colombotos (1969) also found that certain socioeconomic and religious backgrounds correlated with the presence of particular personal values in a large sample of physicians.

Process: Achieving Understanding

The second phase of a proposed intervention concerns the development of rapport. Five verbal interventions can serve as a core set of basic skills to establish rapport: reflection, legitimation, support, partnership, and respect (Epstein, Campbell, Cohen-Cole, McWhinney, & Smilkstein, 1993). Reflection refers to the clinician's explicit recognition of the client's emotion, whenever it emerges. Legitimation refers to explicit statements by the clinician that validate the emotional response. Supportive statements emphasize the clinician's desire to help. Partnership connotes cooperation between the clinician and the client. Respect refers to the clinician's recognition of the client's worth. These verbal responses could be applied to a variety of situations, such as those involving families and groups.

Another method, called the patient-centered approach, validates the client. The patient-centered method is an attitude of mind and a moral position rather than a technique. It is an attitude of openness and receptivity rather than detachment and dominance. The method is based on the fact that clients provide clues to their feelings, fears and expectations. The appropriate response is behavior that encourages clients to tell their stories. The outcome of the session or sessions is to ask clients whether their expectations, feelings and fears have been understood. The patient-centered method is justified by the willingness of clinicians to share their power, show their human face, and respond to suffering, pain or discomfort (Epstein et al., 1993).

Another method, a systems approach, points out how clinicians can improve their communication with clients by taking into account their families and social networks. The systems approach does not always require that the clinician interact with individuals other than the client. It is important, however, that the clinician maintain alliances with other individuals in the client's social network. A systems approach provides the clinician with an opportunity to examine shared and unshared values and beliefs among members of a family or group (Epstein et al., 1993).

A final method, self-awareness, assumes that the clinician's own background is a major influence on the methods of intervention. The way clinician's deal with personal issues will be similar to the way they deal with related professional issues. Greater awareness of personal biases, sensitivities, strengths, and weaknesses will facilitate an intervention and affect its degree of success.

The quality of communication between clinician and client has been shown to relate to compliance, the quality of service given and the client's satisfaction with the service. Studies of the doctor–patient relationship have shown that values play a significant role in the type of communication established. For example, societal norms still place a premium on aggressive communication styles by males. Males have the freedom to be either aggressive or affiliative in their communication styles. Thus, male physicians have greater freedom than female physicians in selecting strategies to affect patient compliance (Burgoon, Birk, & Hall, 1991). Data indicate that male physicians can be verbally aggressive without negatively affecting the physician–patient relationship. Street and Buller (1988) found that physicians were less communicatively dominant, more nonverbally responsive as listeners, and more egalitarian in their interactions with middle-aged and older patients than in their encounters with younger clients. Patients who wrote down questions to ask their physicians while in the waiting room had greater perceptions of control, were more satisfied with the visit, and were more satisfied with the information they received than those who did not (Thompson, Nanni, & Schwankovsky, 1990). Clients apparently respond to any indication of interest and concern on the part of a helper.

Much of the process of establishing rapport and the quality of the relationship between clinician and client appears to be nonverbal (Beier & Young, 1984). It has been said that many physicians know how to talk in a warm and friendly way without really being patient-centered or interested in patient's problems or wishes. Davis (1988) notes that it is easier to control verbal behavior than nonverbal behavior. The nonverbal aspects of affective behavior have a strong predictive influence on the quality of rating of psychosocial care (Bensing, 1991).

Beisecker and Beisecker (1993) compared two metaphors describing physician–patient relationships. Paternalism focuses on obligations of both parties; consumerism focuses on the rights of each side. Paternalism directs the physician to be beneficent; consumerism assumes the physician to be self-centered. Paternalism implies that a basic foundation of trust exists between two parties; consumerism replaces trust with accountability and legal responsibility. Paternalism directs the patient to grant uncritical acceptance to the physician's orders; consumerism cautions the patient to give or withhold informed consent. The two metaphors assume that different hierarchies of values govern the relationship. Paternalism assumes that the patient's and the doctor's specific health care desires must be subordinated when they conflict with values derived from the principles of good medical care. Consumerism asserts that values derived from principles of good medical care must be interpreted and operationalized in reference to the patient's personal health care values and desires. The two metaphors presume different types of interpersonal relationships between physicians and patients.

Beisecker and Beisecker (1993) pointed out that mutual dissatisfaction and relational conflict can occur when a physician and a patient employ different metaphors. Consider the situation in which a paternalistic physician interacts with a consumeristic patient. Attempts by the physician to assume decision making for the patient and to shield him or her from unpleasant consequences will be interpreted by the patient as attempts to control the interaction and manipulate them. To the physician, the consumeristic patient will appear uncooperative and distrustful. Such a relationship is doomed to failure because each party is operating from a different perspective. The starting point for negotiating metaphors must occur the first time the clinician and client meet.

Wyatt (1991), in an extensive review of the literature on physician–patient relationships, concluded that physicians are looking for effective ways of eliciting patient concerns and improving patient satisfaction with their medical treatment in order to prevent malpractice suits, to persuade people to follow their medical advice, and to feel better about their work. As Dossey (1993) notes, it is usually only the patient's beliefs that are considered when a particular therapy is given. Yet, the beliefs of the patient are only one side of the coin. Physicians' beliefs can exert powerful effects. For example, if physicians strongly favor a therapy, they can "talk up" its effects to the patient. This can inflate the patients' expectations.

The effects of suggestion are well known. Evidence suggests that a physician's beliefs can alter the results of double-blind studies. In a double-blind study of the use of vitamin E in treating angina pectoris, an enthusiastic physician who believed in vitamin E found it significantly more effective than a placebo (Toone, 1973), while in two similar studies conducted by skeptics, vitamin E showed no effect (Anderson, 1974; Gillian, Mondell, & Warbasse, 1977). A study to test the effectiveness of meprobamate, an early minor tranquilizing drug, conducted simultaneously at several metropolitan psychiatric outpatient clinics, found that the effectiveness of the drug over a placebo correlated with physician attitudes and beliefs about it (Uhlenhuth et al., 1966).

Research has shown that, in the case of physicians, styles of communication tend to be somewhat fixed. Physicians confronted with stressful, ambiguous, and difficult tasks, tend to apply a set formula to the tasks. Consequently, flexibility regarding patients' needs are limited (Humphrey, Littlewood, & Kamps, 1992). An analysis of over 90 surgeons suggested that the surgeons had a predictable cancer philosophy that they applied to all patients, irrespective of individual differences (Taylor, 1988).

These studies of physicians' communication styles have a lesson to convey regarding the effect of the clinician's beliefs and values on clients. Values are conveyed by what is said and not said, and by emphasis. Thus, the communication style of the clinician often is, itself, an unintended intervention (Bruhn, 1986).

Outcome: Managing Values

Fraser (1989) has suggested that professionals do not intervene to "solve problems." Real solutions are achieved by rearranging attitudes and values. We learn to manage our values better. Value management encourages team building,

---

Clinical Focus 7.2

Men's New Family Roles

The therapeutic implications of men's changing family roles is a ripe area for research. Therapists can help men espousing new family roles in several ways: (1) therapists need to be clear about their own values, by giving attention to the sources of difficulties confronting men espousing new roles, such as blame and self-doubt; and (2) by offering support to men who are trying to create a new world for themselves. First, however, therapists need to recognize the limitations of therapy in solving issues of individual and social change. Perhaps therapists can be most helpful by helping clients find and maintain support groups. Issues such as the changing family roles of men need study to determine factors that facilitate and impede adjustments to new roles and the impact of these changes on other family members.

---

interdependent problem solving and accommodation to change. The development of shared interests helps to keep conflicts at a low level and to avoid win/lose situations. Value management is based on the appropriateness of a decision at a particular point in time. Change requires that we continually reevaluate our decisions to minimize crises and conflicts. Viewed in this way, an intervention that has provided a client with insight into how to manage the interaction between change and values better, has been successful (see Clinical Focus 7.2).

Mediation is an intervention strategy that often results in the ability to manage the potential for conflict positively and to create opportunities for creative problem solving. Mediation is effective when there is no great imbalance in bargaining power between parties or when there is no clear right or wrong position. The goal of mediation is not consensus or partial agreement between people, but the understanding and acknowledgement by each participant of the other's way of viewing a situation. Issues of values and principles are more difficult to mediate than issues of interests or needs (Messing, 1993). Wiseman (1990) stated that what frequently is needed, rather than an external choice, is an internal shift in understanding. Reconnecting people to their values and to information they have screened out gives them greater potential for making choices and decisions. Making decisions gives people the freedom to exert power in their own lives. As Grebe (1992) pointed out, the mediator should actively increase the good of clients. A successful intervention could be said to be one in which clients leave believing they can manage their values more effectively.

Helping relationships extend along a continuum from information giving to counseling and psychotherapy, and, as a result, have a range of outcomes. Information giving is primarily cognitive, counseling and psychotherapy are primarily affective, and conflict resolution is primarily information giving. Consultation is another form of intervention that differs from the helping relationships previously mentioned. Consultation is useful for seeking solutions to the complex issues and problems that people and organizations face. Consultants offer assistance by intervening, that is, by bringing about change in a deliberate way.

Follow-up: Intervention Effects

The final phase, and perhaps the most neglected aspect, of intervention is follow-up. Too often, therapists do not regard follow-up to be part of the therapeutic process. Consultants usually believe their job has been completed when they submit a final report to their clients. Follow-up is often regarded as a task for researchers, not a final step in the intervention process. Without follow-up, however, clinicians never know what worked and what did not work in an intervention. As a result, they often replicate their failures as well as their successes.

Clinicians may not want to follow their clients or patients for several reasons: (1) it extends the time expectations the clinician had for the relationship; (2) the clinician may not feel responsible for what happens after the formal relationship is considered terminated; (3) the clinician may not want to know or be confronted with what didn't work and spend time dealing with those issues; (4) the initial agreement between the clinician and client may not include follow-up; (5) follow-up does not give a clear time termination of the clinician–client relationship; (6) the clinician does not have the time or resources to follow clients.

Some clients do not want to be followed. The boundaries between the intervention period and what might be considered intrusiveness may be a factor for both client and clinician. Also, the kind and amount of information that might be obtained at follow-up is limited; therefore, depending on the type and extent of intervention, the information may be minimally useful to the clinician.

Newman (1993) believed that consultants have a basic ethical responsibility to ensure that the services they provide have efficacy. She stated that the situational determinants of most consulting interventions and the separation that exists between research and practice deter intervenors from determining the effects of their advice. Flaherty (1979) pointed out that an evaluation of outcome should be tied to a needs assessment completed at the initial agreement between the clinician and client. The effectiveness of the outcome, therefore, will be determined by how well, or to what extent, the client's needs were met.

One of the ultimate objectives of most intervention programs is to effect behavioral change. The most direct method of assessing behavioral change is by observing the client's behavior following an intervention. Logistically, this may be difficult for the clinician. Therefore, such alternative approaches are suggested as simulations and role-plays, evaluation by supervisors and peers, satisfaction questionnaires, evaluation using agency records, attitude scales, telephone interviews, and/or focus groups.

Ulschak and Snow Antle (1990) referred to evaluation as the dessert after the meal. It lets us know how well we have done. Follow-up evaluation should be included in the initial contract between the clinician and the client.

Resolving Value Conflicts

A cooperative process of conflict resolution generally involves three phases: (1) expression of initial positions; (2) exploration of underlying values; and (3) choosing mutually satisfying solutions. The effective resolution of conflict depends upon the explicit expression of the conflicting positions. Once the positions have been expressed, they must be explored. Last, solutions need to be considered and selected. As Heitler (1990) stated, a symmetry in communication must be achieved by listening, accepting, teamwork, generating options, and selecting a solution.

The health of any given system, be it an individual, family, group, or organization can be seen as a function of its ability to negotiate conflicts. The role of the clinician, be it therapist, consultant, or mediator, is to be a coach or teacher, to facilitate the process between the conflicting parties to apply problem-solving skills to solve a common problem. This may involve the clinician in teaching new problem-solving skills and giving feedback when the clients fall back into old ways. Thus, the clinician helps to model and shape new behavior patterns. It is important that these new ways of solving problems fit the value systems and life situations of the clients. Clinicians should not insist on their particular way of solving problems, lest the clients return to say, "I tried it your way and it didn't work."

Clinicians undoubtedly will, to varying degrees, be involved in resolving value conflicts either between themselves and their client(s), or within the group or organization in which they are intervening. Two important factors are necessary in resolving value conflicts: the two conflicting parties must have some positive regard for each other, and the conflicting parties must engage in a discussion of values independent from the issue which is generating the disagreement (Druckman, Broome, & Korper, 1983; Druckman & Broome, 1991). It is not productive to attempt to resolve differences in value embedded in a topic or subject. Therapeutic or other settings are not appropriate contexts in which to resolve significant differences in values. Values are not usually bargained or traded; however, it should be recognized that not all therapists can work with all types of clients. Clinicians must know their limitations, not ascribe them to deficiencies in their clients (Odell & Stewart, 1993).

Primary Prevention

Sociologists are usually observers, commentators, and researchers of human society. They study how and why people behave as they do. We have often done better with observation than with explanation and intervention. Intervention is not a mainstream role of sociology. Yet, it could be argued that to comment on society entails an obligation to improve it. Clinical sociologists should become involved in primary prevention because it is proactive and is aimed at high-risk groups that have not yet been affected by the condition to be prevented. Only through prevention can sociologists apply what they have learned about human behavior to reduce the incidence of societal problems.

The field of public health has long been concerned with the prevention of disease. Public health strategies are relatively simple. The first is to identify a noxious agent and attempt to remove, or neutralize it. The second strategy is to strengthen the resistance of the host to the noxious agent. The third strategy is to prevent transmission of the noxious agent to the host. Treating drinking water kills noxious agents. Vaccinating children against common childhood diseases has been successful in reducing death rates among children. Finally, preventing the noxious agent from reaching the host is effective, whether it involves killing disease-bearing mosquitoes and thereby reducing the incidence of malaria, or recommending the use of condoms to prevent transmission of the AIDS virus (Albee & Ryan-Finn, 1993).

In the early years of the 20th century, public health experts began to turn their attention to the prevention of mental disorders. If public health approaches were successful at preventing organic diseases, they should be effective in preventing mental disorders. The beginning efforts to prevent mental and emotional disorders were attempts to teach poor mothers to be better parents since a correlation was observed between crime and poverty. A correlation between slovenly housekeeping and mental conditions also was observed. Gradually, children's mental health clinics were established to instill better parenting skills (Albee & Ryan-Finn, 1993).

Repeatedly, epidemiological studies have shown that very poor people are at highest risk for many pathological physical and mental conditions. As people escape from poverty, rates of disease decline. The compelling evidence that lower social class, irrespective of racial and ethnic background, is associated with high rates of mental and physical disorders, still is not fully realized in our society. Poverty and powerlessness are major causative factors of physical and mental diseases and social problems. Economic security is beneficial to mental health.

An association has been demonstrated between political values and attitudes toward primary prevention. Political conservatives tend to blame victims for their problems, and generally, are not supportive of prevention efforts. Most prevention-ists are environmentalists who believe social and physical environmental experiences in early life, such as child abuse, neglect, sexual abuse, and poor parenting often are reflected in adult maladjustment. They regard mental disorders as difficulties in interpersonal and intrapersonal relationships. Thus, primary prevention programs tend to focus on changing environments and relationships to reduce the damaging consequences by teaching social coping skills, enhancing self-esteem, and encouraging the use of social support groups.

Critics of primary prevention often argue that there have been no reliable studies to support the impact of intervention and sustained change. The majority of current societal problems have multiple etiologies. Therefore, to be effective primary prevention programs must be interdisciplinary.

Epidemiology, public health, sociology, psychiatry, psychology, economics, and political science are but a few of the disciplines whose knowledge and skills are needed for intervention. The interdisciplinary nature of problems and solutions makes it difficult to establish a one-to-one cause-and-effect relationship that clearly ascribes success or failure, and consequently makes it difficult to know what can or cannot be done to replicate successes and avoid future failures in intervention.

Clinical sociologists have the opportunity to become partners in disease prevention and health promotion. People's behavior and the conditions of life that influence behavior now are recognized to be the major health issue of our society. The social environment is as important as the physical environment in causing our societal problems. Therefore, we need to shift our perspectives and strategies of intervention significantly. Most successful approaches to disease prevention and health promotion combined the principles of community organization and citizen involvement. These principles arise from a pooling of theory from many disciplines, ranging from biomedicine to communications.

Three themes unify these disciplinary views about community and individual-based social and behavioral change. First is the emphasis on the powerful social forces that influence individuals' behavior. Communities shape individuals' behavior, both symbolically and tangibly, by transmitting values and norms. As systems of exchange and influence, communities establish behavioral limits for people (Bracht, 1990). Second, communities may be mobilized to act as change agents to achieve social and behavioral outcomes. Mobilizing communities to act as change agents legitimizes values and norms for desirable behavior and creates an acceptable social climate in which to live. Third, early and sustained participation by community members and leaders is necessary for the realization of community ownership and program maintenance.

The community health promotion approach, when combined with supplementary clinical and/or individual approaches, has a number of advantages. Such an approach cuts across most sectors of the community, affect the social milieu of individuals, is well integrated into the total community, ensures the longevity of change, is comprehensive, and reflects shared responsibility (Bracht, 1990).

Not all social and health problems require a community approach, but local values and norms shape individual attitudes and behaviors. Therefore, it seems reasonable that change would require a synthesis of social system and individual levels of intervention.

Prevention and Promotion Ethics

Clinical sociologists may raise questions about a conflict between their active involvement in prevention and promotion activities and their value neutrality as sociologists. Prevention activities usually are seen as organized intrusion which involves issues of power. Providing active primary prevention helps permit preventers to enter the value domains of others, even when not requested. This could put the preventers on a collision course with individual or group values if the preventers present preventive information as their own ideas or values. Information offered to clients as the result of research or the combined opinions of experts, and left up to the clients to accept or reject, does not constitute values imposed by clinicians. Social and economic costs, positive and negative, are a consequence of any change in a person's life. Clients need to evaluate preventive information against these costs and competing priorities in their lives. The presentation of preventive information by clinical sociologists does not violate the principle of value neutrality. Belief in emphasizing the strengths of clients is the basis of primary prevention. Primary prevention can be no better than the knowledge, skills, and values of its practitioners (Bloom, 1993).

Promotion activities suggest that professionals deal with ethical issues before they become conflicts. Forrow and his associates (Forrow, Arnold, & Parker, 1993) note that when ethical issues are discussed, they tend to be seen as unique to a particular case or situation rather than as general issues of ethics or values. Therefore, many discussions of ethics occur in crisis situations when emotions run high. Clinical sociologists as citizens and interventionists have a responsibility to participate in discussions, for example, on the question of rationing health care. Likewise, a clinical sociologist seeing HIV positive patients for individual counseling, has a responsibility to inform patients about the risks of spreading their disease to others as well as to inform patients about actions that can slow HIV progression to full-blown AIDS.

Loewy (1989) pointed out that professionals are obliged to concern themselves with issues of prevention and promotion. They are obliged to speak out for issues of pollution, immunization, safety, and social conditions. This obligation emerges from the professional's citizenship. Clinical sociologists cannot evade the obligation to make value choices. When values, obligations, and loyalties conflict, safeguarding and caring for clients has first claim on the clinical sociologist's actions and choices.

Clinical sociologists are neither compelled to subjugate their personal moral views, nor entitled to impose such views on others. Problems can be resolved by frank and compassionate discussion, which enables clients to make their own choices and reach their own conclusions. Clinical sociologists who cannot resolve their differences with their clients should refer them to other, equally competent clinicians. Either arguing or simply complying with client wishes is a moral abrogation of responsibility.

Trickett (1992) states that primary prevention and health promotion raise new questions and have spurred new professional roles. Prevention and promotion activities are not simple extensions of previous ways of thinking and acting. Rather they require reframing how we think about intervention and ethics. Just as gene therapy raises new contextual issues about the morality of genetic engineering, prevention and promotion generate a variety of ethical questions regarding "doing no harm" and the relationship of preventive activity when implemented, to the social context.

Summary

Our values talk back to us. If we are observant, we can see other's reactions to our values and become aware of our reactions to the values of others. We use our values when we choose our mates and friends. Values also are the core of professional practice. As professionals, we choose our clients by showing them our values. When clients come to us, as professionals for help, guidance, or advice, we go through a mutual process of getting acquainted. This is often called "intake, diagnosis, or defining the problem." We decide whether we can work together by evaluating each other. The more alike our values, the greater our chances for the successful outcome of our relationship.

Sociologists espouse a professional tenet which says that they should stay "value neutral" in their work. This is not unique to sociology, it also is espoused by counselors and psychotherapists. However, no human being or society is value-free. Knowingly or unknowingly, clinicians introduce their own values into a situation. When we intervene in the lives of individuals, families, groups, organizations, institutions, communities, or larger social systems, we introduce changes in values.

Intervention is a process with stages or phases. The first stage involves selecting a client, who in turn, selects a clinician for a specific purpose. Schön (1983) says that this initial stage depends upon an agreement about ends, defining the nature and limits of the problem and the expected outcome of an intervention. When the ends cannot be stated clearly, there is no problem to solve. The second stage involves the process of problem solving. Values become very important at this point because they determine how a problem can be solved. Values help define the limits of our boundaries of a problem, the players, and acceptable options for its solution. Intervention involves as much "art" as "skill," and much of the art centers around the client's involvement in all facets of the intervention. The ultimate success of an intervention (stage 3), depends upon whether clients can manage their values better. Most problems are not solved by attempting to do away with them, but by learning to manage oneself better in relationship to the problem. Real solutions are achieved by rearranging values and attitudes. The fourth and final stage of an intervention is determining its effects. Follow-up, if not a part of the initial agreement between clinician and client, is often overlooked. Yet, only by following clients do we know what did and didn't work with respect to an intervention. It is through feedback and evaluation that clinicians gain insights into how to prevent similar problems.

Prevention is a new role for the clinical sociologist, who is more often an observer, commentator, or analyst than an active clinician. It is only by applying what has been learned that high-risk behavior can be modified. If the purpose of health interventions is to improve the quality of life, the application of professional skills toward the alleviation of disease-generating conditions in society is a moral and ethical imperative.

Involvement in prevention may raise ethical conflicts among clinical sociologists, since many preventive activities are intrusive and confrontational. Yet, it is impossible to avoid value-laden problems. The challenge is to be aware of value differences and find nonthreatening ways in which clients can explore and adjust their values to make their lives more satisfying.

References

Albee, G.W., & Ryan-Finn, K.D. (1993). An overview of primary prevention. *Journal of Counseling and Development, 72,* 115–123.

Anderson, T.W. (1974). Vitamin E in angina pectoris. *Canadian Medical Association Journal, 110,* 401–406.

Bayles, M. (1983). Obligations to clients. In N. Abrams & M.D. Buckner (Eds.), *Medical ethics* (pp. 107–112). Cambridge, MA: MIT Press.

Becker, M.H. (1993). A medical sociologist looks at health promotion. *Journal of Health & Social Behavior, 34,* 1–6.

Beier, E.G., & Young, D.M. (1984). *The silent language of psychotherapy* (2nd ed.). New York: Aldine.

Beisecker, A.E., & Beisecker, T.D. (1993). Using metaphors to characterize doctor-patient relationships: Paternalism versus consumerism. *Health Communication, 5,* 41–58.

Bensing, J. (1991). Doctor-patient communication and the quality of care. *Social Science & Medicine, 32,* 1301–1310.

Bidwell, C.E., & Vreeland, R.S. (1977). Authority and control in client-serving organizations. In R.L. Blankenship (Ed.), *Colleagues in organizations: The social construction of professional work* (pp. 360–370). New York: Wiley.

Bloom, M. (1993). Toward a code of ethics for primary prevention. *The Journal of Primary Prevention, 13,* 173–182.

Bracht, N. (Ed.) (1990). *Health promotion at the community level*. Newbury Park, CA: Sage.

Bruhn, J.G. (1986). Time in therapeutic relationships: Myths and realities. *Southern Medical Journal, 79*, 344–350.

Burgoon, M., Birk, T.S., & Hall, J.R. (1991). Compliance and satisfaction with physician–patient communication: An expectancy theory interpretation of gender differences. *Human Communication Research, 18*, 177–208.

Colombotos, J. (1969). Social origins and ideology of physicians. *Journal of Health & Social Behavior, 10*, 16–29.

Cyert, R., & March, J. (1963). *A behavioral theory of the firm*. Englewood Cliffs, NJ: Prentice-Hall.

Davis, K. (1988). *Power under the microscope*. Dordrecht, Holland: Foris.

Dossey, L. (1993). *Healing words*. New York: Harper-Collins.

Druckman, D., & Broome, B.J. (1991). Value differences and conflict resolution: Familiarity or liking? *Journal of Conflict Resolution, 35*, 571–593.

Druckman, D., Broome, B.J., & Korper, S.H. (1983). Value differences and conflict resolution: Facilitation or delinking? *Journal of Conflict Resolution, 32*, 489–510.

Epstein, R.M., Campbell, T.L., Cohen-Cole, S.A., McWhinney, I.R., & Smilkstein, G. (1993). Perspectives on patient-doctor communication. *The Journal of Family Practice, 37*, 377–388.

Flaherty, E.W. (1979). Evaluation of consultation. In J.J. Platt & R.J. Wicks (Eds.), *The psychological consultant* (pp. 213–242). New York: Grune & Stratton.

Forrow, L., Arnold, R.M., & Parker, L.S. (1993). Preventive ethics: Expanding the horizons of clinical ethics. *Journal of Clinical Ethics, 4*, 287–294.

Fraser, R.A. (1989). Social decision-making and the use of value management. *Ekistics, 56*, 171–174.

Gillian, R., Mondell, B., & Warbasse, J.R. (1977). Quantitative evaluation of vitamin E in the treatment of angina pectoris. *American Heart Journal, 93*, 444–449.

Gilligan, C. (1982). *In a different voice: Psychological theory and women's development*. Cambridge, MA: Harvard University Press.

Grebe, S.C. (1992). Ethics and the professional family mediator. *Mediation Quarterly, 10*, 155–165.

Heitler, S. (1990). *From conflict to resolution*. New York: Norton.

Humphrey, G.B., Littlewood, J.L., & Kamps, W.A. (1992). Physician/patient communication: A model considering the interaction of physicians' therapeutic strategy and patients' coping style. *Journal of Cancer Education, 7*, 147–152.

Jenkins, C.D. (1992). Assessment of outcomes of health intervention. *Social Science & Medicine, 35*, 367–375.

Kaplan, R.M. (1985). Behavioral epidemiology, health promotion, and health services. *Medical Care, 23*, 564–583.

Kelly, T.A., & Strupp, H.H. (1992). Patient and therapist values in psychotherapy: Perceived changes, assimilation, similarity, and outcome. *Journal of Consulting & Clinical Psychology, 60*, 34–40.

Kilby, R.W. (1993). *The study of human values*. New York: University Press of America.

Kluckhohn, C. (1961). *Variations in value orientations*. Evanston, IL: Row Peterson.

Langenhoven, M.L., Rossouw, J.E., Jooste, P.L., Charlton, D.O., Swanepoel, A.S.P., Rossouw, L.J., Jordaan, P.C.J., & Steyn, M. (1991). Change in knowledge in coronary heart disease risk factor intervention study in three communities. *Social Science & Medicine, 33*, 71–76.

Liedtka, J.M. (1991). When values collide: Value conflict in American health care. *Business & Professional Ethics Journal, 40*, 3–28.

Loewy, E.H. (1989). *Textbook of medical ethics*. New York: Plenum.

Maccoby, E.E. (1980).–Social development. New York: Harcourt Brace Jovanovich.

Messing, J.K. (1993). Mediation: An intervention strategy for counselors. *Journal of Counseling & Development, 72*, 67–72.

Newman, J.L. (1993). Ethical issues in consultation. *Journal of Counseling & Development, 72*, 148–156.

Nystrom, P. (1989). *Ethical values as organizational identities: Hospitals and businesses.* Paper presented at a meeting of the National Academy of Management, Washington, DC.

Odell, M., & Stewart, S.P. (1993). Ethical issues associated with client values conversion and therapist value agendas in family therapy. *Family Relations, 42,* 128–132.

Schön, D.A. (1983). *The reflective practitioner.* New York: Basic Books.

Seubert, V.R. (1991). Sociology and value neutrality: Limiting sociology to the empirical level. *The American Sociologist, 22,* 210–220.

Sieber, S.D. (1981). *Fatal remedies: The ironies of social intervention.* New York: Plenum.

Simon, H. (1972). *The sciences of the artificial.* Cambridge: MIT Press.

Street, F.L. Jr., & Buller, D.B. (1988). Patients' characteristics affecting physician-patient nonverbal communication. *Human Communication Research, 15,* 60–90.

Taylor, K.M. (1988). Telling bad news: Physicians and the disclosure of undesirable information. *Sociology of Health & Illness, 10,* 121–132.

Thompson, S.C., Nanni, C., & Schwankovsky, L. (1990). Patient-oriented interventions to improve communication in a medical office visit. *Health Psychology, 9,* 390–404.

Toone, W.M. (1973). Effects of vitamin E: Good and bad. *New England Journal of Medicine, 289,* 689–698.

Trickett, E.J. (1992). Prevention ethics: Explicating the context of prevention activities. *Ethics & Behavior, 2,* 91–100.

Uhlenhuth, E.H., Rickels, K., Fisher, S., Park, L.C., Lipman, R.S., & Mock, J. (1966). Drug, doctor's verbal attitude and clinical setting in the symptomatic response to pharmacotherapy. *Psychopharmacologia, 9,* 392–418.

Ulschak, F.L., & Snow Antle, S.M. (1990). *Consultation skills for health care professionals.* San Francisco: Jossey-Bass.

Warwick, D.P., & Kelman, H.C. (1973). Ethical issues in social intervention. In G. Zaltman (Ed), *Processes and phenomena of social change* (pp. 377–417). New York: Wiley.

Wiseman, J.M. (1990). *Mediation therapy.* Lexington, MA: Lexington.

Wyatt, N. (1991). Physician–patient relationships: What do doctors say? *Health Communication, 3,* 157–174.

Zola, I.K. (1975). In the name of health and illness: On some socio-political consequences of medical influence. *Social Science and Medicine, 9,* 83–87.

Recommended Readings

Bruhn, J.G., Levine, H.G., & Levine, P.L. (1993). *Managing boundaries in the health professions.* Springfield, IL: Charles C Thomas.

Little has been written about turf, territoriality, and boundaries in the health professions. This book grew out of the authors' observations and experiences in health science centers. The chapters detail boundary issues in general and how they apply to the health professions in particular. Attention is given to the effects of organizational change on boundary management and how to more effectively manage changing and complex boundaries. A rich bibliography, case studies, and guidelines for managing boundaries are provided.

Bruhn, J.G., & Henderson, G. (1991). *Values in health care: Choices and conflicts.* Springfield, IL: Charles C Thomas.

This book is concerned with values as they apply to health care. Among the 12 chapters are topics such as health as a value, prevention as a value, pain and suffering, choice as a value, healing as a value, values and ethics in conflict, and professionalism. This volume is intended for students in medicine, nursing, and allied health as well as a resource for fields not directly associated with hands-on patient care.

Gentry, W.D. (Ed.) (1984). *Handbook of behavioral medicine*. New York: Guilford.

This book reflects the interdisciplinary nature of behavioral medicine. In addressing the general issues of compliance, decision making, and etiology common to all health–illness relationships, this volume provides a model for interdisciplinary analysis. It is intended as a sourcebook for researchers and educators who are interested in the interactive nature of biomedical and social behavioral aspects of behavior. This is one of the best sources of the state-of-the-art of behavioral medicine.

Gochman, D.S. (Ed.). (1988). *Health behavior: Emerging research perspectives*. New York: Plenum.

The primary objective of this book is to identify and establish health behavior as an important area of basic research. The 23 chapters are carefully organized in terms of specific health behaviors or specific health problems, e.g., determinants of health behavior; personal, family, social, cultural, and institutional. The book is intended for students and researchers in the social and behavioral sciences as well as in the health professions. It presents state-of-the-art health behavior research and outlines a challenging future research agenda.

Hansen, J.C. (Ed.). (1982). *Values, ethics, legalities and the family therapist*. Rockville, MD: Aspen.

This volume focuses on the ethical, value, and professional conflicts in family therapy. Of particular interest is the chapter on counselor–therapist values and therapeutic style. Specific value issues, such as sexism, sexuality, minorities, handicapped, religion, abortion and sterilization, dual careers, and death and dying, are discussed. The chapters on family law and ethical conflicts in clinical decision-making are especially good.

Kottler, J.A. (1993). *On being a therapist*. San Francisco: Jossey-Bass.

This book provides an excellent overview of the job of a therapist. The process of therapy flows in two directions. Can the clinician be an active instigator of the therapeutic process without, in turn, being affected by its effects? The reciprocal power between participants in the therapy process is discussed along with the implications of the therapist as a model. The book is written for all practitioners of therapy, especially students preparing for a career in therapy.

Matarazzo, J.D., Weiss, S.M., Herd, J.A., Miller, N.E., & Weiss, S.M. (Eds.). (1984). *Behavioral health: A handbook of health enhancement and disease prevention*. New York: Wiley.

This book is a collection of the most significant behavioral and biomedical findings on disease prevention and health enhancement. It sheds new light on the complex links between behavior and health, examines the social and cultural factors involved in health promotion, and explores behavioral health issues by life-cycle stages—prenatal, neonatal, adolescence, adulthood, and advanced age. It also examines the kind of training health professionals currently receive in disease prevention and health promotion.

Ostrow, D.G. (Ed.). (1990). *Behavioral aspects of AIDS*. New York: Plenum.

The chapters in this volume summarize available behavioral information, describe its application to clinical problems and discuss research challenges. The contributors are all involved in their own research or clinical work on HIV and AIDS. Of particular interest are the health care delivery issues in mental health, public health, consultation–liaison psychology, and the training and support of health care professionals dealing with the psychiatric aspects of AIDS. This is a rich resource for teachers, researchers, and clinicians.

Raithbone-McCuan, F., & Hashimi, J. (1982). *Isolated elders: Health and social intervention.* Rockville, MD: Aspen.

A framework for conceptualizing nine subgroups within the elderly population, this book identifies some areas for intervention and prevention. The areas covered include: the Hispanic and black elderly, the rural elderly, the chronically ill, elder abuse, older veterans, Alzheimer's patients, and older and elderly women. Many of these areas lack an empirical knowledge base, and little intervention outcome research has been carried out to demonstrate the effectiveness of services offered to these various groups. This book identifies gaps in our knowledge for research and intervention.

Afterword
An Agenda for Action

Throughout this book we have described the kinds of problems and issues that interest clinical sociologists and illustrated how sociologists work to bring about desired change. The scope of the field is broad and the number of complex problems needing intervention continues to increase. Therefore, the future of clinical sociology holds a plethora of new challenges and opportunities. Our purpose here is to establish a structure and agenda for the further development of clinical sociology and discuss possible directions for the field in the next decade.

A Framework for Change

Establishing a framework for the future of clinical sociology requires an understanding of the demographic trends and prevailing attributes of the U. S. population which will influence the services required.

The population of the United States is projected to increase by 56 million by the year 2038 (U.S. Bureau of the Census, 1989). Several factors will also contribute to the changing nature of the demographic profile. Eight trends seem to be the most important: an aging population, the baby boom generation, a declining younger population, racial and ethnic diversity, changes in the family unit, redefinition of individual and societal roles, increased interest in personal and environmental health, and an information based society.

Perhaps the most striking trend is the overall aging of the population. The median age of the population in 1987 was at an all-time high of 32.1 years. By the year 2000, however, the very large baby boom cohort will be over age 35 and will push up the median age. Thirty million Americans were aged 65 and over in 1987, a number expected to increase by 4 million in 1995. Due to the small birth cohorts of the Depression era who will now be reaching their mid-60s, the 65 and over group will increase by only 2.5 million between 1995 and 2005. After 2010, however, it will grow rapidly to 52 million in 2020 as the members of the baby boom reach age 65. Just as the overall U.S. population is aging, the elderly are aging. While 9.6% of the elderly population was over age 85 in 1987, this percentage will grow steadily to 15.5% in 2010 (U.S. Bureau of the Census, 1989).

As the baby boomers settle into middle age, they have started their own families and produced a baby boom echo. They are changing recreation habits and moving into the years when they will begin to consume more health services. As one of the best educated generations in America they will be more prevention oriented.

The population under 5 was around 18.4 million in 1990 and will shrink to around 16.9 million in 2000, and remain around that level until 2050. The high school population (ages 14 to 17) should remain in the 13 to 14 million range during the period 1995 to 2010. The college-age population (ages 18 to 24), which has been declining since 1980, is expected to decline further by 3 million in 1995. It is expected to rebound somewhat between 2000 and 2010, but it will never be as large as it is now (U.S. Bureau of the Census, 1989).

America continues to absorb new waves of immigrants. In 1980 the Hispanic American population was about half the size of the African American population. By 2005 the two populations will be virtually equal in size and will together represent 26% of the U.S. population. This increase will be driven by a fertility rate of 2.5 and annual immigration of approximately 400,000. The Hispanic American population is also not following a traditional pattern of societal integration. Language, geographic concentration, cultural differences, and religion all limit the ability and willingness of Hispanic Americans to merge into the dominant culture.

Many African Americans remain outside of the mainstream. There has been considerable discussion over the past decade of the emergence of a permanent underclass. Much of this analysis has focused on the life changes for a major part of the African American population.

While other ethnic groups will grow over the next decade, their impact will not be as significant as that of the Hispanic American and African American populations. Regional differences will be even more significant and will impact health care and social services, the educational system and labor market.

The last two decades have produced a remarkable change in the demography of the family. The family with two married adults with children is no longer the definition of what constitutes a family. Considering both mortality and divorce rates, there is a 50% chance that married partners will not be together for a 25th anniversary. There is a one in three chance that American children will spend at least part of their lives in one-parent households. That chance increases to two in three for African American children of (U.S. Bureau of the Census, 1989). Another dimension of the changing family is more women in the labor force. In 1950 the labor force participation rate for women was 23.8%, and by 1985 it had grown to 54.3% and it is expected to continue to increase. These factors have implications for the education and provision of health, mental health, and social services for children and for adults as well.

Individuals are taking on a greater share of responsibility for their health and quality of life. The AIDS epidemic will continue to grow. The effect of the environment will continue to be a concern, especially when it clashes with economic growth, and issues related to medical ethics will be of increasing concern. Finally, major changes in the way people work, communicate, and recreate will be brought on by changes in information technology. Technological "haves" and "have nots" will develop. In some urban areas every individual will be using computers at home and at work by the year 2000. Information technology will become increasingly important as a teaching and learning mode. As Walz, Gazda, and Shertzer (1991) point out, America will move from a "mass society" toward a dynamic, ever-changing mosaic society.

An Agenda for Action

This framework for change provides numerous challenges to sociology as well as opportunities for practitioners of sociology in the next decade. There are, as Handy (1994) pointed out, clear limits to management, control, and planning. Societal issues have become world issues with great complexities that prevent easy solutions. We are now consumed with attempting to manage and treat the unintended consequences of social change. One of the major challenges to sociology in the next decade will be to help provide solutions and not merely point out problems. The opportunity for sociologists to put their skills and expertise to practical use will be limitless.

The area of prevention as it applies to crime and delinquency, mental health, and health in general, offer numerous roles for clinical sociologists ranging from planning, advocacy, and education to program implementation and evaluation to therapeutic intervention such as counseling. Cigarette smoking and AIDS are examples of health problems which involve micro-, meso-, and macrolevels and need the skills of multiple professionals, but sociologists in particular because of their expertise in small groups and social structure. The current need for the expertise of clinical sociologists to work on prevention ranges from public health to public schools to public media.

The area of human abuse and domestic violence involves micro-, meso-, and macrolevels, and the skills of counselors, arbitrators, educators, consultants, planners, and researchers. The prevention and control of violence and the rehabilitation of offenders requires macroplanning, social structure interventions, and shaping of public policy on a societal level. Indeed, as Sanders (1994:3) pointed out in his study of gangs and gang violence, "gangs are dynamic ... both quantitative and qualitative data were taken from situations of violence based on observations, interviews and written reports. The goal was to obtain an overall picture of the situations of gang violence—an ethnography of situations." Clinical sociologists are needed to help plan interventions to curb the spread of violence in all forms in our society and worldwide.

The breaking down of barriers related to differences of ethnicity, race, gender, physical and mental ability and so forth, and the emphasis on equal opportunity and diversification have also brought about the need to educate people about culture and value differences worldwide, ranging from neighborhoods to work-places to international trade alliances. As the world becomes more accessible, people who are different from one another have a greater chance for interacting. This has both positive and negative repercussions. Alliances, coalitions, and unions can cross differences to benefit all. When differences are accentuated, discounted, and people are taunted violence and crime can occur. With their expertise in conflict resolution, cultural mediation, and political arbitration, clini-cal sociologists can provide insights and help to plan programs to help maximize the benefits of increased diversification of the world.

Clinical sociologists can help to shape public policy. Working parents and one-parent families are creating a nationwide need for day care facilities for children. There is a need to examine how we can use day care time to better educate children and experiment with innovative approaches in such education.

There is also a role for clinical sociologists in the media; specifically, in studying how different media shape behavior and how programs can be used to shape and change behavior. Recently the cigarette advertising directed toward youth has been attacked by the federal government as knowingly wooing young people into a life of addiction. Clinical sociologists have an opportunity to help direct media to effect positive outcomes for our youth.

Almost 5% of Americans are incarcerated or on probation due to crime. We persist in building prisons to deal with their overcrowding and release prisoners early because new prisons are not being built fast enough. Yet we do not fully understand why crime of all types is increasing at national and international levels. There is a great need for planning, research, and innovative programs to seek alternatives to punishment. Rehabilitation does not seem to work, possibly because what we label *rehabilitation* is not such. Prevention would seem to be a more cost and time effective alternative to rehabilitation and incarceration. There are nu-merous roles for clinical sociologists in prison reform (Soto, Behrens, & Rose-mont, 1990). Our country has been unsuccessful in developing an equitable, accessible, and affordable system for delivering health services. Lobbies and special interest groups powerfully resist change and the loss of power. The cost and complexities of health services continue to increase. There is an opportunity for clinical sociologists to become involved in political negotiations to bring about modifications in our health care structure. Skills in coalition building, value arbitration, and sharing power will be needed to break current trends. Clinical sociologists, as service providers, have valuable contributions to make in this arena.

There are new challenges for managers to create healthy workplaces. Several demographic shifts are magnifying the power of the worker. The shrinking workforce, the diversification of the workforce, the growing service economy, and the increasing technology of the workplace all require teamwork, more attention to customers, and underscore the importance of a people-oriented, relationship-driven workplace. There must be greater personal and professional development of employees, respect for individual differences, and an ability to be flexible and resilient to change. Clinical sociologists can provide the skills to help shape healthy workplaces with their understanding of organizations, intergroup relations, leadership and followership, and rewards and sanctions. There is a current need for consultants to private and public industry and business to effect workplace transitions.

Competencies for the Twenty-First Century

There is an opportunity to define a set of new competencies required of clinical sociologists to practice in the next decade (Sugars, O'Neil, & Bader, 1991). These competencies are:

Counseling on Ethical Issues

Ethical issues are of importance in sociological practice whatever one's role or scope of practice. These extend beyond the ethics which bind the practitioner–client relationship. Ethical issues may be imbedded in the client's problem or arise in the course of exploring alternative solutions to problems. Treatment and intervention involves ethical values. There is no treatment or intervention that does not have some possible adverse reaction. These need to be discussed with clients before, not after, the fact. A client may be considering having an abortion; a client may be debating about whether to reveal an affair to their spouse; a client may be an abuser, or a thief. All of these involve both the ethics surrounding the issue or problem and the ethics which surround the client–practitioner relationship. The increasing use of electronic records also present major challenges in maintaining and assuming confidentiality. A clinical sociologist should establish relationships with colleagues with whom ethical issues can be discussed as well as regularly attending conferences on the changing nature of ethical issues.

Managing Information Technology

Clinical skills, communication skills, and accurate information influence the effectiveness of an intervention. The computer is a valuable tool in the practice of clinical sociology. Databases can provide information related to referral sources for a client's specific needs. The computer can provide an efficient way to integrate information from many sources in serving a client, including billing data. Clinical sociologists in the future must be computer literate. Indeed, in some instances interactive displays could be used for testing or teaching skills or concepts to clients.

Promoting Healthy Behavior

Clinical sociology practice also involves some teaching and modeling of healthy behavior by the practitioner. As consumers have become increasingly empowered, many expect a more active role on the part of the practitioner in providing information and discussing alternatives. Some consumers place a high priority on health promotion. Wellness programs, exercise regimens, dietary concerns, and a growing array of self-help and self-diagnostic and treatment technologies all testify to consumers' active involvement in their own health. Similar efforts are being made to create healthy workplaces and organizations. As Rosen (1991:viii) has said, "Healthy people make healthy companies ... it means letting go ... of the old concepts of control and supervision ... and embracing the concepts of honesty and trust which lead to the empowerment of every employee." Healthy behavior, be it of individuals or organizations, is newly valued.

Expanded Accountability

Clinical sociologists in the future will increasingly be accountable to third parties in their practice which will set out parameters for acceptable intervention and billing. There will need to be more consultation between parties prior to treatment and intervention to prevent the client from having unfulfilled expectations and becoming a victim while seeking help. The practitioner will also become a victim of the increased bureaucratization of public, governmental, and third-party paperwork. It will be essential that clinical sociologists become instrumental in improving accountability.

Teamwork to Integrate Services

Sociologists usually practice by themselves. However, current and future problems can rarely be solved by the expertise of a single discipline. Furthermore, teamwork is often more cost-effective. Most of the problems confronting our society require that we cross disciplinary boundaries in order to arrive at workable solutions. Clinical sociologists will need to utilize their knowledge of small groups in helping them work together with colleagues in other disciplines.

Understanding the Physical Environment

Many social as well as physical problems have environmental cofactors. Toxic and nuclear wastes pose long-term hazards to groundwater and soil. Lead-based paint and asbestos insulation still found in older buildings cause permanent infant neurological defects and pulmonary disease respectively. Electromagnetic radiation has been posited as a cause of brain cancer, etc. Air pollution and cigarette smoking, or second-hand smoke from cigarettes, have been suggested as causes of cancer of the lung. It is important for clinical sociologists to conduct an "environmental scan" of their clients to assess how, and in what way, the physical environmental relates to a client's problem and the possible solutions.

Helping Shape Public Policy

Clinical sociologists need to participate in advocacy and dialogue regarding the availability, accessibility, and affordability of health and human services, programs designed to prevent violence and abuse, educational and preventive services to children and other groups. Too often we criticize rather than provide input before policy is shaped. We have vested interests as citizens as well as interests as professionals. We should be up-front about these interests and voice our concerns. Considerations for quality of life, extension of life, and death are becoming more complicated. The extension of life, using all measures does not work in all settings as patients, family and society explore more equitable distribution for social resources. All professionals will be looked to for guidance and direction regarding measures of quality and ways to continuously improve the operations and accountability of how we deliver health and human services. Clinical sociologists will need to take leadership positions to help insure there is a voice from all segments of society.

Issues of Identity

We need to help clarify and, thus, advance the field of clinical sociology. We can do this by providing greater formalization and cohesion to the field. We need more activism as clinical sociologists. We need to demonstrate our validity by greater contributions to the literature, workshops, and initiating community projects that tackle social problems. We need to develop our discipline by letting colleagues and related disciplines know what we do and the results of our work by publishing case studies and participating in meetings of professional organizations at all levels.

We could help to clarify our identity if we made our techniques and methodologies more widely known. With ties to a broader communication network of colleagues and peers, clinical sociologists can benefit from, as well as contribute to, the available pool of techniques and methods used to solve common social problems. Indeed, opportunities to apply for grants to support programs should increase as methodologies are known, strengthened, and gain greater credibility.

But most clinicians are not prolific writers, even though they have much to contribute to the field through experience, case histories, and consultations. There needs to be more clinical research from the perspective of clinical sociology, beginning with careful, detailed case reports at various levels. Clinical workers need to write more about what they do. The perfection of techniques and applications and filling the gaps in knowledge can emerge from such reports. Clinically based articles help in identifying areas for study and research, as well as provide validation for and promote theory developments. Part of the socialization of sociologists with an applied preference should include greater reinforcement of the need for and benefits from clinical contributions to the literature. This is important because it helps to build a strong link between science and application, and demonstrates the continuity of theory, application, and social change mentioned above. Moreover, the discipline should reinforce this behavior.

Perhaps the underlying theme in the call for a sharper identity is the need for the legitimization of clinical sociology. We should not need to "sell" the field or appeal for opportunities to call attention to the work of clinical and applied sociologists. Our work should illustrate the field—what we do, how we do it, what its effects are—and the contribution will become obvious. Clinical sociologists, therefore, must be the ones to sharpen clinical sociology's identity. There are no quick fixes to solidify the identity of the field; it takes time, experience, persistence, and an ability to make changes and accommodate new needs.

The future of clinical sociology is not in establishing new degree programs or certifications to create elitism or separatism. Its future is in the encouragement of the application of sociological knowledge and the increased sharing of these applications. All sociology students should be encouraged to think about the relevance of sociological theory and concepts to practical problem solving.

We can be too introspective about the profession of clinical sociology. In a field as broad as sociology, there are bound to be diverse and sometimes conflicting views of core values and priorities. Indeed, diversity is good, but there must be some commonly agreed upon principles, values, and methodologies if a field is to have credibility and recruit new members. The multiplicity of views poses a predicament for practitioners who must choose among multiple roles and approaches to practice, or to devise their own way of combining them. There is some degree of confusion and unease among professionals generally, because they cannot always account for processes they have come to see as central to professional competence. And it is difficult to describe and teach an applied field. We should not be concerned with defending ourselves as applied scientists, as clinical sociologists, or as professionals. The importance of a profession lies in its contribution to society, not in the degree of success we have in trying to get colleagues who adhere to a more "basic" or traditional scope of work, to accept us and our work.

Directions for the Field

Gollin (1990) states that the future of sociology will be tied to its utility. While on the one hand employment opportunities for sociologists in academic settings will be limited, those sociologists who go outside of academe are likely to be viewed as marginal. Economic cutbacks in universities and in the world have put pressure on various disciplines to be accountable. Sociology is perceived to be, as yet, a generalist field without clearly definable outcomes and its graduates are often perceived to have indefinable skills. Gollin feels that there will be continuing pressures on sociology to become a practice-oriented profession. Eitzen (1991) identified three major changes he feels prophesies a bright future for sociology. These are structural changes in society resulting in greater diversity as well as diversity within sociology; increasing constraints on research funding from private and public sources and the transformation of the world economy.

Demographic changes in U.S. society and continuing social movements toward a more open, equal, and participative society have created a more diverse society. Sociologists are students of change and the struggle between cooperation and conflict. Yet as observers and commentators sociologists have not been active participants in helping to shape and direct change and options for controlling its effects. Sociologists have also not been leaders in interdisciplinary teaching and research. Finally, sociologists have resisted intervening in societal change and have mainly commented on the consequences of change, especially its negative effects. As a result, sociology is often perceived as a "hands off" field. This type of career is often unattractive to students who want to make a difference in their career and are drawn to disciplines where they can learn through "hands on" experience.

This was reinforced in Ruggerio and Weston's (1994) study of sociological practitioners' views of the most important issues facing the discipline of sociology now and in the future. The use of sociological principles and theories to help solve a variety of societal and organizational problems, the resolution of disciplinary concerns, and the training, licensure/certification, and marketing of sociologists were the major issues identified. It is perhaps ironic that sociologists, who are usually observers and commentators on change and its effects, now have to deal with the pressures of change on their own discipline.

Gollin (1990) and Borgatta and Cook (1988) pointed out that many areas that used to be almost exclusively the domain of sociologists, such as marriage and the family, industrial sociology, and social psychology, have been preempted by other disciplines. Bulmer (1990) notes that there have been many areas where there have been successes in sociology, e.g., sociology of mental illness, sociology of education, and political sociology, but sociologists have done a poor job of marketing their findings. He points out that the greatest obstacle to the recognition of sociology's successes is the self-doubt of sociologists of the practical use of sociology, Berk (1988) and Borgatta and Cook (1988) stressed that in the future sociologists need to become more concerned with the application of knowledge and the consequences of their work, as well as becoming proactive with respect to the formation of social policy.

The yield for the field of clinical sociology for the future lies in the hands of clinical sociologists themselves. There is no shortage of needs to address. There is no limit to the field or the satisfactions for engaging in actions that are intended to bring about positive change. Obviously there is a shortage of people power to work on the multiplicity of problems needing attention. Therefore, one of the challenges to clinical sociology in the future is to develop more clinical sociology programs. Most college and university students today want to take on careers that are challenging and where they can see whether they have made a difference. Many professional careers are removed from the origins of problems. Clinical sociologists have chosen to be more than observers of and commentators on the life of society; they have chosen to intervene to help correct wrongs and injustices. There is no limit to the number of problems that await action. John Schaar has said it well: "The future is not a result of choices among alternative paths offered by the present, but a place that is created—created first in mind and will, created next in activity. The future is not some place we are going to, but one we are creating" (Walz, Gazda, & Shertzer 1991:78).

References

Berk, R.A. (1988). How applied sociology can save basic sociology. In E.F. Borgatta & K.S. Cook (Eds.). *The future of sociology* (pp. 57–72). Newbury Park, CA: Sage.

Borgatta, E.F., & Cook, K.S. (Eds.). (1988). *The future of sociology*. Newbury Park, CA: Sage.

Bulmer, M. (1990). Successful applications of sociology. In C.G.A. Bryant & H.A. Becker, (Eds.), *What has sociology achieved?* (pp. 117–142). London: Macmillan.

Eitzen, S.D. (1991). Prospects for sociology into the 21st century. *The American Sociologist, 22*, 109–115.

Gollin, A. (1990). Whither the profession of sociology? *The American Sociologist, 21*, 316–320.

Handy, C. (1994). *The age of paradox*. Boston, MA: Harvard Business School Press.

Rosen, B.H. (1994). *The healthy company*. New York: Putnam.

Ruggerio, J.A., & Weston, L.C. (1994). Results of a practitioner survey and comparison with the themes of articles published in the *ASA Footnotes*: Major issues facing the discipline of sociology. *Clinical Sociological Review, 12*, 17–28.

Sanders, W.B. (1994). *Gangbangs and drive-bys: Grounded culture and juvenile gang violence*. New York: Aldine De Gruyter.

Soto, M.A., Behrens, R., & Rosemont, C., Eds. (1990). *Healthy people 2000: Citizens chart the course.* Washington, DC: National Academy Press.

Sugars, D.A., O'Neil, E.H., & Bader, J.D., Eds. (1991). *Healthy America: Practitioners for 2005.* Durham, NC: Pew Health Professions Commission.

U.S. Bureau of the Census, (1989, January). *Current population reports, projections of the population of the United States by age, sex and race; 1988–2080,* Washington, DC: Department of Commerce.

Walz, G.R., Gazda, G.M., & Shertzer, B. (1991). *Counseling futures.* Ann Arbor, MI: ERIC Counseling and Personnel Services Clearinghouse.

Recommended Readings

Stacey, R.D. (1992). *Managing the unknowable: Strategic boundaries between order and chaos in organizations.* San Francisco, CA: Jossey-Bass.

Stacy shows how planning is based on directing complex, often chaotic interactions that take place in organizations. He explains how chaos can inspire creativity, describes role contradiction and conflict. He offers guidelines in building the skills necessary to handle unknowable futures, including advice on establishing self-organizing teams, encouraging multiple cultures, and improving group learning skills.

Handy, C. (1994). *The age of paradox.* Boston, MA: Harvard Business School Press.

Handy documents new developments in technology, global economics, and efficiency and their impact on organizations, careers, and life-styles. He proposes ideas of how individuals and organizations can navigate through the brave new world. The end of lifelong careers gives us the freedom to explore new organizations. Fewer full-time positions create more flexibility. Knowledge as a commodity offers the possibility of a more egalitarian society. He discusses the unintended consequences of change—the paradoxes. He points out how these paradoxes can be managed.

Karasek, R., & Theorell, T.Z. (1990). *Healthy work: Stress, productivity, and the reconstruction of working life.* New York: Basic Books.

With declining productivity becoming a major economic problem and job-related stress a major health concern, these authors are concerned with the quality of working life. They explain the linkages between the environment, the worker, and health, and point out the psychosocial characteristics that foster both productivity and health. They advocate a redesign of jobs to build a learning-based organization.

Glossary

Adaptation: The adjustment of individuals or social systems to conditions and to changing conditions.

Antecedent conditions: Conditions or events that occur before, and may have a causal influence on, subsequent events or conditions.

Archival data: Information kept as records of organizations and institutions such as courts, justice, medical, or school systems.

Assessment: The process of gathering information about a case for the purpose of planning and developing a program of change or problem solution.

Baseline: The measured preintervention status or condition of a case.

Biopsychosocial perspective: A point of view that studies human behavior as the complex interaction of biological, psychological, and social factors.

Boundary: Physical, social, and psychological barriers that limit movement or thought. That which divides a system from its environment.

Client-centered approach: A humanistic approach to working with clients that is nonjudgmental and emphasizes respect for clients' autonomy.

Closed systems: Systems that do not interact with their environment, that do not exchange information, material, and/or activity with their environments or other systems.

Concomitant variation: When changes in the measured value of one variable are associated with changes in the measured value of another variable.

Confidentiality: A component of ethical practice that requires that clinicians safeguard information obtained from clients, students, or research subjects except, perhaps, when doing so may result in harm.

Cultural sensitivity: An awareness of the nuances of one's own and other cultures.

Ecosystem: A system in which living things are interrelated with each other and with their shared environment.

Empowerment: To give authority or delegate moral or physical actions to a group.

Epidemiology: A field of inquiry directed at determining the distribution and etiology of disease. The epidemiologist attempts to determine who develops a specific disease and why.

Equifinality: A property of open systems that refers to systems' independence from their initial states. That is, two systems with the same initial states may produce different outcomes; two systems with different initial states may arrive at the same outcome.

Experimental design: A research design that requires that subjects be randomly selected and randomly assigned to treatment conditions, that an investigator carefully control presentation of experimental conditions, and that among the conditions there be a no-treatment control group, established as similar to treatment groups, against which the effects of the treatment will be compared.

Feedback: The return of information material, and/or energy to the system as input.

Focal system: The system under study.

Genogram: An intergenerational schematic of a family used as a tool in assessment with individuals and families.

Hawthorne effect: When clinicians or investigators knowingly or unknowingly change the situation or behavior they wish to observe or study.

Health promotion: Strengthening parameters of living (behavioral, physiological, genetic, etc.) to minimize the risk of health problems.

Idiographic explanation: Explanation of a unique case or situation.

Impact evaluation: The assessment of both the intended and unintended effects of an intervention or treatment program.

Input: The information, energy, and/or material introduced into a system from its environment.

Intervenor: The person who introduces a technique or method to introduce change.

Intervention: A technique or method to introduce a change in behavior or environment.

Intervention outcome: The results or effects of introducing a technique or method to bring about change.

Key respondents: Identified members of a group under observation who agree to talk to the observer about the group and its activities.

Macro–micro continuum: The organization of sociological phenomena on a continuous scale ranging from large-scale social systems (macrosociological) to individuals and small primary groups (microsociological).

Macrosociology or Macrolevel: The sociological study of large-scale social systems such as whole societies or cultures or social institutions.

Mediation: The act of interposing or serving as an intermediary.

Microsociology or Microlevel: The sociological study of individuals and/or small primary groups.

Mesosociology or Mesolevel: The sociological study of midlevel collections of people in secondary groups such as organizations and social networks.

Model: A representation or likeness of something that is real which is used for the purposes of analysis and understanding.

Niche: The place or function an entity occupies within an ecosystem.

Nomothetic explanation: Explanation based on general principles of classes of events.

Nonsummativity: A property of open systems that indicates that the system is more than the sum of its parts and that the system cannot be understood simply by analysis of its parts.

Open systems: Systems that interact with their environment; they exchange information, material, and energy with their environment.

Output : Information and other resources introduced into the environment from a system and available to other systems within the environment.

Personal values: The code of beliefs and criteria for decision making that mold individual behavior.

Placebo effect: An intervention or treatment that has no specific, direct, effect, e.g., taking a sugar pill instead of a medication.

Presenting problem: The initial problem as stated by clients.

Primary prevention: Averting the occurrence of an action or disease at the principal site; for example, by not smoking cigarettes or by immunization.

Process evaluation: A part of program evaluation that assesses those things that have to do with whether the program is being executed as planned.

Program monitoring: A part of program evaluation that takes place while program implementation is underway that is designed to determine if the program is moving toward the planned objectives.

Quasi-experimental designs: Research designs that attempt to approximate the experimental design but cannot meet all the requirements, especially random assignment to treatment and control groups.

Random assignment: The unbiased assignment of subjects to treatment groups strictly according to chance; the assignment of subjects to groups such that each subject has an equal chance of being assigned to any group.

Random selection: The unbiased sampling of cases from a population such that each element of a population has an equal chance of being selected.

Social system approach: Seeing human behavior and that of social groups as the result of multiple interacting internal and external factors.

Social systems model: A way of looking at the interrelationships between people and their environments.

Social values: Values that affect the individual's relationship to society, such as the ideals of caring for others, respect toward others, sharing, helping, etc.

Sociological spectrum: The Macro–Micro Continuum: The ordering of sociological phenomena on a continuous scale from large scale to smaller scale social action.

Stakeholders: Persons who are affected by a program and/or evaluation of that program.

Steady state: The state that occurs when the whole system is in balance; the system is maintaining a viable relationship with its environment and its functions are being performed in such a way as to ensure its continued existence.

Superordinate goal: A goal introduced with the aim of reducing tension and conflict in a group and to lead to the integration of the group.

Synergy: The combined action of all the parts of a healthy system.

System: A set of elements that are functionally interrelated such that the action or state of any element affects all the other elements and the system as a whole.

Theory: A set of well-established propositions or statements that explain some class of events of phenomena.

Value system: An enduring organization of beliefs concerning preferable modes of conduct along a continuum of relative importance; they are perceptual filters.

Values: A value is an assessment of worth. Good, bad, right, wrong, should, ought are value words that express moral judgments of what is desirable, preferable, important, and appropriate.

Values clarification: Enabling one to take off the blinders of prevailing mores and examine values without pressures or influences.

Value-free: The illusion that an individual is free from bias or subjective assumptions about others.

Value conflict: Dissonance between sets of values held by an individual, between individuals, groups, etc.

Wholeness: A property of systems that indicates that all parts of a system are functionally interrelated and the system functions as a whole.

Index